Concept of Computer & 'C' Programming

CONCEPT OF COMPUTER
&
'C' PROGRAMMING

By

Dr. Krishan Kumar Goyal
Associate Professor
Faculty of Computer Application
Raja Balwant Singh
Management Technical Campus,
Agra, Uttar Pradesh

M.K. Sharma
Senior Lecturer
Deptt. of Computer Science,
Amrapali Institute of Management
and Computer Applications,
Haldwari, Uttarakhand

Dr. M.P. Thapliyal
Reader, Deptt. of Computer Science,
HNB Garhwal University Srinagar,
Garhwal, Uttarakhand

UNIVERSITY SCIENCE PRESS
(An Imprint of Laxmi Publications Pvt. Ltd.)
An ISO 9001:2015 Company
BENGALURU • CHENNAI • GUWAHATI • HYDERABAD • JALANDHAR
KOCHI • KOLKATA • LUCKNOW • MUMBAI • RANCHI
NEW DELHI

CONCEPT OF COMPUTER AND 'C' PROGRAMMING

Printed and bound in India
Typeset at : Shubham Composer, Delhi
First Edition : 2010, *Reprint* : 2015, 2016, *Second Edition* : 2021
ISBN : 978-93-80386-40-9

Published in India by

UNIVERSITY SCIENCE PRESS
(An Imprint of Laxmi Publications Pvt. Ltd.)
An ISO 9001:2015 Company
113, GOLDEN HOUSE, GURUDWARA ROAD, DARYAGANJ,
NEW DELHI-110002, INDIA
Telephone : 91-11-4353 2500, 4353 2501
Fax : 91-11-2325 2572, 4353 2528
www.laxmipublications.com info@laxmipublications.com

Branches

✆	Bengaluru	080-26 75 69 30	
✆	Chennai	044-24 34 47 26,	24 35 95 07
✆	Guwahati	0361-254 36 69,	251 38 81
✆	Hyderabad	040-27 55 53 83,	27 55 53 93
✆	Jalandhar	0181-222 12 72	
✆	Kochi	0484-237 70 04,	405 13 03
✆	Kolkata	033-22 27 43 84	
✆	Lucknow	0522-220 99 16	
✆	Mumbai	022-24 93 12 61	
✆	Ranchi	0651-224 24 64	

C—
Printed at:

Contents

PREFACE

This book **'Concept of Computer & 'C' Programming'** contains some special features to aid you on your path to learn about fundamental concepts of computer and later programming with C in easy way. Each chapter provides concrete examples and explanation of concepts. You will get knowledge of new concepts like Grid computers, Storage area network, Bluetooth etc., in this book. Numerous sample programs illustrate C's features and concepts, so that you can apply them in your computer lab with ease. Each chapter ends with section containing common questions relating to the chapter with reference to old year questions asked in university exams. It contains objective questions and exercises. That tests your knowledge of the concepts and helps you to prepare for aptitude test conducted by various software companies at the time of recruitment. You won't learn Computer Fundamentals and C just by reading this book, however. If you want to be a good computer programmer, you've got to write programs in lab sessions. You can use Lab exercises for that. We recommend that you attempt each exercise. Writing C code is the best way to learn C. Some advance features like interact with hardware, assembly programming in C and small Virus programs are key features of this book that lead you to be a system programmer using C. Unlike most other C books, this book offers many sample programs and exercises with clear explanations and answers, which makes the concepts of the C language easier to be understood. After reading this book, you'll be able to write C programs on your own.

STRUCTURE OF THE BOOK

Chapter 1 introduces you to the computer, its parts, different generation of computers, about programming languages and the basic software and hardware of computers.

Chapter 2 is a basic introduction about computer organization. You will learn about input, output and other devices like memory, disk, CDROM.

Chapter 3 will teach you about operating system and its use with application and a know how of MSDOS, WINDOWS, which help you to get functional knowledge of these operating systems. Introduction to internet and basic terms of internet will help to be a part of global software industry.

Chapter 4 will start your journey toward programming, you will learn about algorithms and flow charts that are basics before writing actual code.

Chapter 5 demonstrates the entire procedure of writing, compiling, linking, and running a C program as well several important concepts, such as constants, variables, expressions, and statements. Four data types, char, int, float, and double, are introduced in detail. Also, the rules of naming a variable are explained. You will learn also how to receive input from the keyboard, and print output on the screen with the help of a set of C functions, such as getc(), getchar(), putc(), putchar(), and printf().

Chapter 6 emphasizes operators and control-flow statements like if in C. In this chapter you will use arithmetic, assignment operators, the unary operator, increment/decrement operators, relational operators, and the cast operator with the help of sample programs. We will explore more operators, such as logical operators, bitwise operators, the size of operator, and the ?: operator, which are frequently used in C. With if you will learn decision making and to control the program use loops like for, while, or do-while statements. You will learn how to use switch, break, continue and goto statement in your programs.

Chapter 7 describes how to use arrays in your program. Several types of arrays like single, double and three dimensions provided by C are introduced.

Chapter 8 some more tricks about input and output functions of 'C'.

Chapter 9 the very important part of C, yes the functions. How to declare, how to call and how to pass values in functions, you will get a good practice of that all in this chapter. Recursion and its application are part of this chapter. Use of command-line arguments to the main() function are also taught in this chapter.

Chapter 10 discusses structures, unions. You learn to access structure members, and pass structures to functions with the help of pointers. Nested and forward-referencing structures are also discussed in this hour. Next you will learn how to describe the union data type, and the difference between union and structure. The applications of unions are demonstrated in several examples.

Chapter 11 is an introduction to pointers, teaches you how to reference variables with pointers. Concepts such as left value and right value are also introduced. Applying Pointers, teaches you how to perform pointer arithmetic operations, access elements in arrays with pointers, and how to pass pointers to functions.

Chapter 12 is based on dynamic memory allocation and file handling, explains the concept of allocating memory dynamically. C functions, such as malloc(), calloc(), realloc(), and free(), are introduced with regard to the dynamic memory allocation. You will also learn the concepts of the file and the stream in C. The basics of disk file input and output are introduced in this first part. The following C functions, along with several examples are introduced in this like fopen(), fclose(), fgetc(), fputc(), fgets(), fputs(), fread(), fwrite(), and feof() are introduced to show how they can help you get random access to disk files.

Appendix is there to show you some advance concepts like Virus programming, working with system and assembly programming in C and having good collection of error finding and objective questions, based on software industry question papers, that will help you to prepare yourself for booming software industry.

—Authors

Acknowledgement

During the course of writing this book, we had long discussions with many savants of the field on several topics, issues, they all deserve our sincere thanks. Without their pragmatic professional tips this book would not have seen the light of day. To name a few and mention some of their contributions.

The Hon'ble Vice Chancellor of Gharwal University Prof. M.S.M. Rawat, an academic of international repute, has been the guiding force in our endeavor.

There has been a galaxy of experts of informatics and computer science who have been instrumental in bringing out this volume like. Dr. Durgesh Pant, Prof. D.K. Joshi, Prof. M.M.S Rauthan, Dr. Harish Kumar, Dr. K.S. Bhatia.

We sincerely thank Mr. Sanjay Dhingra (CEO) and Mr. Narendra Dhingra(Secretary) , Amrapali Group of Institutions (Haldwani) for their endless encouragement, and invaluable support.

Without extended our hearty thanks to our family members Vandana , Vama and Suhani Sharma, Mrs. Pushpa Thapliyal, Nitin and Deepti for their love and support we can not end this acknowledgement.

At last many-many thanks to our lovable students whose queries and support during lectures gave us encouragement to write this book.

—Authors

SYLLABUS

COMPUTER & 'C' PROGRAMMING
(UP and Uttarakhand Technical University)

UNIT 1

Introduction to computer : Computer hardware components, Disk storage, memory, keyboard, mouse, printers, monitors, CD etc., and their functions, Comparison of hardware components.

UNIT 2

MS_DOS, WINDOWS, Functional knowledge of these operating systems, Basic commands of DOS, Managing files and directories, Introduction to internet, Basic terms in internet, TCP/IP.

UNIT 3

Programming in C : History, Introduction to C programming, Structure of C program, Compilation and execution, Debugging tech, Data types and size, variables, modifiers, identifiers, keywords, symbolic constants, storage classes (automatic, external, registar, static), Enumerations, command line, Macros, The C preprocessor.

UNIT 4

Operators all with precedence table, Control statements if else, break, goto, continue Loops, Functions built in, user defined call by value, call by reference, recursive function, multiple programs arrays, Linear array, multi, passing array to functions, arrays and strings.

UNIT 5

Structure and Union definition and use, self refer structure, pointers, pointer to pointer, dynamic memory calloc, malloc, array of pointers, functions of pointers, structure and pointers, File handling in C Opening, closing, creating data files, read write functions, unformatted data files.

1

INTRODUCTION TO COMPUTER

1.1 DEFINITIONS OF COMPUTER

What is a Computer?

A computer is an electronic device that executes the instructions in a program to process raw facts or figures known as data and convert them into information.

"One who computes, a calculator, reckoner, specifically a person employed to make calculations in an observatory, in surveying, etc." *(Oxford English Dictionary, 1926).*

"An apparatus built to perform routine calculations. "*(Grolier Multimedia Encyclopedia, 1993).*

"A usually electronic device for **storing** and **processing data** (usually in binary form), according to **instructions** given to it in a **variable program**" *(The Concise Oxford Dictionary, 9th Edition).*

The definitions clearly categorizes computer as an electronic device although the initial computers were mechanical and electromechanical, definition is also pointing towards the two major areas of computer application, data processing and computer assisted operations. Another important confluence of the definitions is the fact that the computer can perform only those operations/calculations which can be expressed in Logical or Numerical terms.

In the year 2007, when you are learning Information and Communication Technology (ICT), a new definition can be :

A PC is a **general-purpose** information processing device. It can take information from a person (through the keyboard and mouse), from a device (like a floppy disk or CD) or from the network (through a modem or a network card) and process it. Once processed, the information is shown to the user (on the monitor), stored on a device (like a hard disk) or sent somewhere else on the network (back through the modem or network card).

1.2 FUNCTIONS OF A COMPUTER

A computer has four major functions :

Accepts data	**Input**
Processes data	**Processing**
Produces output	**Output**
Stores results	**Storage**

So a computer is a general purpose, user programmable, (A program is a Meaningful Group of instructions written in a specific language aimed to do a specific task) electronic gadget capable of doing the following tasks :

1. Data Processing (Numeric & Non Numeric) with a high degree of accuracy at a pretty high speed.
2. Storage of huge amount of information with reasonably high access speed (Like Information in Banks, Railway).
3. Communication Gateway. (Link to the World using Internet).

1.3 JOHN VON NEUMANN COMPUTER ARCHITECTURE

Most of today's computer designs are based on concepts developed by John von Neumann referred to as the Von Neumann architecture. Von Neumann proposed that there should be a unit performing arithmetic and logical operation on the data. This unit is termed as Arithmetic Logic Unit (ALU). A control unit directs the ALU to perform specific arithmetic or logic function on the data. Therefore in such a system, by changing the control signal the desired operation can be performed on data. Main components of a von Neumann computer Architecture or block diagram of a computer is:

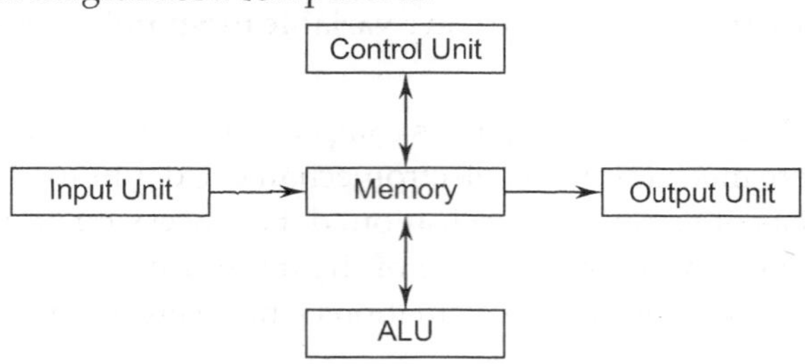

Fig. 1.1 *Block diagram of a computer*

The Arithmetic Logic Unit (ALU) and the Control Unit (CU) together are termed as the **Central Processing Unit (CPU).** The CPU is the most important component of a computer's hardware. The ALU performs the arithmetic operations such as addition, subtraction, multiplication and division, and the logical operations such as: "Is A > B?

How can the instructions and data be put into the computers? The instruction and data need to be supplied by external devices known as input unit like keyboard. Main responsibility of input unit will be to put the data in the form of signals that can be recognized by the computer. Similarly, we need another component that will show the results in proper format and form. This component is known as output unit like monitor. These components are referred together as input/output (I/O) components.

1.4 APPLICATIONS OF COMPUTERS IN YOUR LIFE

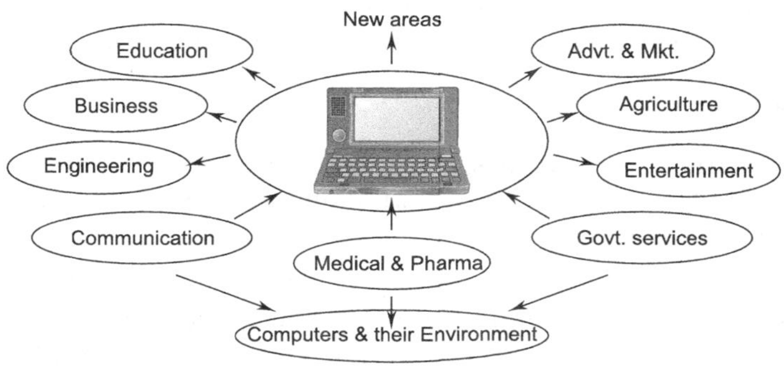

Fig. 1.2 *Application areas of computers*

Even if you never touch a computer, computer technology still has an impact on your life. For example, your student record is kept on a computer, your bank statement is printed by a computer, the special effects in movies and TV commercials are produced by computers, and so on. We can say that computers have various impacts in society like:

1. Ordinary Arithmetic Operations.
2. Logical Operations like **comparing** two items.
3. Special type of arithmetic operations like **addition of two very very large integers** (achieved through **Special Application Programs**).
4. Manipulating floating point numbers.
5. Sorting of Data like preparation of merit list.
6. Manipulating Pictures & Graphics.
7. Multimedia (Audio, Video, Graphics, Video Games etc.) Manipulations.
8. Ability to create, format, send & receive messages.
9. Art(Computers are extensively used in dance, photography, arts and culture. The fluid movement of dance can be shown live via animation. Photos can be digitized using computers).
10. Business (Nowadays, computers are totally integrated into business. The main objective of business is transaction processing, which involves transactions with suppliers, employees or customers. Computers can make these transactions easy and accurate. People can analyze investments, sales, expenses, markets and other aspects of business using computers).

1.4.1 Computers in Education

The capability of interacting with learners using multimedia methods makes computers a powerful tools for enhancing the process of learning. In addition, computers also play an important role in searching information and school or college administration. Some of good use of computers in education are :

Computer Assisted Learning (CAL)

Computer assisted learning is a term which refers to the use of computers in assisting learning. For example, a teacher may use a graph plotting software to demonstrate the behavior of different functions in a mathematics lesson; a kid student may use an animated nursery rhymes to learn and sing rhymes. A chemistry tutorial program can teach students chemical bonding on monitor screen in 3D form to enhance skills of the students.

Information searching

Dictionaries, encyclopedias, maps and other specialized references are now available in CD-ROMs. Many of them also include multimedia capabilities. You can easily search any topic in that CD in less time.

The World Wide Web is a system of interlinked hypermedia documents that enables users to find and retrieve information by navigating the web sites. Google search engine is a example of web search, where you can search information on any topic.

1.4.2 Computers in Games

Computer games is another area of computer application. You can play electronic golf or cricket at home. You can play chess with the computer as your opponent.

In computer games, the players become characters in situations they know only a little about. The characters will then encounter different phases of the adventure, and only successful problem solving with the given resources and information will move them one step ahead to accomplish the required mission.

Simulation games allow players to explore artificial environments, imaginary or based on the real world. The players can experience the consequences of their actions.

1.4.3 Computers in Edutainment

Edutainment comes from two words: Education and Entertainment. It means the combination of education with entertainment. Most of the edutainment software use multimedia elements to entertain users while they learn.

Computer for special effects in movies

The characters in Jurassic park or anaconda were computer generated. About 25, 0000 storyboards have been prepared for this movie. The animators have to animate each and every move the characters made.

A film director may need scenery that does not exist in real life. For example, a scene with the Tower Bridge (in England) appearing in Victoria Harbour (in Hong Kong). With the help of computers, pictures of Victoria Harbour can be combined with the digital image of the Tower Bridge to produce this special scenery.

1.4.4 Computers in Business Applications

Computers are widely used in business nowadays. They are part of designing, marketing, production, transitions etc. Some of their uses are in banking, supermarkets and transaction payments.

Computers in banks (ATM)

An ATM is a terminal specially designed for self-service banking. A typical ATM has the following input and output devices. It provides routine banking services 24 hours a day, 7 days a week. It helps banks save human resources, hence reducing their labor cost. An ATM machine can be used to :

- withdraw cash.
- transfer money from one account to another.
- pay bills.
- check account balances.
- request cheque books and bank statements.
- change personal identification number.

Computers for Internet banking

Internet banking is a latest facility for customers, if you have internet connection and internet banking account in SBI, PNB, HDFC bank or ICICI bank, you can :

- transfer money from one account to another.
- pay bills for school, telephone, electricity on line.
- check account balances and transaction history.
- access previous account statements.
- request cheque books.
- initiate stop payment requests.
- change personal identification number.
- trade stocks, view major indices and get stock quotes.
- view currency exchange and interest rates.
- place fixed-time deposits and change maturity instructions.
- apply for credit cards and various types of loans.

1.4.5 Computers in Supermarket

UPC & POS

UPC (Universal Product Code) is a system for uniquely identifying different products. Each product has its own unique code number on its label represented by a pattern of light and dark bars. It is commonly known as Bar code.

POS (Point of Sale) It is a special-function terminal. In retail stores, it is a combination of an electronic cash register and a bar code scanner or reader.

1.4.6 Computers in Office Applications

The advance of computer technology supports a range of improved office activities. The applications of computers in various general office works are:

Office automation

Office automation is the use of hardware, software and networks to enhance general office works such as communication among employees, and documents typing and filing. A verity of office automation software is available in market like : Word processing software, Spreadsheet software, Database management software, Presentation software, Accounting software etc.

1.4.7 Computers in Industrial Applications

Now a days more and more engineers and architects are designing products with computers. Some uses of computers in design, manufacturing and transportation are :

Computer-Aided Design (CAD)

Computer-aided design is a term that refers to the use of computers and graphics-oriented software to aid in the design process. CAD systems allow engineers to create two-dimensional or three-dimensional electronic objects. They also enable the designers to view the objects from different perspectives. For example, the engineer of Honda or Maruti while designing a vehicle model use a 3D-CAD system. The system allows the engineer to view the models at different angles. The architect is designing a building model can use a CAD system. Its use in designing electronic systems is known as *electronic design automation* (EDA). In mechanical design it is known as *mechanical design automation* (MDA) or *computer-aided drafting* (CAD), which includes the process of creating a *technical drawing* with the use of *computer software*.

Computer-Aided Manufacturing (CAM)

Computer-aided manufacturing is a term that refers to the use of computers to control equipment drilling, welding and milling in the manufacturing process. Like in Vehicle welding the computer controls the welding robot when and where to spot weld on the vehicle being assembled. The computer-controlled robot can perform tasks with precision and it is more accurate than a human. The computer-controlled equipment can perform dangerous and repetitive tasks for humans. The computer-controlled equipment reduces production costs because it does not require any annual leave, sick leave and other fringe benefits.

CAM has been considered a *numerical control* (NC) programming tool, wherein two-dimensional (2-D) or three-dimensional (3-D) models of components are generated in CAD. As with other "Computer-Aided" technologies, CAM does not eliminate the need for skilled professionals such as manufacturing engineers, NC programmers, or machinists.

1.4.8 Computers in Scientific Applications

Computers are used extensively in science. For example, meteorologists use computers to study the formation of tornadoes. Computers can also be used to simulate automobile accidents on screen. Some good uses of computers are modeling, simulation, and weather forecasting.

Computer modeling

Computer modeling is the use of computers to create abstract models of real life objects, organisms, situations, or systems. A computer model is not static, you can feed data in and examine how it behaves under certain conditions.

Computer simulation

A computer simulation refers to the use of computers to execute a model. It is represented by a computer program that gives information about the object, situation or system being examined. It is much cheaper to use a simulator to train pilots rather than using the real planes or ships.

1.4.9 Computers in Weather Forecasting

A weather observatory collects a lot of weather data from satellites, weather balloons, airplanes in flight, ground weather stations and overseas reports everyday. It is impossible for the scientists over there to process and analyze them manually. Hence, high-speed computers play a significant role. They can process the gathered data and easily give the next few days' weather forecasts. A supercomputer takes less than one hour to produce a 24-hour forecast using a 20 km by 20 km grid high-resolution numerical weather prediction model. A normal PC will take more than 5 months to perform the same calculation.

1.5 PERSONAL COMPUTER AND CHARACTERISTICS OF COMPUTER SYSTEM

As a student of Information Technology (IT) when you mention the word "technology," most people think about **computers.** Virtually everywhere around you, you will find some computerized component. The appliances in our homes have microprocessors built into them, as do your televisions, washing machine etc. Even modern cars have a computer. But the computer that everyone thinks of first is typically the **personal computer,** or **PC.**

1.5.1 Defining a PC

A PC is a **general-purpose** information processing device. It can take information from a person (through the keyboard and mouse), from a device (like a floppy disk or CD) or from the network (through a modem or a network card) and process it. Once processed, the information is shown to the user (on the monitor), stored on a device (like a hard disk) or sent somewhere else on the network (back through the modem or network card).

Fig. 1.3 *A PC*

We have lots of special-purpose processors in our lives. An MP3 Player is a specialized computer for processing MP3 files. It can't do anything else. A GPS is a specialized computer for handling GPS signals. It can't do anything else. A Game boy is a specialized computer for handling games, but it can't do anything else. A PC can do it all because it is general-purpose.

A PC is a general purpose tool built around a microprocessor. It has lots of different parts like memory, a hard disk, a modem, etc., that work together. "General purpose" means that you can do many different things with a PC. You can use it to type documents, send e-mail, browse the Web and play games.

1.5.2 Main Components of Desktop Computer

Central processing unit (CPU). The microprocessor "brain" of the computer system is called the central processing unit. Everything that a computer does is overseen by the CPU.

Memory. This is very fast storage used to hold data. It has to be fast because it connects directly to the microprocessor. There are several specific types of memory like RAM, ROM in a computer:

Random-access memory (RAM). Used to temporarily store information that the computer is currently working with.

Read-only memory (ROM). A permanent type of memory storage used by the computer for important data that do not change.

Basic input/output system (BIOS). A type of ROM that is used by the computer to establish basic communication when the computer is first turned on.

Caching. The storing of frequently used data in extremely fast RAM that connects directly to the CPU.

Virtual memory. Space on a hard disk used to temporarily store data and swap it in and out of RAM as needed.

Motherboard. This is the main circuit board that all of the other internal components connect to. The CPU and memory are usually on the motherboard. Other systems may be found directly on the motherboard or connected to it through a secondary connection. For example, a sound card can be built into the motherboard or connected through PCI.

Power supply. An electrical transformer regulates the electricity used by the computer.

Hard disk. This is large-capacity permanent storage used to hold information such as programs and documents.

Operating system. This is the basic software that allows the user to interface with the computer.

Integrated Drive Electronics (IDE) Controller. This is the primary interface for the hard drive, CD-ROM and floppy disk drive.

Peripheral Component Interconnect (PCI) Bus. The most common way to connect additional components to the computer, PCI uses a series of **slots** on the motherboard that PCI cards plug into.

SCSI. Pronounced "scuzzy, " the **small computer system interface** is a method of adding additional devices, such as hard drives or scanners, to the computer.

AGP. Accelerated Graphics Port is a very high-speed connection used by the graphics card to interface with the computer.

Sound card. This is used by the computer to record and play audio by converting analog sound into digital information and back again.

Graphics card. This translates image data from the computer into a format that can be displayed by the monitor.

1.5.3 Input/Output Devices

No matter how powerful the components inside your computer are, you need a way to interact with them. This interaction is called **input/output** (I/O). The most common types of I/O in PCs are:

Monitor. The monitor is the primary device for displaying information from the computer.

Keyboard. The keyboard is the primary device for entering information into the computer.

Mouse. The mouse is the primary device for navigating and interacting with the computer.

Removable storage. Removable storage devices allow you to add new information to your computer very easily, as well as save information that you want to carry to a different location.

Floppy disk. The most common form of removable storage, floppy disks are extremely inexpensive and easy to save information to.

CD-ROM. CD-ROM (compact disc, read-only memory) is a popular form of distribution of commercial software. Many systems now offer CD-R (recordable) and CD-RW (rewritable), which can also record.

Flash memory. Based on a type of ROM called **electrically erasable programmable read-only memory** (EEPROM), Flash memory provides fast, permanent storage. CompactFlash, SmartMedia and PCMCIA cards are all types of Flash memory.

DVD-ROM. DVD-ROM (digital versatile disc, read-only memory) is similar to CD-ROM but is capable of holding much more information.

Joy Stick. Joysticks are often used to control video games, and usually have one or more push-buttons whose state can also be read by the computer. A popular variation of the joystick used on modern video game consoles is the analog stick.

Light pen. A **light pen** is a *computer input device* in the form of a light-sensitive wand used in conjunction with a computer's *cathode-ray tube* (CRT) display.It allows the user to point to displayed objects or draw on the screen in a similar way to a *touchscreen* but with greater positional accuracy.

Track Ball. A **trackball** is a *pointing device* consisting of a *ball* held by a socket containing sensors to detect a rotation of the ball about two axes—like an upside-down *mouse* with an exposed protruding ball.Users roll the ball to position the on-screen *pointer*, using their *thumb*, *fingers*, or commonly the *palm of the hand* while using the fingertips to press the mouse buttons.

Scanner. An **image scanner**—often abbreviated to just **scanner**, is a device that optically scans images, printed text, handwriting or an object and converts it to a *digital image*.

Commonly used in offices are variations of the desktop *flatbed scanner* where the document is placed on a glass window for scanning.

CONNECTIONS : PORTS

Parallel. This port is commonly used to connect a printer.

Serial. This port is typically used to connect an external modem.

Universal Serial Bus (USB). Quickly becoming the most popular external connection, USB ports offer power and versatility and are incredibly easy to use.

FireWire (IEEE 1394). FireWire is a very popular method of connecting digital-video devices, such as camcorders or digital cameras, to your computer.

CONNECTIONS: INTERNET/NETWORK

Modem. This is the standard method of connecting to the Internet.

Local area network (LAN) card. This is used by many computers, particularly those in an Ethernet office network, to connected to each other.

Cable modem. Some people now use the cable-television system in their home to connect to the Internet.

Digital Subscriber Line (DSL) modem. This is a high-speed connection that works over a standard telephone line.

Very high bit-rate DSL (VDSL) modem. A newer variation of DSL, VDSL requires that your phone line have fiber-optic cables.

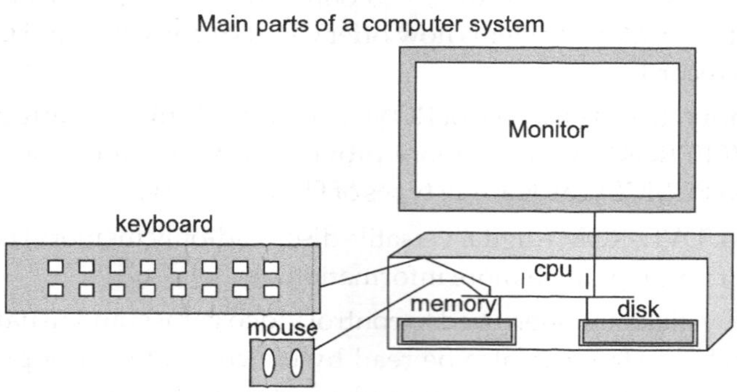

Fig. 1.4 *Parts of a computer*

1.6 CHARACTERISTICS OF COMPUTER SYSTEM

The main characteristics of computers are capability of processing information with speed, reliability, accuracy and having huge storage capacity.

1.6.1 Speed

The processing speed of computers is in the range of millions to billions of instructions per second. In other words, the time required to execute an instruction can be measured in nanoseconds or picoseconds. For example, it may take you about five minutes to find the location of a book in the library by searching the index cards. However, if you use a computerized library system to search the book's location, it may only take you about a few seconds, depending on how fast you can type. Normally, the computer only takes less than a second to process your request.

Computer operations are measured in milliseconds, microseconds, nanoseconds, and picoseconds.

Units of time	*Abbreviation*	*Fraction of a second*
Millisecond	*ms*	Thousandth: 0.001
Microsecond	μs	Millionth: 0.000001
Nanosecond	*ns*	Billionth: 0.000000001
Picoseconds	*ps*	Trillionth: 0.000000000001

1.6.2 Reliability

Computer is an electronic device built with integrated circuits that are more reliable. They have a low failure rate. Computers are most suitable to handle repetitive tasks because they do not take tea breaks and false leaves like you, and they never complain. For example, the automatic teller machines (ATM) are in operation 24 hours a day, 7 days a week, all the 365 days of the year.

1.6.3 Accuracy

Computers can generate accurate results, provided that the input data is correct and the program of instructions is reliable. They are not affected by emotion and do what they are programmed to do. Hence, they can produce consistent and accurate result like mark sheets of your university exams. If inaccurate data is entered, the computers will generate incorrect results. This is known as "Garbage In Garbage Out" **(GIGO)** but you can make it "Good In Good Out" also.

1.6.4 Storage

Imagine, if you can, how many filing-cabinet drawers would be required to hold the thousands of student records kept by your school. It would take a lot of space to store data and information in paper form. However, computers can store them on several disks that take up less space than the boxes. A diskette of 1.44 MB capacity can store 300 pieces of composition of 500 words each. You can store three 3 hours movie in a single DVD.

1.7 HISTORY OF COMPUTERS

1.7.1 Abacus (about 200 B.C.)

The abacus was a mechanical aid used for counting. Addition, subtraction, division and multiplication can be performed on a standard abacus. The frame of the abacus has a series of vertical rods on which a number of wooden beads are allowed to slide freely. A horizontal beam separates the frame into two sections, known as the upper deck and lower deck.

1.7.2 Charles Babbage's Difference Engine (1833)

Charles Babbage (1791-1871) designed this engine in an attempt to mechanize the computation of mathematical tables. He used the principle of the method of differences, *i.e.*, adding increments (=differences) to intermediate results.

1.7.3 Charles Babbage's Analytical Engine (1871)

Babbage abandoned the Difference Engine, to pursue a better idea, a general purpose computer for automatically solving mathematical equations. The Analytical Engine would be able to carry out any mathematical operation by use of stored programs. One could modify its behavior by altering two boxes of punched cards.

1.7.4 Babbage's Idea and Modern Computers

Babbage's engine separates a "store" from a "mill". These correspond to the two most important components of a modern computer the **main memory** and the **central processing unit**(CPU). A modern stored-program machine can execute any sequence of instructions stored in its memory.

1.8 GENERATION OF COMPUTERS

From abacus to PC, PDA or tiny computers, computers can be divided in given below generations :

1.8.1 First Generation (1940–1958)

First generation computers were built by using vacuum tubes. A vacuum tube is, reasonably enough, a sealed glass tube containing a vacuum in which are present several electronic elements like the cathode, anode, grid, and filament. John Atanasoff developed an electronic switch based on vacuum tubes, and used this in a special purpose computer that had capacitors as memories (essentially the same principle as modern dynamic RAM).

ENIAC (Electronic Numerical Integrator and Calculator) was developed at the Moore School of Engineering as a specialized programmable computer for computing ballistics tables for the Army. It was programmed by changing wires in patch panels, and flipping switches. John von Neumann became involved with ENIAC and saw the need for storing the program in the machine itself, resulting in the EDVAC (Electronic Discrete Variable Calculator) design. EDSAC (Electronic Delay Storage Automatic Calculator) was based closely on the EDVAC design and was the first true stored program computer to become operational.

The IBM 709 was the last of the major vacuum tube computers. It was faster than others, which had 4K 36- bit words of core memory. During this period, IBM also sold a model 650, which had a magnetic drum memory, but was low enough in cost that many were sold to universities—it was the basis for the first computers user community.

Vacuum tubes, however, are large, require a lot of power, and produce a lot of waste heat. In fact, for one rather large vacuum tube machine, it was once estimated that if its four turbine-powered air conditioners were to fail, the heat buildup in 15 minutes would be sufficient to melt the concrete and steel building containing it. It has also been estimated that if a modern computer were built with vacuum tubes, it would be the size of the Empire State Building.

1.8.2 Second Generation (1959–1964)

The transistor, invented in 1948, performed the same basic function as the vacuum tube, but with much lower voltage and current, and very little waste heat. By using a material called a semiconductor, which conducts electricity when a charge is applied to it and acts as an insulator when then the charge is removed, an electronic switch can be built. Computers of this era mostly used magnetic core memory, although registers were built from transistor circuits—eventually leading to modern solid-state memories.

Still, a computer equivalent to a modern day microprocessor, built with transistors, would have occupied several floors of the Empire State Building. A typical machine of the period had 16K 32-bit words of core, and filled a large room.

The TX-0 was the first computer built with transistors. The PDP-1 was an 18-bit machine that resulted in a family of similar machines which culminated in the PDP-15. You can see a PDP-1, still playing Space War (the world's first video game), at the Computer Museum in Boston. IBM was also building a small machine for business, the 1401, which used BCD arithmetic (base 10, represented by 4-bit words) where operations were carried out digit-serially on values of arbitrary length. This same sort of scheme would later become the basis of most pocket calculators.

1.8.3 Third Generation (1965–1970)

The concept behind the third generation of computers was integrated circuit (IC), an IC can be formed by crossing two semi conducting materials on a silicon substrate. The important point about the integrated circuit is that multiple transistors can be formed on a single substrate. Thus, a logic circuit that occupied a whole PC board can be reduced to fit on a single chip of silicon. In an IC transistors can be connected directly on the chip, they can be smaller and need less power to communicate. Thus, IC's require less power, and generate less waste heat. So the IC revolutionized computer design in two ways by shrinking the size of computers, and by making the memory technology compatible with the processing technology.

The "successor" to the PDP-8 and PDP-15 was the PDP-11, a 16-bit machine that could directly access 64KB and indirectly up to 256KB. The successor to the PDP-11 and PDP-10 was the VAX (Virtual Architecture eXtension), a 32-bit machine drawing on the experience of both families.

1.8.4 Fourth Generation (1971–present year)

Very Large Scale Integration (VLSI) was simply the next step beyond IC, to built thousands of transistors on a chip and to develop a new chip named microprocessor that lead to microcomputer. Intel developed the first microprocessor, the 4-bit 4004, in 1971, as a basis for a desktop calculator. In the next year, they produced the 8008, an 8-bit microprocessor to control a terminal. Fortunately for Intel, the terminal manufacturer chose not to use the 8008—thus forcing Intel to look for other uses for the device. Intel followed the 8008 with the 8080, a more powerful 8-bit system and the 8085 which required fewer support chips. The 80186 and 80286 are extensions of the 8086 16-bit processor. The 8088 is an 8086 with an 8-bit external data path. The 80386 is a 32-bit extension of the family and the 80486 adds floating point and virtual memory support to the processor. The Pentium family added cache memory and pipelined execution. Subsequent generations of the Pentium like P2, P3, P4 have continued to increase on-chip cache and pipeline depth the P4 has a 20-stage branch pipe as well as adding special features such as multimedia instructions.

1.9 CLASSIFICATION OF COMPUTERS

Computers can be classified under three main classes, the main factor behind classification are technology used, size, speed, cost and applications. Although with development in technology the distinction between these is becoming obsolete. Yet it is important to classify them as it is sometimes useful to differentiate the key elements and architecture among the classes of computers. Some of the type of computers are :

- Microcomputers or PC
- Minicomputers
- Mainframe computers
- Supercomputers
- Distributed or Grid computers

1.9.1 Microcomputers or PC

Computers for personal use come in all shapes and sizes, from tiny PDAs (personal digital assistant) to desktop or laptop PC (personal computer) towers. More specialized models are announced each week for users.

A microcomputer's main part is a microprocessor. The first microcomputers were built around 8-bit microprocessor chips. What do we mean by an 8-bit chip? It means that the chip can retrieve instructions/data from storage, manipulate, and process an 8-bit data at a time or we can say that the chip has a built-in 8-bit data transfer path. It was very slow. Today we have 32-bit or 64-bit microcomputers having very fast processing speed.

Most of the popular microcomputers are developed around Intel's chips like Pentium 4 or 5, while most of the minis and, super minis are built around Motorola's 68000 series chips. With the advancement of display and VLSI technology now a microcomputer is available in very small size. Some of these are laptops, notebook or PDA computers. Most of these are in small size but equivalent capacity of an older mainframe. The market for the smallest PCs is expanding rapidly. Software is becoming available for the small types of PC like the **palmtop (PPC) and handheld (HPC).** This new software is based on new operating systems like Windows CE (for Consumer Electronics) or Symbion. You may find simplified versions of the major applications you use. One big advantage for the newer programs is the ability to link the small computers to your home or work computer and coordinate the data using Bluetooth wireless technology. So you can carry a tiny computer like a PalmPilot around to enter new phone numbers and appointments and those great ideas you just had. Then later you can move this information to your main computer.

With a Tablet PC you use an electronic stylus to write on the screen, just like with a pen and paper, only your words are in digital ink. The Tablet PC saves your work just like your wrote it (as a picture), or you can let the Hand Recognition (HR) software turn your rough hand written text into regular text.

A **workstation** is part of a computer network and generally would be expected to have more than a regular desktop PC of most everything, like memory, storage space, and speed. Today we are living in the world of networking, a workstation PC can be a part of network, controlled by a **Server.**

1.9.2 Minicomputers

The **minicomputer** has become less important since the PC has gotten so powerful on its own. In fact, the ordinary new PC is much more powerful than minicomputers used in past. Originally this size was developed to handle specific tasks, like engineering and CAD calculations, that tended to tie up the main frame.

The term minicomputer originated in 1960s when it was realized that many computing tasks do not require an expensive contemporary mainframe computers but can be solved by a small, inexpensive computer. Initial minicomputers were 8 bit and 12 bit machines but by 1970s almost all minicomputers were 16 bit machines. The 16 bit minicomputers have the advantage of large instruction set and address field; and efficient storage and handling of text, in comparison to lower bit machines.

With the advancement in technology the speed, memory size and other characteristics developed and the minicomputer was then used for various stand alone or dedicated applications. The minicomputer was then used as a multi-user system like with Unix, which can be used by various users at the same time. Gradually the architectural requirement of minicomputers grew and a 32-bit minicomputer, which was called supermini, was introduced. The supermini had more peripheral devices, large memory and could support more users working simultaneously on the computer in comparison to previous minicomputers.

1.9.3 Mainframe Computers

The **mainframe** is the workhorse of the business world. A mainframe is the heart of a network of computers or terminals which allows hundreds of people to work at the same time on the same data. Earlier mainframe computers were generally 32-bit machines or on the higher side. These are suited to big organizations, to manage high volume applications. Few of the popular mainframe series are IBM, HP, etc. Mainframes are also used as central host computers in distributed systems like as Unix / Linux server.

1.9.4 Supercomputers

The **supercomputer** is the top of the heap in size, power and expense. These are used for jobs that take massive amounts of calculations, like weather forecasting, engineering design and testing, serious decryption, economic forecasting, etc. These are amongst the fastest machines in terms of processing speed and use multiprocessing techniques, where a number of processors are used to solve a problem. Lately ranges of parallel computing products, which are multiprocessors sharing common buses, have been in use in combination with the mainframe supercomputers. The supercomputers are reaching upto speeds as well over 25000 million arithmetic operations per second. India also has its supercomputer name Param. Supercomputers are mainly being used for weather forecasting, computational fluid dynamics, remote sensing, image processing, biomedical applications, etc. In India, we have one such mainframe supercomputer system- CRAY XMP-14, which is at present, being used by Meteorological Department.

India has11 supercomputers from the top 500 supercomputers in the world. Here are some names like mammoth supercomputers that serve our nation. SahasraT supercomputer is located at Supercomputer Education and Research Centre (SERC) facility at Indian Institute of Science in Bangalore.

1.9.5 Distributed or Grid Computers

The power needed for some calculations is more than even a single supercomputer can manage. In distributed computing using a PC grid many computers of all sizes can work on parts of the problem and their results are pooled. A number of current projects like **openmosix** rely on volunteers with computers connected to form a grid. The projects that need distributed computing are **highly technical** like **SETI** (Search for Extra-Terrestrial Intelligence.) used for signs of intelligent communication in radio signals coming from space.

REVIEW QUESTIONS

1. What kind of information can a computer generate (what forms can the information take)?
2. Draw a Block Diagram of computer mentioning the functions of each unit in brief. **(UTU, MCA 2006-07)**
3. Briefly explain the utility and working of CPU.
4. Write some popular applications of computers.
5. What are fourth generation computers?
6. Where we can use a super computer and why?
7. What is a PDA?
8. Name some mobile operating systems.
9. What is optical storage device?
10. Draw and describe block diagram of a computer.
11. What are the names of the different parts of the computer?
12. What is each part of a computer used for?
13. Name some input devices.
14. Name some output devices.
15. Name some storage devices.

2

COMPUTER ORGANIZATION

2.1 INTRODUCTION TO I/O

The computer will be of no use if it is not communicating with the external world. Thus, a computer must have a system to receive information from outside world and must be able to communicate results to external world. A computer system uses Input/Output devices to communicate with user. In short we use I/O devices for that.

2.2 INPUT DEVICES

Input devices are used by a user to input information (data) into the computer for processing or storage, as well as give commands to the computer. Examples of input devices are keyboards, scanners, touch screens, digital cameras, Microphones etc.

Keyboards

The keyboard is one of the most common input devices for computers. The layout of the keyboard is like that of the traditional QWERTY typewriter, there are some extra commands and function keys used to perform various user given commands. The keyboard provides facility to input data and commands to computer in text form. You can enter text in any language using a keyboard. Pressing a key on the keyboard generates a code that represents the character associated with the key.

The two main codes associated with computers are **ASCII** and **EBCDIC.** ASCII is a seven bit code, so characters generated by the keyboard are made available as a seven bit code (a total of 128 different combinations). ASCII stands for *American Standard Code for Information Interchange.* EBCDIC stands for *Extended Binary Coded Decimal Interchange Code.*

Scanners

Scanners are devices which scan documents containing text or graphics and convert them into digital form to store bitmap (picture image). The image may be in black and white, gray scale, or color depending upon the features of the scanner. The quality of a scanner refers to how many pixels (dots) per inch it can detect and reproduce in the final bitmap image.

Hand Held Scanners

Hand held scanners are generally cheap and used in market to read bar codes or in a post office by a speed post clerk. A hand held scanner is held within the hand and is moved slowly down the document scanning it as it moves.

Flatbed Scanners

Flatbed scanners allow documents or images to be placed on a flat scanning surface. It works like a photocopier machine, by moving a light along the entire length of the document or image it produce digital image. Using scanner driver software and application programs like paint or photo editor you can save the scanned image as a file. Some of popular forms of image files are .bmp, .jpg, .gif etc. Flatbed scanners come in different sizes, like A4 or A3 paper sizes, with varying resolutions.

Fig. 2.1 *Flatbed scanner*

Sheet Feed Scanners

The document is fed into the scanner, and is digitized as it passes through the scanner. It has the advantage of small size and lower cost, but has limits on the size of paper and speed of scanning. One problem with sheet fed scanners is they cannot scan books. The mechanisms used in sheet fed scanners is generally not as good as flatbed scanners.

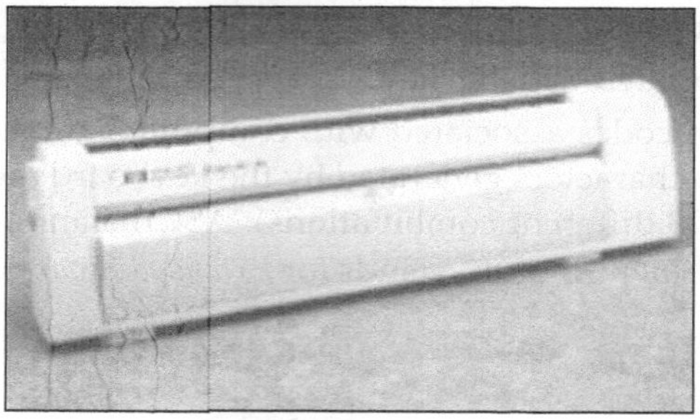

Fig. 2.2 *Sheet feed scanner*

Digital Cameras

These are cameras which convert the captured photograph directly into a digital image and store it locally inside the camera memory chip and later on you can transfer that images to a computer.

The number of pictures that can be stored depends upon the memory available within the camera and the size of each image. Digital cameras are easy to use and operate, even by new users. At present, they tend to be expensive and have limited software support for email and faxing. Software included with the Digital Camera includes download capability between the camera and PC, and image editing software for editing the images on the PC. You can use USB data cable to attach a digital camera with your PC.

Fig. 2.3 *Digital camera*

Touch Screen

Most of you must have ATM card of a bank like State bank of India or HDFC or PNB. When you operate an ATM machine, there is a touch screen. You have to touch your desired operation using your finger. So you can input your commands to ATM machine just touching the screen.

Magnetic Ink Character Recognition (MICR)

Magnetic Ink Character Recognition (MICR) devices are generally used by the banking industry to read the account numbers on cheques or on drafts directly and does the necessary processing to prevent frauds.

Optical Mark Recognition (OMR)

Optical Mark Recognition (OMR) devices can sense marks on computer readable papers. This kind of device is used by academic and testing institutions to grade aptitude tests like CPMT, PMT, where candidates mark the correct alternatives on a special sheet of paper. Even in your Technical University you have to fill up the OMR sheet given in front of your answer sheet. The optical mark recognition devices then directly read these answer sheets and the information sent to a computer for processing. Using OMR we can produce results of thousands of students within few days.

Optical Bar Code Reader (OBR)

Optical Bar Code Reader (OBR) scans a set of vertical bars of different widths for specific data and are used to read tags and merchandise in stores, medical records, library books, etc. These are available as hand held devices. Go to any good departmental store in your city and you will find a small handy OBR there.

Microphone

If you want to record your voice or any other sound to use in a software application the device used is Microphone. You can purchase a headphone with microphone for a PC and connect it through a sound card inside your PC. A software say Window sound recorder will help you to record and get .wav files.

2.3 OUTPUT DEVICES

The output normally can be produced in two ways either on a display unit/device known as softcopy or on a paper known as hardcopy. Other kinds of output can be speech or sound output.

Monitor

The most visible and familiar output device is Monitor, some times known as VDU (Visual Display Unit). On a monitor display is made up of a series of dots called 'pixels' whose pattern produces the image. Each dot on the screen is defined as a separate unit, which can be directly addressed. Since each dot can, be controlled individually there is much greater flexibility in drawing pictures. The density of pixels define the quality of picture. There is role of Graphics card also to produce pictures on monitor. Common graphics card are CGA, VGA, SVGA etc.

There are three categories of display screen technology are :

1. Cathode Ray Tube (CRT)

The main components of a CRT terminals are the electron gun, the electron beam controlled by an electromagnetic field and a phosphor coated display screen. CRT monitor used in Desktop PC 's and most common in schools, shops, railway terminals. CRT monitor can be Black & White and color. Now a days TFT screen monitors are also available in market with flat screen and slim body with light weight.

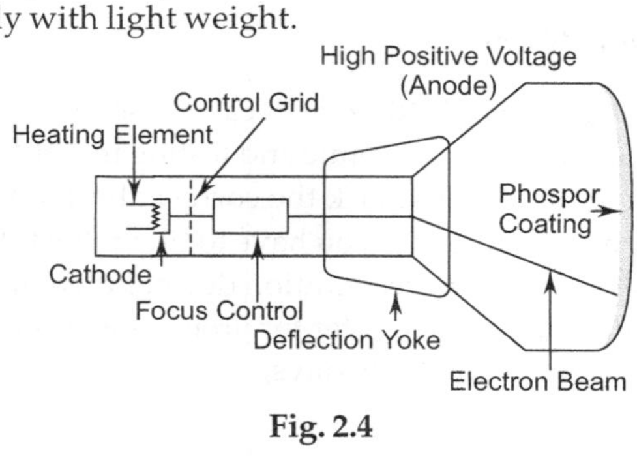

Fig. 2.4

Monitor Screens

Monitor screens are devices used to display information from the computer. In fact, Television sets include monitor screens, though in general, the monitor screens used in computer systems are of a much higher quality.

Monitors come in various sizes, commonly starting at 14", then 15", as well as 17" and 19". This is the size of the viewable screen measured across the diagonal from corner to corner. The larger the size the more expensive the monitor. Larger sizes are required for higher resolutions.

Resolution

Resolution refers to the number of dots displayed in the X (across) and Y (down) co-ordinates. Typical screens are capable of displaying 640 × 480 dots. Larger screens are required for higher resolutions, for example, 1024 × 768 resolutions displayed on a 14" screen look very small, but the same resolution on a 17" screen is much easier to read. The following table shows some common resolutions.

Standard	*Resolution, x, y, colors*
CGA	640 × 200 × 2
EGA	640 × 350 × 16
VGA	640 × 480 × 256
SVGA	800 × 600 × 256
XGA	1024 × 768 × 65536

Refresh Rate

Another term used with monitors is **refresh rate.** This refers to the number of times per second that the image is redrawn on the monitor screen. A refresh rate of 60Hz means the images is redrawn 60 times a second. Typical refresh rates are 60Hz, 72Hz and 75Hz. Higher refresh rates are required for larger resolutions, else the viewer tend to notice the image on the screen flicker. The images on the screen have to be refreshed at a reasonable rate (greater than 50Hz), otherwise the human eye perceives the image as flickering.

Dot Pitch

This is the distance in millimeters between the phosphor triads. Typically it is .28 mm, and the smaller the better, resulting in a much crisper sharper display. Obviously, the smaller dot pitch monitors like .26 mm are very expensive.

2. Liquid Crystal Display (LCD)

First introduced in watches and clocks in 1970s, LCD is now applied to display devices. The major advantage of LCD is the low energy consumption. The CRT (Cathode Ray Tube) is replaced by liquid crystal to produce the image. This also have color capability. These are commonly used in portable devices like Palmtop, Laptop or Mobile handsets screens.

3. Projection Displays

The personal size screen of the previous displays is replaced by a large screen upon, which images are normally used for large group presentation. These systems can be connected to computer and whatever appears on the computer terminal gets enlarged and projected on a large screen. These are popularly used in seminars, classrooms, marketing or public presentations.

Printers

Printers are used for producing output on paper. There are a large variety of printing devices, which can be classified according to the print quality and the printing speeds. There are two main classifications of printers.

1. Impact

In impact printers, the print head mechanism strikes an inked ribbon located between the print head and the paper. The general features of impact printers are :

- uses force by applying hammer pins to strike the paper
- slow speed in characters per second
- prints on most paper types
- transparencies can not be used
- multiple copies may be printed at once using carbon paper.

The two main types of impact printers are **Dot-Matrix** and **Daisy-Wheel.**

Dot-Matrix Printers

Dot matrix printers are suitable for draft copies and home use, where quality of the finished type is not an issue like to print bills, reports or tickets in railway reservation system. Dot matrix printers have tended to become cheap, but now are being quickly overtaken by cheap LaserJet and Inkjet printers, which offer higher printing speeds and superior quality, as well as good color.

Daisy-Wheel Printers

Daisy wheel printers use a spoke wheel with characters placed at the end of each spoke. A print hammer is used to strike the desired character onto the ink ribbon and then the paper. The spoke wheel of characters is rotated around until the desired character is under the print hammer, then the print hammer is fired which strikes the character, pushing it against the ink ribbon, and onto the paper, creating the character. Different fonts are available by changing the print wheels. Daisy wheel printers were commonly found in typewriters

2. Non-Impact

With non-impact printers, the print head does not make contact with the paper, and no inked ribbon is necessary. The general features of non-impact printers are :

- print head does not make contact with the paper
- higher speed in characters per second is possible
- prints on most paper types but better quality obtained with better paper
- transparencies can be print easily.

The three main types of non-impact printers are Desk or Laser jet, ink-jet and thermal.

Laser-Jet Printers

Laser jet printers are very common today. This is a high quality, high speed, and high volume technology, which works in non-impact fashion on plain paper or pre-printed forms. Printing is achieved by deflecting laser beam on to the photosensitive surface of a drum and the latent image attracts the toner to the image areas. The toner is then electro statically transferred to the paper and fixed into a permanent image. Speeds can range from 10 pages a minute to about 200 pages per minute. This technology is relatively expensive but is becoming very popular because of the quality, speed and noiseless operations. Mostly used by desk top publishing shops.

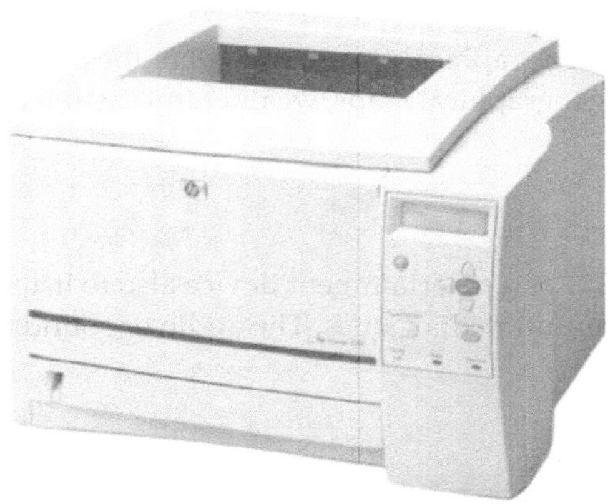

Fig. 2.5 *Laser Printer*

Ink-Jet Printers

Ink-Jet printers are part of home computers for low cost printing. They offer good quality at an affordable price. In Ink-Jet printer ink is forced through a small nozzle producing a small droplet of ink, which is propelled towards the screen surface to produce the image. Print quality is high, speed is slow, typically about 100 cps but good results may require special non-absorbing paper, overhead transparencies require special material to print.

Thermal Printers

Thermal printers are generally used in low cost printers and fax machines. The print head contains high temperature heat elements arranged in a matrix when the print head is pressed against the paper, the heat elements burn small holes in the paper to form the character. Some thermal printers use a silvery grey paper, which is an aluminum surface coating. When the print head burns away this layer, it exposes a dyed layer underneath. One application for thermal printers is the production of bar codes on products.

Fig. 2.6 *Thermal Printer*

Plotters

To produce large size graphical outputs on paper the plotters are used. Plotters are used to take print outs of geographical maps, weather forecasting data or architectural design of an building.

Speakers

You can use you PC as a entertainment device also to listen your favorite songs, to watch movies or to play multimedia games. The audio or sound can be hear with the help of PC speakers.

2.4 POINTING DEVICES

A variety of pointing devices are used to move the cursor on the screen to click a Icon or file in GUI operating systems like Windows. The most commonly used pointing devices are Mouse, Joystick, Trackball, Glidepad etc.

Mouse

Mouse is most popular and common pointing device to work with a PC or on Internet. A Scroll mouse has three buttons to click and one ball to move the cursor in a desired direction when you move the mouse on surface. Buttons on the mouse can be clicked or double-clicked to perform tasks, like to select an icon on the screen or to open the selected document.

There are new mice in market now known as Optical Mouse that don't have a ball. They use a laser to sense the motion of the mouse instead.

Trackball

Instead of moving the whole mouse around, the user rolls the trackball only, which is on the top or side. It does not need as much desk space as a mouse. Is not as tiring since less motion is needed. Requires fine control of the ball with just one finger or thumb. Repeated motions of the same muscles is tiring and can cause carpal tunnel syndrome.

Glidepad

Uses a touch sensitive pad for controlling cursor. The user slides finger across the pad and the cursor follows the finger movement. For clicking there are buttons, or you can tap on the pad with a finger. The glidepad is a popular alternate pointing device for laptops. It does not need as much desk space as a mouse. It can readily be built into the keyboard. It has finer resolution. That is, to achieve the same cursor movement onscreen takes less movement of the finger on the glidepad than it does mouse movement.

2.5 I/O MODULE

In a computer system, the role of microprocessor is to control both the Input and Output devices. There are separate units to control input and output signals. An I/O module works as a mediator between the processor and I/O devices. It controls the data exchange between the external devices and main memory; or external devices and CPU registers.

Therefore, an I/O module provide an interface internal to the computer which connect it to CPU and main memory and an interface external to the computer connecting it to external device or peripheral. The I/O module should not only communicate the information from CPU to I/O device, but it should also co-ordinate these two. In addition since there are speed differences between CPU and I/O devices, the I/O module should have facilities like buffer (storage area) and error detection mechanism.

The input/output module interfaces (I/O module) is normally connected to the computer system on one end and one or more Input/Output devices on the other. Normally, an I/O module can control one or more peripheral devices. An I/O module is needed because of following reasons :

(*a*) Diversity and variety of I/O devices makes it difficult to incorporate all the peripheral device logic (like. its control commands, data format etc.) into CPU. This in turn will also reduce flexibility of using any new input or output device.

(*b*) The I/O devices are normally slower than that of memory and CPU, therefore, it is suggested not to use them on high-speed bus directly for communication purpose.

(*c*) The data format and word length used by the peripheral may be quite different than that of a CPU.

In computer system there can be two types of I/O interface :

1. Parallel Interface
2. Serial Interface

Parallel Interface

In parallel interface multiple bits can be transferred simultaneously. The parallel interfaces are normally used for high-speed peripherals such as tapes and disks. A common parallel interface is printer.

Serial Interface

In serial interface only one line is used to transmit data, therefore, only one bit is transferred at a time. Serial interface is used for serial printers and terminals. The most common serial interface is RS-232-C. Mouse are usually connected on serial port. Serial ports work slower than parallel ports.

2.6 CPU OR MICROPROCESSOR

The computer you are using to read any document or to write your C program uses a **microprocessor** to do its work. The microprocessor is the brain of any normal computer, whether it is a desktop machine, a server or a laptop. The microprocessor you are using might be a Pentium, a K6, a PowerPC, a Sparc or any of the many other brands and types of microprocessors, but they all do approximately the same thing in approximately the same way.

A microprocessor is also known as a CPU or central processing unit, is a complete computation engine that is fabricated on a single chip. The first microprocessor was the Intel 4004, introduced in 1971. The 4004 was not very powerful, all it could do was add and subtract, and it could only do that 4 bits at a time. But it was amazing that everything was on one chip. Prior to the 4004, engineers built computers either from collections of chips or from discrete components (transistors wired one at a time). The 4004 powered one of the first portable electronic calculators.

The first microprocessor to make it into a home computer was the Intel 8080, a complete 8-bit computer on one chip, introduced in 1974. If you are familiar with the PC market and its history, you know that the PC market moved from the 8088 to the 80286 to the 80386 to the 80486 to the Pentium to the Pentium II to the Pentium III to the Pentium 4. All of these microprocessors are made by Intel and all of them are improvements on the basic design of the 8088.

Name	*Year*	*Transistors*	*Microns*	*Clock speed*	*Data width*	*MIPS*
8080	1974	6,000	6	2 MHz	8 bits	0.64
8088	1979	29,000	3	5 MHz	16 bits8-bit bus	0.33
80286	1982	134,000	1.5	6 MHz	16 bits	1
80386	1985	275,000	1.5	16 MHz	32 bits	5
80486	1989	1,200,000	1	25 MHz	32 bits	20
Pentium	1993	3,100,000	0.8	60 MHz	32 bits64-bit bus	100
Pentium II	1997	7,500,000	0.35	233 MHz	32 bits64-bit bus	~300
Pentium III	1999	9,500,000	0.25	450 MHz	32 bits64-bit bus	~510
Pentium 4	2000	42,000,000	0.18	1.5 GHz	32 bits64-bit bus	~1,700
Pentium 4 "Prescott"	2004	125,000,000	0.09	3.6 GHz	32 bits64-bit bus	~7,000
Core i5-750	2009	774,000,000	0.045	2.67 GHz	64 Bit	42,820
Core i7-970	2010	1170,000,000	0.032	3.2 GHz	64 Bit	147,600

- The **date** is the year that the processor was first introduced. Many processors are re-introduced at higher clock speeds for many years after the original release date.
- **Transistors** is the number of transistors on the chip. You can see that the number of transistors on a single chip has risen steadily over the years.
- **Microns** is the width, in microns, of the smallest wire on the chip. For comparison, a human hair is 100 microns thick. As the feature size on the chip goes down, the number of transistors rises.
- **Clock speed** is the maximum rate that the chip can be clocked at. Clock speed will make more sense in the next section.
- **Data Width** is the width of the ALU. An 8-bit ALU can add/subtract/multiply/etc. two 8-bit numbers, while a 32-bit ALU can manipulate 32-bit numbers. An 8-bit ALU would have to execute four instructions to add two 32-bit numbers, while a 32-bit ALU can do it in one instruction. In many cases, the external data bus is the same width as the ALU, but not always. The 8088 had a 16-bit ALU and an 8-bit bus, while the modern Pentiums fetch data 64 bits at a time for their 32-bit ALUs.
- **MIPS** stands for "millions of instructions per second" and is a rough measure of the performance of a CPU. Modern CPUs can do so many different things that MIPS ratings lose a lot of their meaning, but you can get a general sense of the relative power of the CPUs from this column.

The Functions of the CPU

The CPU (Central Processing Unit) performs the following tasks by executing Instructions of some specific program stored in Main Memory :

- Controlling all peripheral devices.
- Communicating with all types of Devices
- Recognizing user commands
- Inputting Data
- Producing Output (on screen/or on printer) after obtaining Data from Main/Secondary Memory.
- Performing arithmetic & logical operations. As per Specified Instruction(s) of the executing program.

Microprocessor Instructions

Even the incredibly simple microprocessor shown in the previous example will have a fairly large set of instructions that it can perform. The collection of instructions is implemented as bit patterns, each one of which has a different meaning when loaded into the instruction register. Humans are not particularly good at remembering bit patterns, so a set of short words are defined to represent the different bit patterns. This collection of words is called the **assembly language** of the processor. An **assembler** can translate the words into their bit patterns very easily, and then the output of the assembler is placed in memory for the microprocessor to execute.

Here's the set of assembly language instructions that the designer might create for the simple microprocessor as an example:

- **LOADA mem** – Load register A from memory address
- **LOADB mem** – Load register B from memory address
- **CONB con** – Load a constant value into register B
- **SAVEB mem** – Save register B to memory address
- **SAVEC mem** – Save register C to memory address
- **ADD** – Add A and B and store the result in C
- **SUB** – Subtract A and B and store the result in C
- **MUL** – Multiply A and B and store the result in C
- **DIV** – Divide A and B and store the result in C
- **COM** – Compare A and B and store the result in test
- **JUMP addr** – Jump to an address
- **JEQ addr** – Jump, if equal, to address
- **JNEQ addr** – Jump, if not equal, to address
- **JG addr** – Jump, if greater than, to address
- **JGE addr** – Jump, if greater than or equal, to address
- **JL addr** – Jump, if less than, to address
- **JLE addr** – Jump, if less than or equal, to address
- **STOP** – Stop execution

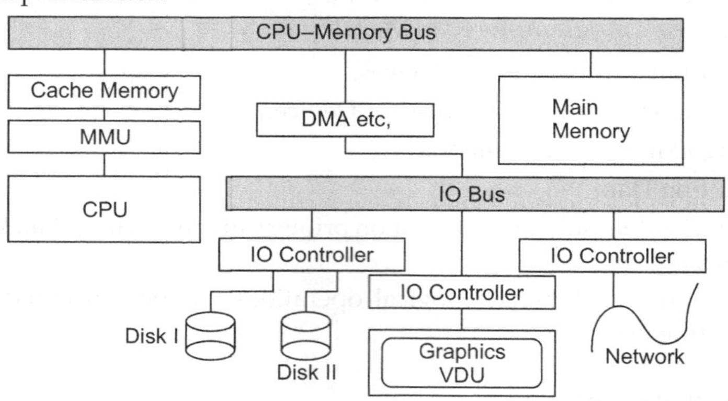

Fig. 2.7 *Computer Architecture*

The CPU Bus

Address Bus. Group of lines that is used to carry address information from the CPU to the concerned device(s). Address is one that helps the CPU to select one among many devices. Hence it is **unidirectional.**

Data Bus. The group of lines used to carry data/information from the device to CPU & vice versa. It is always *bi-directional.*

Control Bus. The group of lines that enables the CPU to control various activities by *sending* appropriate commands as well as monitor status of the concerned device e.g. *Read Signal, Write Signal, Status Set Signal.*

Each bus consists of a number of lines, which is represented in a compact manner.

2.7 MEMORY

All of the components in your computer, such as the CPU, the hard drive and the operating system, work together as a team, and memory is one of the most essential parts of this team. From the moment you turn your computer on until the time you shut it down, your CPU is constantly using memory.

The Functions of Main/Physical Memory

1. Acts as the temporary storage brain of the Computer System.
2. Stores inputted commands, data, program as well as intermediate & final results.
3. CPU stores data into it and retrieves data as well as Instructions from it.
4. It is composed of several locations, each location size is normally one byte or its integer multiple. (1 byte = 8 Bits = 1 Character).
5. It is finite sized (typical capacity 256 Mbytes(MB)), Electronic, Volatile and Random Access (Time taken to access any location is identical) and relatively costly.
6. The main memory can be viewed as a very large sized, one dimensional matrix/array, a column vector. Time taken to access any element/location happens to be the same.
7. Some part of it is non volatile like Read Only Memory, some of it is Read Write Memory [RWM] commonly termed as RAM (Random Access Memory).
8. Now a days Main Memory is connected to the CPU through a high speed electronic Memory known as the Cache Memory.

Although memory is technically any form of electronic storage, it is used most often to identify fast, temporary forms of storage. If your computer's CPU had to constantly access the hard drive to retrieve every piece of data it needs, it would operate very slowly. When the information is kept in memory, the CPU can access it much more quickly. Most forms of memory are intended to store data temporarily.

When you think about it, it's amazing how many different types of electronic memory you encounter in daily life. Many of them are :

- RAM
- ROM
- Cache
- Dynamic RAM (DRAM)
- Static RAM (SRAM)
- Flash memory
- Memory Sticks
- Virtual memory

- Video memory
- BIOS

You already know that the computer you have has memory. What you may not know is that most of the electronic items you use every day have some form of memory also. Here are just a few examples of the many items that use memory, Like :

- Cell phones
- PDAs
- Game consoles
- Car
- VCD /DVD Players
- TVs

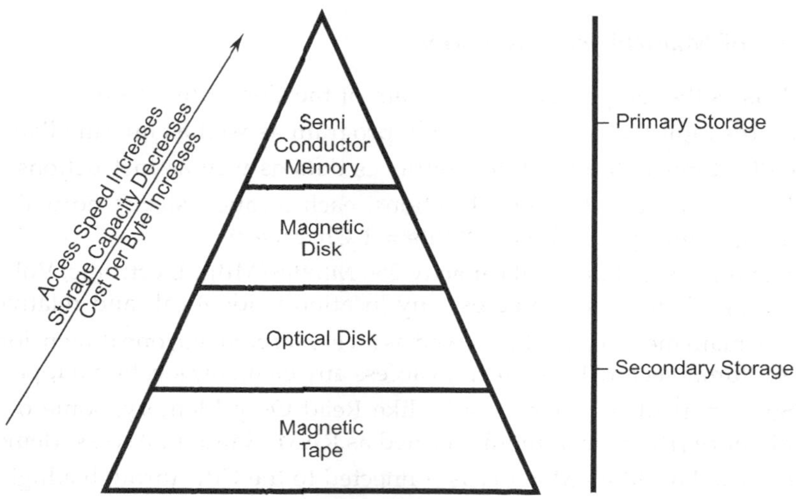

Fig. 2.8 *Memory Triangle*

As you can see in the diagram above, the CPU accesses memory according to a distinct hierarchy. Whether it comes from permanent storage (the hard drive) or input (the keyboard), most data goes in **random access memory** (RAM) first. The CPU then stores pieces of data it will need to access, often in a **cache**, and maintains certain special instructions in the **register.**

Let's take a look at a typical scenario of working of memory in computers :

- You turn the computer on.
- The computer loads data from **read-only memory** (ROM) and performs a **power-on self-test** (POST) to make sure all the major components are functioning properly. As part of this test, the **memory controller** checks all of the memory addresses with a quick **read/write** operation to ensure that there are no errors in the memory chips. Read/write means that data is written to a bit and then read from that bit.
- The computer loads the **basic input/output system** (BIOS) from ROM. The BIOS provides the most basic information about storage devices, boot sequence, security, **Plug and Play** (auto device recognition) capability and a few other items.

- The computer loads the **operating system** (OS) from the hard drive into the system's RAM. Generally, the critical parts of the operating system are maintained in RAM as long as the computer is on. This allows the CPU to have immediate access to the operating system, which enhances the performance and functionality of the overall system.
- When you open an **application,** it is loaded into RAM. To conserve RAM usage, many applications load only the essential parts of the program initially and then load other pieces as needed.
- After an application is loaded, any **files** that are opened for use in that application are loaded into RAM.
- When you **save** a file and **close** the application, the file is written to the specified storage device, and then it and the application are purged from RAM.

In the list above, every time something is loaded or opened, it is placed into RAM. This simply means that it has been put in the computer's **temporary storage area** so that the CPU can access that information more easily. The CPU requests the data it needs from RAM, processes it and writes new data back to RAM in a **continuous cycle.** In most computers, this shuffling of data between the CPU and RAM happens millions of times every second. When an application is closed, it and any accompanying files are usually **purged** (deleted) from RAM to make room for new data. If the changed files are not saved to a permanent storage device before being purged, they are lost.

Byte Organized Memory VS. Multi Byte CPU

In your computer the main memory is byte organized but modern day CPUs can handle multi byte words (usually integral multiples) say 4 bytes. In such a case one of the two following storage pattern is followed :

Little Endian : Lower Memory Address holds lower order byte.(Intel Convention).

Big Endian : Lower Memory Address holds Higher Order byte.

2.8 RAM

Random Access Memory (RAM) is the best known form of computer memory. RAM is considered "random access" because you can access any memory cell directly if you know the row and column that intersect at that cell.

The opposite of RAM is **serial access memory** (SAM). SAM stores data as a series of memory cells that can only be accessed sequentially (like a cassette tape). If the data is not in the current location, each memory cell is checked until the needed data is found. SAM works very well for memory **buffers,** where the data is normally stored in the order in which it will be used (a good example is the texture buffer memory on a video card). RAM data, on the other hand, can be accessed in any order.

Design of RAM

Similar to a microprocessor, a memory chip is an **integrated circuit** (IC) made of millions of transistors and capacitors. In the most common form of computer memory, **dynamic**

random access memory (DRAM), a transistor and a capacitor are paired to create a **memory cell,** which represents a single bit of data. The capacitor holds the bit of information—a 0 or a 1 (see How Bits and Bytes Work for information on bits). The transistor acts as a switch that lets the control circuitry on the memory chip read the capacitor or change its state.

A capacitor is like a small bucket that is able to store electrons. To store a 1 in the memory cell, the bucket is filled with electrons. To store a 0, it is emptied. The problem with the capacitor's bucket is that it has a leak. In a matter of a few milliseconds a full bucket becomes empty. Therefore, for dynamic memory to work, either the CPU or the **memory controller** has to come along and recharge all of the capacitors holding a 1 before they discharge. To do this, the memory controller reads the memory and then writes it right back. This refresh operation happens automatically thousands of times per second.

DRAM & SRAM

SRAM uses a completely different technology. In static RAM, a form of flip-flop holds each bit of memory. A flip-flop for a memory cell takes four or six transistors along with some wiring, but never has to be refreshed. This makes static RAM significantly faster than dynamic RAM. However, because it has more parts, a static memory cell takes up a lot more space on a chip than a dynamic memory cell. Therefore, you get less memory per chip, and that makes static RAM a lot more expensive. So static RAM is fast and expensive, and dynamic RAM is less expensive and slower. So static RAM is used to create the CPU's speed-sensitive cache, while dynamic RAM forms the larger system RAM space.

DIMM/DIP

Memory chips in desktop computers originally used a pin configuration called **dual inline package** (DIP) or **dual inline memory module** (DIMM). This pin configuration could be soldered into holes on the computer's motherboard or plugged into a socket that was soldered on the motherboard. This method worked fine when computers typically operated on a couple of megabytes or less of RAM, but as the need for memory grew, the number of chips needing space on the motherboard increased.

The solution was to place the memory chips, along with all of the support components, on a separate **printed circuit board** (PCB) that could then be plugged into a special connector (**memory bank**) on the motherboard. Most of these chips use a **small outline J-lead** (SOJ) pin configuration, but quite a few manufacturers use the **thin small outline package** (TSOP) configuration as well. The key difference between these newer pin types and the original DIP configuration is that SOJ and TSOP chips are **surface-mounted** to the PCB. In other words, the pins are soldered directly to the surface of the board, not inserted in holes or sockets.

Memory chips are normally only available as part of a card called a **module.** You've probably seen memory listed as 8x32 or 4x16. These numbers represent the number of the chips multiplied by the capacity of each individual chip, which is measured in **megabits** (Mb), or one million bits. Take the result and divide it by eight to get the number of megabytes on that module. For example, 4x32 means that the module has four 32-megabit chips. Multiply 4 by 32 and you get 128 megabits.

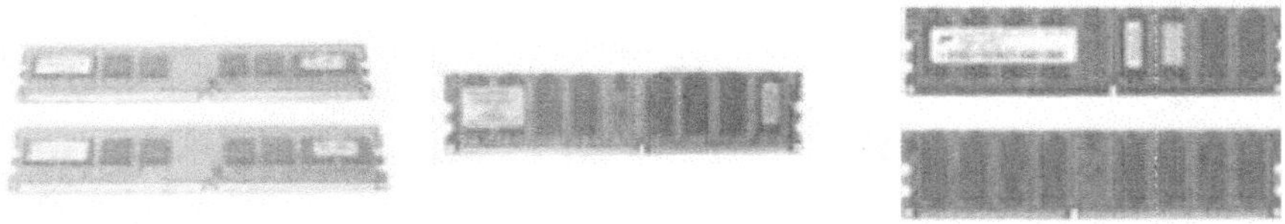

Fig. 2.9 *RAM chips*

2.9 ROM

Read-only memory (ROM), also known as **firmware,** is an integrated circuit programmed with specific data when it is manufactured. ROM chips are used not only in computers, but in most other electronic items as well.

ROM Types

There are five basic ROM types:

- ROM
- PROM
- EPROM
- EEPROM
- Flash memory

Each type has unique characteristics, but two things in common:

- Data stored in these chips is **nonvolatile,** it is not lost when power is removed.
- Data stored in these chips is either **unchangeable** or requires a special operation to change (unlike RAM, which can be changed as easily as it is read).

  This means that removing the power source from the chip will not cause it to lose any data.

PROM

Creating ROM chips totally from scratch is time-consuming and very expensive in small quantities. For this reason, mainly, developers created a type of ROM known as **programmable read-only memory** (PROM). Blank PROM chips can be bought inexpensively and coded by anyone with a special tool called a **programmer.** PROM chips have a grid of columns and rows just as ordinary ROMs do. The difference is that every intersection of a column and row in a PROM chip has a **fuse** connecting them. A charge sent through a column will pass through the fuse in a cell to a grounded row indicating a value of 1. Since all the cells have a fuse, the initial **(blank)** state of a PROM chip is all 1s. To change the value of a cell to 0, you use a programmer to send a specific amount of current to the cell. The higher voltage breaks the connection between the column and row by **burning** out the fuse. This process is known as **burning the PROM.** PROMs can only be programmed once. They are more fragile than ROMs. A jolt of static electricity can easily cause fuses in the PROM to burn out, changing essential bits from 1 to 0. But blank PROMs are inexpensive and are great for prototyping the data for a ROM before committing to the costly ROM fabrication process.

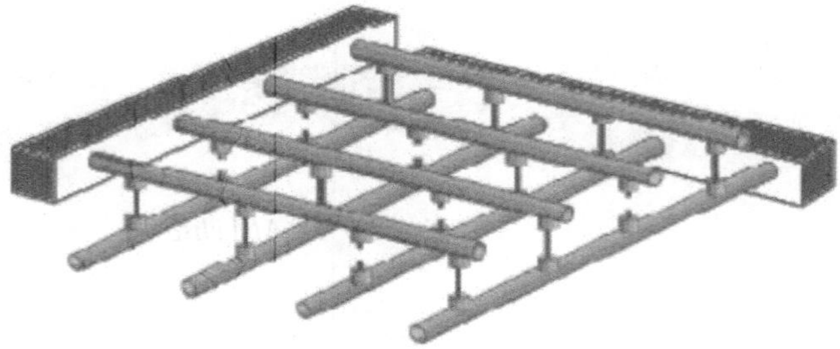

Fig. 2.10 *PROM*

EPROM

Working with ROMs and PROMs can be a wasteful business. Even though they are inexpensive per chip, the cost can add up over time. **Erasable programmable read-only memory** (EPROM) addresses this issue. EPROM chips can be rewritten many times. Erasing an EPROM requires a special tool that emits a certain frequency of ultraviolet (UV) light. EPROMs are configured using an EPROM programmer that provides voltage at specified levels depending on the type of EPROM used.

Once again we have a grid of columns and rows. In an EPROM, the cell at each intersection has two transistors. The two transistors are separated from each other by a thin oxide layer. One of the transistors is known as the **floating gate** and the other as the **control gate.** The floating gate's only link to the row **(wordline)** is through the control gate. As long as this link is in place, the cell has a value of 1. To change the value to 0 requires a curious process called **Fowler-Nordheim tunneling. Tunneling** is used to alter the placement of electrons in the floating gate. An electrical charge, usually 10 to 13 volts, is applied to the floating gate. The charge comes from the column **(bitline),** enters the floating gate and drains to a ground.

This charge causes the floating-gate transistor to act like an electron gun. The excited electrons are pushed through and trapped on the other side of the thin oxide layer, giving it a negative charge. These negatively charged electrons act as a barrier between the control gate and the floating gate. A device called a **cell sensor** monitors the level of the charge passing through the floating gate. If the flow through the gate is greater than 50 percent of the charge, it has a value of 1. When the charge passing through drops below the 50-percent threshold, the value changes to 0. A blank EPROM has all of the gates fully open, giving each cell a value of 1.

To rewrite an EPROM, you must erase it first. To erase it, you must supply a level of energy strong enough to break through the negative electrons blocking the floating gate. In a standard EPROM, this is best accomplished with UV light at a frequency of 253.7. Because this particular frequency will not penetrate most plastics or glasses, each EPROM chip has a quartz window on top of it. The EPROM must be very close to the eraser's light source, within an inch or two, to work properly. An EPROM eraser is not selective, it will erase the entire EPROM. The EPROM must be removed from the device it is in and placed under the UV light of the EPROM eraser for several minutes. An EPROM that is left under too long can become **over-erased.** In such a case, the EPROM's floating gates are charged to the point that they are unable to hold the electrons at all.

EEPROM

Though EPROMs are a big step up from PROMs in terms of reusability, they still require dedicated equipment and a labor-intensive process to remove and reinstall them each time a change is necessary. Also, changes cannot be made incrementally to an EPROM; the whole chip must be erased. **Electrically erasable programmable read-only memory** (EEPROM) chips remove the data using **electric field.**

In EEPROMs:

- The chip does not have to removed to be rewritten.
- The entire chip does not have to be completely erased to change a specific portion of it.
- Changing the contents does not require additional dedicated equipment.

Instead of using UV light, you can return the electrons in the cells of an EEPROM to normal with the localized application of an **electric field** to each cell. This erases the targeted cells of the EEPROM, which can then be rewritten. EEPROMs are changed 1 byte at a time, which makes them versatile but slow. In fact, EEPROM chips are too slow to use in many products that make quick changes to the data stored on the chip.

Flash Memory

Manufacturers responded to this limitation of EEPROM with **Flash memory,** a type of EEPROM that uses **in-circuit wiring** to erase by applying an electrical field to the entire chip or to predetermined sections of the chip called **blocks.** Flash memory works much faster than traditional EEPROMs because it writes data in chunks, usually 512 bytes in size, instead of 1 byte at a time.

Flash memory is used for easy and fast information storage in such devices as digital cameras and home video game consoles. It is used more as a hard drive than as RAM. In fact, Flash memory is considered a **solid state** storage device. Solid state means that there are no moving parts—everything is electronic instead of mechanical.

Here are a few examples of Flash memory:

- Your computer's BIOS chip
- CompactFlash (most often found in digital cameras)
- SmartMedia (most often found in digital cameras)
- Memory Stick (most often found in digital cameras)
- PCMCIA Type I and Type II memory cards (used as solid-state disks in laptops)
- Memory cards for video game consoles

Cache Memory

Computers operate at very high speeds. Current CPU's operate at speeds of 400 million cycles per second or more. What this means is, in every 2.5 nanoseconds, the computer can execute a complete processing loop. This is the speed even a Pentium III base computer.

The problem is, while the computer can operate at this speed, it has to get the program and data to execute from somewhere.

Hard drives are very slow compared to the CPU. RAM is much faster than a hard drive, but still 4-5 times slower than your CPU, so CPU has to wait for fetching data from RAM. The solution of this problem is Cache Ram which is extremely fast and capable of delivering data at or near the speed of the CPU.

In modern computers the process of computer working is first program and data is loaded from the hard drive into RAM. From RAM it is loaded into cache RAM, and from there it is executed by the CPU.

Cache memory is random access memory which work between RAM and CPU as very fast buffer and computer microprocessor can access data more quickly than it can access from regular RAM.

In addition to cache memory, one can think of RAM itself as a cache of memory for hard disk storage since all of RAM's contents come from the hard disk initially when you turn your computer on and load the operating system, you are loading it into RAM and later as you start new applications and access new data. RAM can also contain a special area called a disk cache that contains the data most recently read in from the hard disk.

Importance of Cache Memory

Cache RAM and normal RAM are very similar in the way they work. Cache is just extremely fast, and expensive. That is why there is so very little of cache RAM used compare to RAM because it is expensive. In order to reduce the cost of computers, hard drives are used to store huge amounts of data because they are cheaper than a megabyte of RAM storage.

RAM is much more expensive, over 100 times more expensive than a hard drives. Cache RAM is a lot more expensive than regular RAM. In order to reduce the cost of computers, engineers have designed controllers that load data and instructions from the hard drive when they may be needed into RAM. When they are not needed in RAM, something else is loaded. Then, as the computer runs, whatever is needed for that time is loaded into cache. When the controller does a pretty good job at predicting what is needed, the computer will operate at close to its full speed. When the controllers don't do a good job, things will slow down while the CPU waits for data to be loaded from the hard drive to RAM, and then into the cache before it can continue.

So you can think cache memory as where the computer gets the program and data it needs to execute. If the cache is slower than your CPU, your computer will be slow. But if it is faster, your computer won't speed up. So you want to make sure the cache is fast enough for your computer, but getting faster cache memory is a waste of money. Second, the amount of cache memory also affects the speed of your computer. In general, the more cache, the faster your computer will go. Most computers have a fairly small limit on the amount of cache RAM possible.

2.10 SECONDARY STORAGE OR AUXILIARY MEMORY

As discussed earlier the cost of RAM is very high and the semiconductor RAMs are mostly volatile, therefore, it is highly likely that a secondary cheap media should be used which should show some sort of permanence of storage and should be relatively inexpensive. The magnetic material was found to be inexpensive and quite long lasting material. Therefore, became an ideal choice to do so. Magnetic tape and magnetic disks are commonly used as storage media. With the advancements in the optical technology now the optical disks are trying to make inroads as one of the major external memory.

Magnetic Disk

A magnetic disk is a circular platter of plastic, which is coated with magnetized material. One of the key components of a magnetic disk is a conducting coil named as Head which performs the job of reading and writing on the magnetic surface. The head remains stationary while the disk rotates below it for reading or writing operation.

Diskette/Floppy Disk

A floppy disk is made of a flexible thin sheet of plastic material with a magnetic coating and grooves arranged in concentric circles with tracks. Floppy disk becomes a convenient recording medium to transport information from one location to another. Disk is removable from the reading device attached to the computer and therefore provides unlimited storage capacity. The floppy disks of today are available in two sizes 5.25 inches and 3.5 inches and their capacity ranges from 360 KB to 1.44 MB per disk.

Fig. 2.11 *Floppy disk*

Internal Structure

The head of disk is a small coil and reads or writes on the position of the disk rotating below it, therefore, the data is stored in concentric set of rings refer figure. These are called tracks. The width of a track is equal to the width of the head. To minimize the interference of magnetic fields and to minimize the errors of misalignment of head, the adjacent tracks are separated by inter track gaps. As we go towards the outer tracks the size of a track increase but to simplify electronics same number of bits are stored on each track. The data is transferred from and to the disks in blocks. Block is a section of disk data and is normally equal to a sector. A track is divided into 10-100 sectors and these sectors should be either fixed or variable length sectors. Two adjacent sectors are separated by intra-track gaps. This helps in reducing the precision requirements of sectors. To identify the sector position normally there may be a starting point on a track or a starting and end point of each sector.

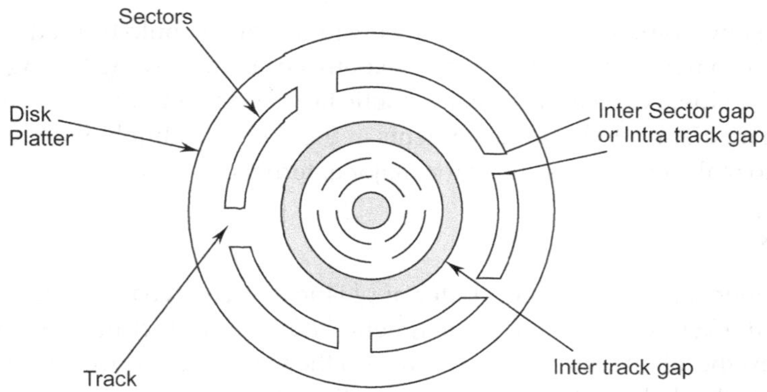

Fig. 2.12 *Internal structure*

Several other kinds of removable magnetic media are in use, such as the popular Zip disk. All of these have a much higher capacity than floppy disks. Some kinds of new computers come without a floppy disk drive at all. Each type of media requires its own drive. The drives and disks are much more expensive than floppy drives and disks, but then, you are getting much larger capacities.

Winchester Disk or Hard Disk

This is a sealed rigid magnetic oxide medium disk, which typically holds 10 GB to 100 GB of data. Hard or Winchester disks are not removable from the drive and since they are sealed dust and other contaminations, which are likely in a floppy disk, are minimized. These provide substantially faster data access compared to floppy disk and provide very large data storage for on-line retrieval.

Internal Structure

Sides : The magnetic coating if applied to both the sides of the platter is called as double sided disks. The data can be recorded on either side of these disks. Some inexpensive disks were initially single sided.

Platters : Some disks have single platter e.g. floppy disks while some disks have multiple platters which are stacked vertically, normally at a distance of an inch. This is known as disk pack. In disk pack one additional term cylinder is defined which is the ring of all co-centric tracks see figure. A disk pack can contain multiple heads mounted with the same arm.

Access Time on Disk

Disk operates in semi-random mode of operation and normally is referenced block wise. The data access time on disk consists of two main components.

Seek time: Time to position the head on a specific track. On a fixed head disks it is the time taken by electronic circuit to select the require head while in movable head disk it is the time required to move the head to a particular track.

Latency time: The time required by a sector to reach below the read/write head. On an average it is half of the time taken for a rotation by the disk.

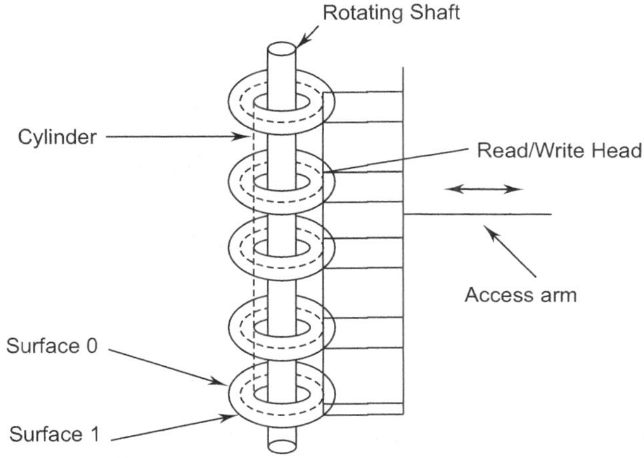

Fig. 2.13 *Hard disk*

Magnetic Tape

Magnetic tapes are mounted on reels or a cartridge or a cassette of tape to store large volumes or backup data. These are cheaper and since these are removable from the drive, they provide unlimited storage capacity. Information retrieval from tapes is sequential and not random. These are not suitable for on-line retrieval of data, since sequential searching will take long time. These are convenient for archival storage, or for backup. The tapes are one of the earliest storage devices. They are low cost, low speed, portable and are still widely used because of their low cost.

2.11 OPTICAL MEMORIES

Optical memories are alternate mass storage devices with huge capacity. The advent of compact disk digital audio system, a non-erasable optical disk, paved the way for the development of a new low cost storage technology. In optical storage devices the information is written using laser beam. These devices which are memories can store large amount of data. We will discuss here three optical memory devices, which are now becoming increasingly popular in various computer applications.

CDROM

The most common size of optical disk is the **CD-ROM,** which stands for **Compact Disk – Read Only Memory.** It looks just like an audio CD. Almost all software is being distributed on CDs now. The price of the drives that read the disks (but can't write one) has dropped low enough that a new system will come with a CD drive unless you go to some effort to avoid it! Such drives will also play your audio CDs, if you have a sound card and speakers.

Fig. 2.14 *CD drive*

The CDs that contain commercial software are of the **Write Once Read Many (WORM)** variety. They can't be changed once they are created. This is where the ROM part comes from. The CD-ROM is useful as a backup medium only when you really need indefinite storage of non-changing material. For data that changes often it is too expensive since a disk can only be used once.What you need for backup storage of changing data are **rewritable** disks. These use a different material for the laser to work on that can be softened and lasered again. The drives and disks are still quite expensive. But prices are dropping fast.

Advantages

1. The optical disk is much **sturdier** than the other media discussed so far. It is physically harder to break or melt or warp.
2. It is **not sensitive** to being touched, though it can get too dirty or scratched to be read.
3. It is entirely **unaffected by magnetic fields.** Plus you can imprint a pretty label right on the disk!

So for software providers, the optical disk is a great way to store the software and data that they want to distribute or sell.

Disadvantages

1. The main disadvantage has been cost. But the cost of a CD-RW drive has dropped drastically and quickly. In 1995 such a drive was around Rs.6000. In the summer of 1997 CD-RW drives were down to just under Rs 4000. In June 2003 a CD-RW that will read at 40X speed, write on CD-R media at 40X speed, and write on re-writable media at 12X, can be bought for under Rs. 3000, So for commercial use, the read/write drives are quite cost effective. For personal use, they are available, but may be quite cheap enough to use for data storage for most users.
2. It is not easy to copy an optical disk without a CD or DVD writer. (This is an advantage as far as commercial software providers are concerned and cause for software piracy also)

2.12 RADIO FREQUENCY IDENTIFICATION (RFID)

Radio Frequency Identification (RFID) is an automatic identification method, relying on storing and remotely retrieving data using devices called RFID tags or transponders. An RFID tag is an object that can be attached to or incorporated into a product, animal, or person for the purpose of identification using radio waves. Chip-based RFID tags contain silicon chips and antennas. Passive tags require no internal power.

Types of RFID Tags

RFID cards are also known as "proximity", "proxy" or "contactless cards" and come in three general varieties: passive, semi-passive (also known as semi-active), or active.

Passive

Passive RFID tags have no internal power supply. The minute electrical current induced in the antenna by the incoming radio frequency signal provides just enough power for the CMOS integrated circuit in the tag to power up and transmit a response. Most passive tags signal by backscattering the carrier signal from the reader. This means that the antenna has to be designed to both collect power from the incoming signal and also to transmit the outbound backscatter signal. The response of a passive RFID tag is not necessarily just an ID number; the tag chip can contain non-volatile EEPROM for storing data. The lack of an onboard power supply means that the device can be quite small: commercially available products exist that can be embedded in a sticker, or under the skin in the case of low frequency RFID tags.

Active

Unlike passive RFID tags, active RFID tags have their own internal power source which is used to power any ICs that generate the outgoing signal. Active tags are typically much more reliable (fewer errors) than passive tags due to the ability for active tags to conduct a "session" with a reader. Active tags, due to their onboard power supply, also transmit at higher power levels than passive tags, allowing them to be more effective in "RF challenged" environments like water (including humans/cattle, which are mostly water), metal (shipping containers, vehicles), or at longer distances. Many active tags have practical ranges of hundreds of meters, and a battery life of up to 10 years. Some active RFID tags include sensors such as temperature logging which have been used in concrete maturity monitoring or to monitor the temperature of perishable goods. Other sensors that have been married with active RFID include humidity, shock/vibration, light, radiation, temperature and atmospherics like ethylene. Active tags typically have much longer range (approximately 300 feet) and larger memories than passive tags, as well as the ability to store additional information sent by the transceiver. The United States Department of Defense has successfully used active tags to reduce logistics costs and improve supply chain visibility for more than 15 years. At present, the smallest active tags are about the size of a coin and sell for a few dollars.

Passports

RFID tags are being used in passports issued by many countries. The first RFID passports ("*e*-passports") were issued by Malaysia in 1998. In addition to information also contained on the visual data page of the passport, Malaysian *e*-passports.

2.13 STORAGE AREA NETWORK (SAN)

In computing, a **storage area network (SAN)** is a network designed to attach computer storage devices such as disk array controllers and tape libraries to servers. As of 2007, SANs are most commonly found in enterprise storage. A SAN allows a machine to connect to remote targets such as disks and tape drives on a network for block level I/O. From the point of view of the class drivers and application software, the devices appear as locally attached devices.

There are two variations of SANs:

1. A network whose essential purpose is the transfer of data between computer systems and storage elements. A SAN consists of a communication infrastructure, which provides physical connections, and a management layer, which organizes the connections, storage elements, and computer systems so that data transfer is secure and robust. The term SAN is usually (but not necessarily) identified with block I/O services rather than file access services.
2. A storage system consisting of storage elements, storage devices, computer systems, and/or appliances, plus all control software, communicating over a network.

Designing SAN

Storage networks are distinguished from other forms of network storage by the low-level access method that they use. Data traffic on these networks is very similar to those used for internal disk drives, like ATA and SCSI.

In a storage network, a server issues a request for specific blocks, or data segments, from specific disk drives. This method is known as block storage. The device acts in a similar fashion to an internal drive, accessing the specified block, and sending the response across the network.In more traditional *file storage* access methods, like SMB/CIFS or NFS, a server issues a request for an abstract file as a component of a larger file system, managed by an intermediary computer. The intermediary then determines the physical location of the abstract resource, accesses it on one of its internal drives, and sends the complete file across the network. Most storage networks use the SCSI protocol for communication between servers and disk drive devices, though they do not use its low-level physical interface. Typical SAN physical interfaces include 1Gbit Fibre Channel, 2Gbit Fibre Channel, 4Gbit Fibre Channel, and (in limited cases) 1Gbit iSCSI. The SCSI protocol information will be carried over the lower level protocol via a mapping layer. For example, most SANs in production today use some form of SCSI over Fibre Channel system, as defined by the FCP mapping standard. iSCSI is a similar mapping method designed to carry SCSI information over IP.

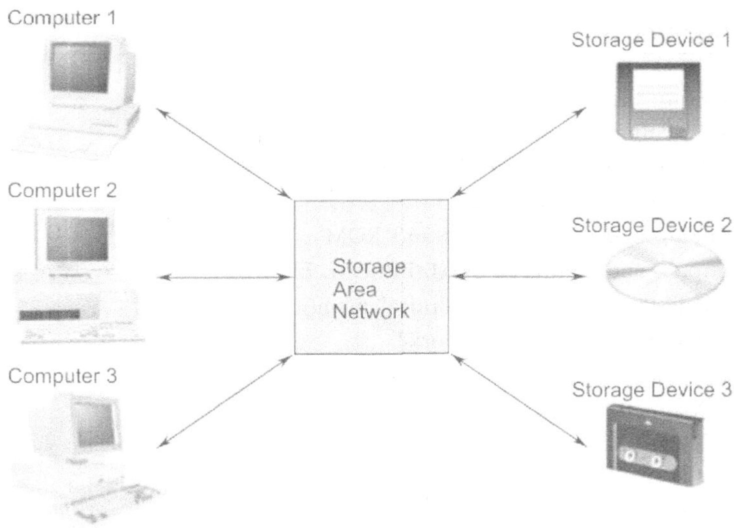

Fig. 2.15 *Storage area network (SAN)*

Benefits

Sharing storage usually simplifies storage administration and adds flexibility since cables and storage devices do not have to be physically moved to move storage from one server to another. Note, though, that with the exception of SAN file systems and clustered computing, SAN storage is still a one-to-one relationship. That is, each device (or Logical Unit Number (*LUN*)) on the SAN is "owned" by a single computer (or *initiator*). In contrast, Network Attached Storage (NAS) allows many computers to access the same set of files over a network. It is now possible to combine the SAN and NAS using a NAS head.

SANs tend to increase storage capacity utilization, since multiple servers can share the same growth reserve. Other benefits include the ability to allow servers to boot from the SAN itself. This allows for a quick and easy replacement of faulty servers since the SAN can be reconfigured so that a replacement server can use the LUN of the faulty server. This process can take as little as half an hour and is a relatively new idea being pioneered in newer data centers. There are a number of emerging products designed to facilitate and speed up this process still further. For example, Brocade Communication Systems offers an Application Resource Manager product which automatically provisions servers to boot off a SAN, with typical-case load times measured in minutes. While this area of technology is still new, many view it as being the future of the enterprise datacenter. SANs also tend to enable more effective disaster recovery processes. A SAN attached storage array can replicate data belonging to many servers to a secondary storage array. This secondary array can be local or, more typically, remote. The goal of disaster recovery is to place copies of data outside the radius of effect of an anticipated threat, and so the long-distance transport capabilities of SAN protocols such as Fibre Channel and FCIP are required to support these solutions.

REVIEW QUESTIONS

1. What are the differences in:
   (*a*) Volatile versus Non-volatile memory.
   (*b*) Static versus dynamic memories
   (*c*) Storage and Memory **(UTU, MCA 2006-07)**
2. Compare and contrast RAM and ROM.
3. Compare and contrast EROM, EPROM, EEPROM.
4. What is the importance of optical memories?
5. What is Storage Area Network?
6. Write about
   (*a*) Magnetic tape
   (*b*) RFID
   (*c*) CD-ROM
7. What is DIMM?
8. Write about Firmware and Human ware. **(UTU, B.tech 2006-07)**
9. Write the utility of cache memory in a computer. **(UTU, MCA 2006-07)**
10. What do you mean by a Bus in a computer system ? Explain Address Bus and Data Bus. **(UTU, MCA 2006-07)**
11. Explain the following with respect to monitor :
    (*a*) Resolution
    (*b*) Refresh rate **(UTU, MCA 2006-07)**

3

Operating Systems and Internet Basics

3.1 COMPUTER SYSTEM

A computer system can be defined as a collection of Hardware, Operating systems, Application software and Users.

Hardware. Basic physical parts of a computer system like Monitor, Keyboard, Hard disk, CPU, memory etc.

Operating systems. To operate or control a computer like Unix, Windows, Linux etc.

Application software. Used to use system resources to perform some task or to solve the computing problems of the users like Word processors, compilers, web browsers, database systems, games etc.

Users. That uses the computer system like People, other machines and other computers on network or Internet.

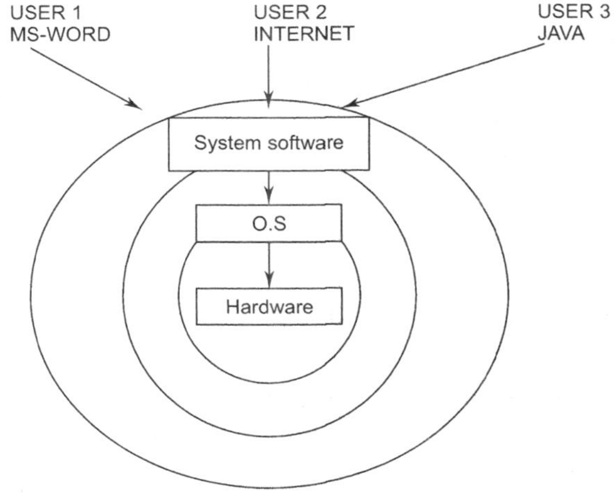

Fig. 3.1 *Computer System*

3.2 OPERATING SYSTEMS

An operating system is an essential component of a computer system. The primary objective of an operating system is to make computer system convenient to use and utilize computer hardware in an efficient manner. An operating system works as a mediator or interface between user and computer.

Fig. 3.2 *Operating system as mediator*

An operating system can be imagine as a large collection of software, which manages resources of the computer system, such as memory, processor, file system and input/output devices. It keeps track of the status of each resource and decides who will have a control over computer resources, for how long and when. You can say operating system works as a manager to control all the user activities and system activities in a computer system. Operating system directly controls computer hardware resources. Other programs rely on facilities provided by the operating system to gain access to computer system resources. Modern operating systems like MSDOS, Unix, Linux, Windows or Solaris perform various functions to control a computer system.

Functions of an Operating System

Operating system has to perform various functions for proper working of a computer system, like:

1. Providing a good user interface for human—machine interaction
2. Allocation of hardware and software components to user.
3. Memory management
4. Process management
5. Secondary storage or Disk management
6. File system management
7. Network management
8. Security management
9. Multitasking, multiprogramming, multi user, multithreading operations
10. Distributed process management

Modern operating systems like Linux, Windows or Solaris perform some more functions to control a computer system like :

Provides Abstractions : Hardware has low-level physical resources with complicated interfaces. OS provides abstractions that present clean interfaces. Goal: make computer easier to use. Examples: Processes, Unbounded Memory, Files, Synchronization and Communication Mechanisms.

Provides Standard Interface : Unix runs on many very different computer systems. To a first approximation can port programs across systems with little effort. Windows has a very simple user interface and it is same worldwide.

Mediates Resource Usage : Modern Operating System allow multiple users to share resources fairly, efficiently, safely and securely. Examples:

- Multiple processes share one processor.
- Multiple programs share one physical memory.
- Multiple users and files share one disk.
- Multiple programs share a given amount of disk and network bandwidth.

3.3 POPULAR OPERATING SYSTEMS

Between the hardware and the application software lies the **operating system.** The operating system is a program that conducts the communication between the various pieces of hardware like the video card, sound card, printer, the motherboard and the applications. Originally the operating system was created by each company that manufactured a processor and motherboard. So each operating system was proprietary, that is, unique to each manufacturer. Now the problem is changing to a new computer meant your software had to be replaced. So there is a need to standardize things so that software could be transferred to the new computer. This required more standardization in operating systems.

MSDOS

The winner in the PC market was **MS-DOS,** Microsoft's **Disk Operating System,** and its twin IBM, PC-DOS, also written by Microsoft. DOS is a commands based operating system and very tiny, you can store MS-DOS in a small floppy or today in your pen drive. It has command using interface and single user also without networking support.

Windows

Windows 95 and **Windows 98** are actual operating systems on their own. The previous versions of Windows use DOS as the operating system and adding a graphical user interface which will do multitasking. But with Windows 95 Microsoft released an operating system that can take advantage of the 32-bit processors.

Windows ME (Windows Millennium Edition) is an upgrade of Windows 98, release date Sept. 14, 2000. The system resources required for this operating system are significantly higher than previous versions of Windows.

Windows NT (the NT apparently came from New Technology) is an operating system for client-server type networks. The latest version of NT has a user interface that is practically identical to Windows 95. Since Windows NT is designed for the higher demands of networks, it has higher demands itself for disk space and memory.

Windows 2000 is an upgrade of Windows NT rather than of Windows 98.

Windows XP is an upgrade to Windows 2000. It comes in two versions—Home and Professional. The Professional version contains all the features of the Home version plus more business features, like networking and security features.

Windows CE is for small devices like your mobile phones, palmtop and handheld computers. This is very tiny versions with a number of major applications are available to run on these devices. You can link your small computer with this to synchronize documents and data.

Apple Macintosh

The **Apple Macintosh** is a multitasking operating system that was the first graphical interface to achieve commercial success. The Mac was an immediate success in the areas of graphics production, and still commands the major share of that market. Apple made a major marketing error when they decided to keep their hardware and software under tight control rather than licensing others to produce compatible devices and programs. While the Apple products were of high quality, they were always more expensive than comparable products that were compatible with Microsoft's DOS operating system. Apple's share of the computer market has dropped to an estimated 2.4% worldwide and 3.48% of the US market. Mac OS X, Version 10.2 (Jaguar) is the current version. Since January 2002, all new Mac computers use Mac OS X.

IBM OS/2

IBM's 32-bit operating system is **OS/2.** This is a popular system for businesses with complex computer systems from IBM. It is powerful and has a nice graphical interface. Programs written for DOS and Windows can also run on this system.

Unix

UNIX is an multi-user operating system developed by Bell Labs to handle complex scientific applications. University networks are likely to use UNIX, as are Internet Service Providers. A lot of people have experience with UNIX from their college work. Many computer old-timers love UNIX and its command line interface. But all those commands are not easy to remember for newcomers. X-Windows is a graphical interface for UNIX that some think is even easier to work with than Windows 98.

Linux

Linux is an operating system similar to UNIX that is becoming more and more popular.

It is a open-source program created by Linus Torvalds at the University of Finland, starting in 1991. Open source means that the underlying computer code is freely available to everyone. Programmers can work directly with the code and add features. They can sell their customized version of Linux, as long as the source code is still open to others. You can find more info at the Linux home site.

Mobile Device Appliance Operating Systems

- Windows CE.NET
- Windows XP Embedded
- Handheld PC
- Pocket PC
- Palm OS

3.4 INTRODUCTION TO DOS

MS-DOS is "Disk Operating System" developed by Microsoft Inc. in 1980 for small PC. That means it is simply "a System for Operating the Disks", but DOS does more than just operate the disks, It enables the user to organize data files, load and execute or run program files, and control the input and output devices attached to the computer. There are other brands of DOS besides the most well known "MS-DOS", PC-DOS, DR-DOS/OPENDOS. Generally speaking, they will all function in the same way, especially at the most simple level.

Booting

To run DOS on a computer, it should be the first program to be executed when the computer is switched on. This led to a problem for the designers, "How can DOS be loaded and executed when there is no DOS program running to load and execute ". Well, just as the fictional Baron Munchausen managed to pull himself up by his own bootstraps, the computer manages this seemingly impossible trick, and the term "bootstrapping", or "booting up" is applied to this process. When you start a computer your ROMBIOS start a process known as booting and you will get a prompt A:\> on screen.

Communicate with DOS

DOS is an entirely text based system. All it provides for the user is a prompt: "C:>" or "A:>", where the user can type in commands from the keyboard. The system is entirely case insensitive, so either "dir" or "DIR" is same.

How Does DOS Organize Disks?

DOS works within a file, directory and disk drive structure. This means that all program and data files are named, and grouped together in named directories on disks. 'Directories' are just lists of files.

How are Files Named?

While newer versions of DOS support longer filenames, the standard DOS filename format remains:

1-8 letter first name, period, 3 letter extension like :

- vama.txt
- suhani.jpg
- vandana.doc

The extension to a file's name is there to allow files of a similar type to be grouped together. All word processor files might have the extension.DOC, while all picture files might have the extension.PIC While these extensions can be specified by the user, many programs have used them to differentiate between formats, and so they have gradually become standardized. For example you would expect a ".TXT" file to be a file containing unformatted text, or a ".BMP" file to be in a bit mapped graphics file format.

To completely specify a file on your computer you must specify its drive and directory path, and its filename. However a file does not always have to be specified in this complete form: If it is in the current directory, then you can just enter its filename.

How are Directories Named?

Every disk drive has a root directory which can have subdirectories which are named in the same format as filenames, (though generally without any extension). The subdirectories can have subdirectories and so on. Like your hard drive disk might contain the following directory structure:

- Mysongs
- Mypictures
- Myprograms
- Myphotos

A directory path name includes the disk drive and all subdirectories needed to specify a directory on a disk. The disk drive is specified by a single letter. Like the floppy disk drive is A and the hard disk drive is C.

The drive letter, is followed by a colon, the directory path names are separated by backward slashes (\), Like in the above example "D:\PICTURES\HOME\VAMA" would be more than likely to contain pictures of my daughter.

How is DOS Used?

When you type anything at the DOS prompt, and press enter, you are telling DOS to run a program. It will first look to see if there is an internal command program which has that name, and if it does not find one, then it will look to see if there is a file on disk with that name. If it finds an external file with the extension.COM (command), or.EXE (executable), then the program is loaded and run. At this point DOS looses control of the computer until the program has ended. However parts of it are still used by the programs as they are running, like to load and save files etc.

DOS Commands

DOS is a command using operating system, that means to perform some task you should type a command that will do your work. In DOS commands can be of two types :

Internal Commands

You can run many of DOS commands with out having files of that commands in.com or.exe format. Some popular internal DOS commands are :

External Commands

External DOS commands are in form of a file, that means to execute an external dos command like format, you must have format.com file on your disk.

Examples of MSDOS Commands

To be functional, each DOS command must be entered in a particular way: this command entry structure is known as the command's "syntax." The syntax "notation" is a way to reproduce the command syntax in print.

SYNTAX

Command Name

The DOS command name is the name you enter to start the DOS program (a few of the DOS commands can be entered using shortcut names). The DOS command name is always entered first. In this book, the command is usually printed in uppercase letters, but you can enter command names as either lowercase or uppercase or a mix of both.

Space

Always leave a space after the command name.

Drive Designation

The drive designation like C: or D: is an option for many DOS commands. However, some commands are not related to disk drives and therefore do not require a drive designation like VER. Whenever you enter a DOS command that deals with disk drives and you are already working in the drive in question, you do not have to enter the drive designator. For example, if you are working in drive C: and you want to use the DIR command to display a directory listing of that same drive, you do not have to enter the drive designation. If you do not enter a drive designation, DOS always assumes you are referring to the drive you are currently working in sometimes called the "default" drive.

ATTRIB(External)

Sets or displays the read-only, archive, system, and hidden attributes of a file or directory.

ATTRIB [d:][path]filename [/S]

ATTRIB [+R | -R] [+A | -A] [+S | -S] [+H | -H] [d:][path]filename [/S]

BACKUP(External)

Makes a backup copy of one or more files. (In DOS Version 6, this program is stored on the DOS supplemental disk.)

BACKUP d:[path][filename] d:[/S][/M][/A][/F:(size)] [/P][/D:date] [/T:time] [/L:[path]filename]

CHDIR (CD) (Internal)

Displays working (current) directory and/or changes to a different directory.

CHDIR (CD) Dir name like C:\>CD mks

CHDIR or CD..

CHKDSK (External)

Checks a disk and provides a file and memory status report.

CHKDSK [d:][path][filename] [/F][/V]

CLS (Internal)

Clears (erases) the screen.

CLS

COPY(Internal)

Use to Copies and appends files.

COPY C:\Java*.java D:\mks

DATE(Internal)

Displays and/or sets the system date.

DATE

DEL/ERASE (Internal)

Deletes (erases) files from disk.

DEL (ERASE) [d:][path]filename [/P]

DELTREE(External)

Deletes (erases) a directory including all files and subdirectories that are in it.

DELTREE [/Y] [d:]path [d:]path[...]

DIR(Internal)

Displays directory of files and directories stored on disk.

DIR d: [/B][/C][/CH][/L][/S][/P][/W]

DISKCOMP(External)

Compares the contents of two diskettes.

DISKCOMP [d:] [d:][/1][/8]

DISKCOPY(External)

Makes an exact copy of a diskette.
DISKCOPY [d:] [d:][/1][/V][/M]

DOSKEY(External)

Loads the Doskey program into memory which can be used to recall DOS commands so that you can edit them.

DOSKEY

EDIT(External)

Starts the MS-DOS editor, a text editor used to create and edit ASCII text files.

EDIT [d:][path]filename [/B][/G][/H][/NOHI]

FDISK(External)

Partition a hard disk to make logical drives like C:, D:, E: to accept DOS files for storage.

FDISK

FORMAT(External)

Formats a disk to set file system for DOS files.

FORMAT C: /S

HELP(External)

Displays information about a DOS command.

HELP [command] [/B][/G][/H][/NOHI]

LABEL(External)

Creates or changes or deletes a volume label for a disk.

LABEL [d:][volume label]

MKDIR/MD (Internal)

Creates a new subdirectory.

MKDIR/MD dir name

PATH(Internal)

Sets or displays directories that will be searched for programs not in the current directory.

PATH

PATH d:\dos;c:\windows

PRINT(External)

prints data files.

PRINT filename

PROMPT(Internal)

Changes the DOS command prompt.

PROMPT $p$dmksharma

RENAME/REN (Internal)

Changes the filename under which a file is stored.

RENAME / REN) oldfile newfile

RMDIR/RD(Internal)

Removes a subdirectory.

RMDIR / RD d:\vama

SCANDISK(External)

Starts the Microsoft ScanDisk program which is a disk analysis and repair tool used to check a drive for errors and correct any problems that it finds.

SCANDISK d:

TIME(Internal)

Displays current time setting of system clock and provides a way for you to reset the time.

TIME

TREE(External)

Displays directory paths and (optionally) files in each subdirectory.

TREE [d:][path] [/A][/F]

TYPE(Internal)

Displays the contents of a file.

TYPE [*d*:][path]filename

UNDELETE(External)

Restores files deleted with the DELETE commands

UNDELETE [d:][path][filename]

VER(Internal)

Displays the DOS version number

VER

XCOPY(External)

Copies directories, subdirectories, and files.

XCOPY d:\path\dirname c:\path\dirname /A

3.5 MS WINDOWS

MS-Windows is the most popular operating having Graphical Using Interface(GUI) for personal computers. Windows provides an environment that enhances DOS in many ways. The major features of Windows are:

GUI Interface

The terms "user interface" originated from the engineering environment. In Early days of computers those who interacted directly with computers had been engineers and programmers, but in present a new kind of users was emerging the non computer literate users like a bank ATM customer, a shopkeeper or a housewife. These users face difficulties in dealing with a computer, they need very simple user interface to work with computers. MS windows graphically display every thing on screen what the computer is doing.

In Windows you have a pointing device known as mouse to point and shoot your actions, you have functionality with screen menus that appear or disappear under pointing-device-control.

In windows you will seen small pictures known as icons that represent files, directories and other application and system entities. Dialog boxes, button, sliders, check boxes and many other graphical objects that let the programmer and user tell the computer what to do and how to do it.

Today's GUIs have expanded basic functionality to support not only graphics but also dimensions, color, height, video and highly dynamic interaction. Modern user interfaces can simulate a very realistic view of a real, three-dimensional world.

Device Independence

Windows presents a device-independent interface to applications. Unlike most of MSDOS applications, a Windows application is not bound to the underlying hardware such as mouse, keyboard or display. Windows shields the applications from this responsibility. The application deals with the Windows API to manipulate any underlying devices.

Multitasking

Windows provides non-pre-emptive multitasking support, Users can have several applications in progress at the same time. Each application can be run in a separate window. You can play a song in window media player while writing your program.

Memory Management

Windows provides better memory management to break the 640KB use of memory by applications in MSDOS. An application has the ability to use the extended memory, share data segments with other applications and swap unwanted segments to disk. Thus a user can run multiple application using virtual memory management.

Network and Advance Plug and Play Support

Using Windows you can connect multiple computers to design a Local Area Network(LAN), A Window machine can be member of intranet or internet easily. Windows Server 2006 or Windows XP can be used to serve other client machines in Network. You can use Digital camera, High speed USB printers, Pen drives or many USB devices with windows as plug and play devices.

Features of Windows XP

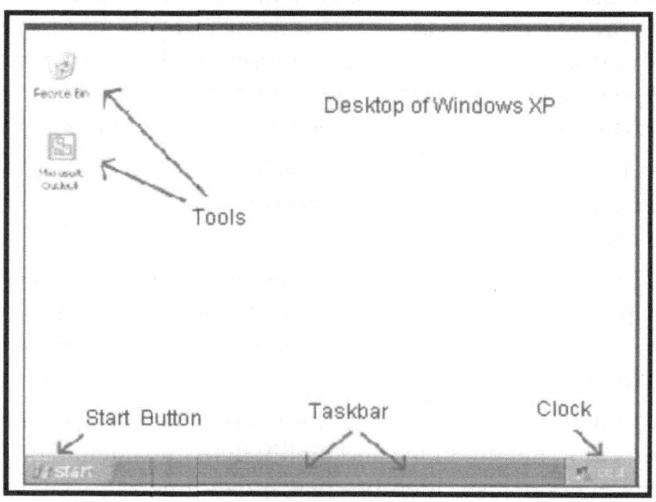

Fig. 3.3 *XP desktop*

Desktop

Windows XP desktop, when you first switch on your machine it usually looks similar to that shown in above figure, although Windows XP by default has a picture for the desktop background. Desktop refers to the main background area, you can customize your desktop by adding background pictures, changing the background color, changing the size of the icons, and more.

Introduction to Icons

Icons are small graphical images that can represent your computer's programs, files, folders and printers amongst other things. To activate the program/file/folder that an icon represents you simply double click (two clicks in quick succession) on it with the left mouse button, this will activate the icon and either start a program or open a file/folder. The icons on your desktop can be renamed by right clicking on them and selecting **rename,** similarly they can be deleted by right clicking and selecting **delete.**

It's possible to create your own icons for programs, files, folders, etc.

Keeping the Desktop Tidy

The more you use Windows XP the more your desktop may start to fill up with icons, either because you install more software or you create your own icons. Windows XP can automatically align and sort your desktop icons to keep the desktop tidy, to achieve this click the right mouse button anywhere on the desktop and a menu will appear, hover the mouse pointer over **Arrange Icons By** and a submenu will appear, from here you can sort your desktop icons by name, size, type and last modified date. Selecting the **Auto Arrange** option will automatically align your desktop icons every time you add one to the desktop.

Start Button

The start button is a very important part of Windows XP, clicking on the start button opens up what is called the start menu, the start menu is used to access your programs, settings, printers and more.

Taskbar

The taskbar is another important part of the Windows XP operating system, one of its main uses is to switch between any open programs or documents.

Clock

The clock sits on the taskbar and displays the system time, hovering the mouse pointer over the clock will reveal the date,You can change date and time to double click on it.

Windows Explorer

An integral part of using your PC is file management, at some point you will want to make a new folder or delete a file. Windows Explorer has been around since Windows 95 and is a very handy tool for managing your files and folders. Windows Explorer is basically the same environment as **My Computer** except it has a folders list shown by default (which can be turned on anyway in the **My computer** environment, making them exactly the same), so all of the tasks in this section can be achieved using either Windows Explorer or the My Computer environment. To Open Windows Explorer there are a few ways to open Windows Explorer, here are 4 different methods:

Method 1

Click on the **START** button, hover your mouse over the **All Programs** (or programs in classic view) and then hover over **Accessories,** finally click on **Windows Explorer.**

Method 2

hold down the **START** button and press the **E** key.

Method 3

click the **START** button, click **run,** type **explorer** into the box and press enter.

Method 4

open **My Computer** and click on the **Folders** button at the top of the **My Computer** environment.

Open Your Drives and Folders

When you have opened Windows Explorer (or opened my computer and then clicked the folders button) you will see something similar to that shown in figure :

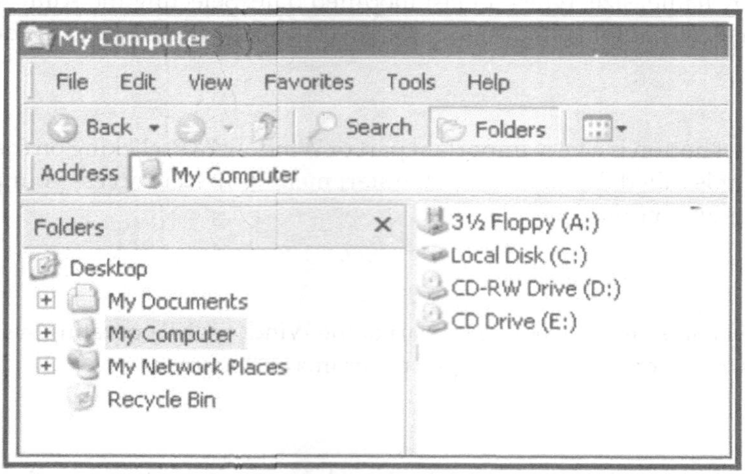

Fig. 3.4 *Windows Explorer*

You can see Windows Explorer is split into two parts, the left hand side which is called the **folders list** and the right hand side, which is where you will be managing your files and folders. First let's concentrate on the **folders list,** you may have noticed the small plus sign (+) next to some of the icons, these indicate that the drive/folder has more folders inside it. Just click on + sign and you can explore the indicated folder.

Creating a New Folder or Folders

There are numerous ways to create a new folder in Win XP, Open Windows Explorer, navigate to the drive or folder in which you want to create your new folder, for our example, we are going to create a new folder in our **pc courses** folder.

The steps are:

1. **right click** anywhere in the white space and hover the mouse over **new**
2. then click on **folder** from the sub-menu that appears below.

You will then be prompted to name the folder, simply type in the name and then press the enter (return) key, we are going to name our folder **mksharma.** Try and be as descriptive as you can when naming folders, and avoid using any punctuation symbols in the names.

Copying, Deleting, and Renaming Files and Folders

First, navigate to the folder where the file or folder is stored, then right click on the file/folder of interest, you will be presented with a menu. Your menu may vary, with at least 3 options:

1. **copy** – clicking on this option will copy the file or folder into (the clipboard) memory, you can then navigate to the folder where you want to copy the file to, right click (as if making a new folder) in the right hand pane and select **paste** from the menu that appears.
2. **delete** – this option will delete the file or folder (send it to the **recycle bin**), Windows XP will prompt you for confirmation first.
3. **rename** – this option allows you to rename the file or folder, simply type in the new name and press the enter (return) key.

3.6 COMPUTER NETWORK

Information and communication technology has changed many aspects of your life. To get information about current trains status for reservation, no need to go to railway station just use Internet or even your mobile phone. Collect money any where any time using ATM bank machines. Transfer information within seconds any where in the world, that is because of computer networks. In today, Computer networks form the backbone of most enterprises like Indian railway, State bank of India,LIC India, IBM or Microsoft around the world.

"A computer network is a collection of inter connected computers and resources to share information in small area or world wide". Computer networks are being used to provide resource sharing between systems separated from a few feet to thousands of kilometers. This technology is leading many corporations to take advantage of the reduced price and increased performance in the workplace like banks. This trend of information sharing in most sophisticated manner has completely revolutionized the concept of communication. It brings with it increased access to people in different fields. Today million of computer network are interlinked together all over the world known as Internet or WWW.

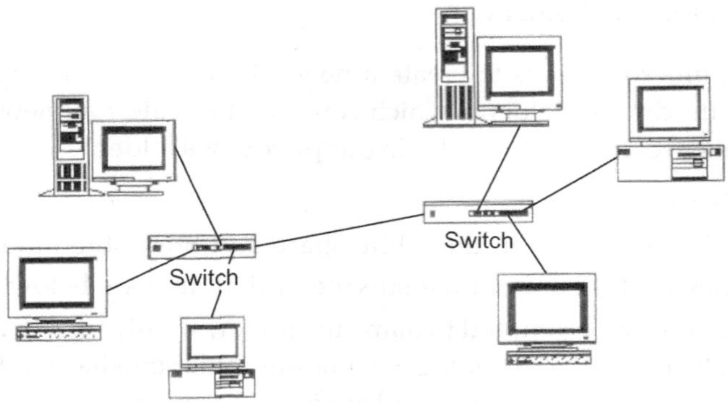

Fig. 3.5 *Computer Network*

3.7 LOCAL AREA NETWORK (LAN)

A LAN is a group of microcomputers or other workstation devices located in the same general area and connected by a common cable or wireless. The characteristics of LAN's are:

- Physically limited area < 2Km
- High bandwidth of data transmission > 1Mhz
- Inexpensive cable media or wireless infrastructure
- Data and hardware sharing amongst users
- Owned by the user or private network
- Simple operating systems like Windows 2000 server, Unix or Linux.
- Use of switches, hubs to connect many clients
- C class IP address schemes

A LAN is used to share resources amongst a group of individuals or company employees. These resources are typically

- Files
- Printers
- Modems
- Application software
- Computing power
- Fax machines

In a local branch of your near by bank, there are computers on LAN, and you can operate your account form any counter of the bank. In a Hotel customer information can be shared by all parts like front office, room service, laundry or restaurant at once using LAN environment. In a University campus where departments are located on various locations LAN can be helpful to share all resources and information without moving form your seat.

3.8 WIDE AREA NETWORK

A Wide Area Network is similar to a LAN, but geographically spread over a wider area. The different segments of the WAN are interconnected by communication links Microwave, VSAT or leased lines. In fact, a WAN often comprises a number of interconnected LAN's at various sites. You can imagine WAN as a network of computer networks situated on various location. The computer network of Indian Railway that is available on different stations all over India, is an example of WAN. Your favorite Internet is also a form of WAN.

The characteristics of a WAN are :

- Cover wide area, a state, a country, a continent or even the world
- Large number of computers, modems and multiple host machines known as servers
- Sophisticated support devices like routers and gateways for interconnecting the various segments of networks
- Based on packet switch and IP address schemes.

3.9 NETWORK PROTOCOLS

This section describes the protocols used in different network topology's. Remember that a protocol defines the rules for sending data from one point to another.

Carrier Sense Multiple Access with Collision Detection (CSMA/CD)

This protocol is commonly used in bus (Ethernet) implementations. Multiple access refers to the fact that in bus systems, each station has access to the common cable. Carrier sense refers to the fact that each station listens to see if no other station is transmitting before sending data. Collision detection refers to the principle of listening to see if other stations are transmitting whilst we are transmitting.

In bus systems, all stations have access to the same cable medium. It is there for possible that a station may already be transmitting when another station wants to transmit. Rule 1 is that a station must listen to determine if another station is transmitting before initiating a transmission. If the network is busy, then the station must back off and wait a random interval before trying again.

Rule 2 is that a station which is transmitting must monitor the network to see if another station has begun transmission. This is a *collision,* and if this occurs, both stations must back off and retry after a random time interval. As it takes a finite time for signals to travel down the cable, it is possible for more than one station to think that the network is free and both grab it at the same time.

CSMA/CD models what happens in the real world. People involved in group conversation tend to obey much the same behavior.

Token Ring

This protocol is widely used in ring networks for controlling station access to the ring. A short message (called a *token*) is circulated around the ring, being passed from station to station (it originates from a controller or master station which inserts it onto the ring).

A station which wants to transmit waits for the token to arrive. When it arrives, it changes it from a token to a *connector message,* and appends its message on the end. This is then placed on the outgoing side of the ring.

Each station passes on received tokens if they have nothing to transmit. They monitor connector messages to see if the message is addressed to them. If connector messages are addressed to them, they copy the message, modify it to signify its receipt, then send it on around the ring. Connector messages which are not addressed to them are passed directly onto the next station in the ring.

When the connector message travels full circle and arrives at the original sending station, it checks the message to see if its been received. It then discards the message and replaces it with a token.

Token Bus

is a popular standard for the token passing LANs. In a token bus LAN, the physical media is a bus or a tree and a logical ring is created using coaxial cable. The token is passed from one user to other in a sequence (clockwise or anticlockwise). Each station knows the address of the station to its "left" and "right" as per the sequence in the logical ring. A station can only transmit data when it has the token. The working of token bus is somewhat similar to *Token Ring*

TCP/IP

TCP/IP is a software-based communications protocol used in networking. Although the name TCP/IP implies that it is a product of combination of two protocols :

1. Transmission Control Protocol
2. Internet Protocol

The term TCP/IP refers not to a single entity combining two protocols, but a larger set of software programs that provides network services such as remote logins, remote file transfers, and electronic mail. TCP/IP provides a method for transferring information from one machine to another. A communications protocol should handle errors in transmission, manage the routing and delivery of data, and control the actual transmission by the use of predetermined status signals. TCP/IP accomplishes all of this.

The architecture of TCP/IP is often called the Internet architecture because TCP/IP and the Internet are very close. TCP/IP is the "language" of the Internet. It is a networking technology developed by the United States Government Defense Advanced Research Project Agency (DARPA) in the 1970s. It is most commonly employed to provide access to the Internet.

3.10 INTERNET

The Internet as you watching today, its origin is the US Defense Department project in 1969. The subject of the project was wartime digital communications. At that time the telephone system was the only communications system in use. A major problem had been identified in its design like its dependence on switching stations that could be targeted during an attack. Only voice can be transmitted through, there was no way to send text data electronically. The Defense Advanced Research Projects Agency (DARPA) launched the DARPA Internet Program to design a computer based digital communication system. In 1975, DARPA declared the project as a success and handed its management over to the Defense Communications Agency. Several of today's internet protocols like TCP or IP were stable by 1980, and adopted throughout ARPANET by 1983. In August 1983, there were 562 registered ARPANET hosts.

Driven largely by the development of the PC and LAN technology, subnetting was standardized in 1985 when RFC 950 was released. LAN technology made the idea of a "catenet" feasible, an internet work of networks. Subnetting opened the possibilities of interconnecting LANs with WANs. Domain naming was stable by 1987 when RFC 1034 was released. Until then, hostnames were mapped to IP address using static tables, but the Internet's exponential growth had made this practice infeasible.

In the early 90s the World Wide Web (WWW) has been one of Internet's most exciting recent developments. The idea of hypertext has been around for more than a decade, but in 1989 a team at the European Center for Particle Research (CERN) in Switzerland developed a set of protocols for transferring hypertext via the Internet. In the early 1990s it was enhanced by a team at the National Center for Supercomputing Applications (NCSA) at the University of Illinois, one of NSF's supercomputer centers. The result was NCSA Mosaic, a graphical, point-and-click hypertext browser that made Internet easy. The resulting explosion in "Web sites" drove the Internet into the public eye.

The real progress of Internet started in the 1990s and today we all are familiar with the strength of Internet as commercial, social and political tool. It has already become part of the international vocabulary, and seems headed for even greater prominence. It has been accepted by the business community like banks, with a resulting explosion of service providers, consultants, books, and media coverage. For the next few years, the Internet will almost certainly be content-driven. Although new protocols like WAP by which you can access Internet on your mobile phone are always under development, we have barely begun to explore the potential of Internet in form of Email, E-commerce, E-governance etc. The most popular form f Internet is the World Wide Web (WWW), with its potential for simple on-line access to almost any information you need at your home. Broad band, Mobile Internet, IPTV are new buzzword in market for fast and easy access for Internet.

3.11 INTERNET ORGANIZATION

The Internet is an organized international collaboration of autonomous, interconnected networks, supports host-to-host communication through protocols and procedures defined by Internet Standards. Nobody really owns or controls the Internet. Rather, participation in the Internet derives from voluntary participation in Internet Standards. Many Internet providers not only adhere to these standards, but make access to their networks available to the public. It is the voluntary interconnection and cooperation of these providers that forms the global Internet. In 1996, approximately 300 service providers are interconnected to form the Internet.

The Internet Society (ISOC) is a professional society that is concerned with the growth and evolution of the worldwide Internet, with the way in which the Internet is and can be used, and with the social, political, and technical issues which arise as a result. The Internet Architecture Board (IAB) is a technical advisory group of the ISOC. It is chartered to provide oversight of the architecture of the Internet and its protocols, and to serve, in the context of the Internet standards. The Internet Engineering Steering Group (IESG) is responsible for technical management of IETF activities and the Internet standards process. As part of the ISOC, it administers the process according to the rules and procedures which have been ratified by the ISOC Trustees. The IESG is directly responsible for the actions associated with entry into and movement along the Internet "standards track," including final approval of specifications as Internet Standards.

InterNIC

InterNIC, the Internet Network Information Center, has two major components. AT&T provides Directory and Database Services, most importantly the Internet White Pages, used by the Whois program to locate people, networks, and domains. Network Solutions, Inc. provides Registration Services, including domain name registration.

3.12 COMPONENTS OF INTERNET

A browser (short for web browser) is a computer program (software) that accesses web pages and displays them on your computer screen. The browser is a client program that is reading files from a web server. The browser sends a request to the server for a specific web page— receives the information in small pieces of information - interprets special commands that format the information and displays the web page. These commands are HTML (Hyper Text Markup Language). It is the browsers job to interpret the HTML, find all the pictures (or other types of media), take all of these pieces and display the information. Browsers are capable of accepting text, pictures, sound, and movies. Browsers use "helper applications" to generate some of these special effects. Quicktime is an example of this: Quicktime is a program and a plug-in that allows playing movies through your browser. The two most popular n browsers available are Internet Explorer from Microsoft and Netscape navigator from Sun.

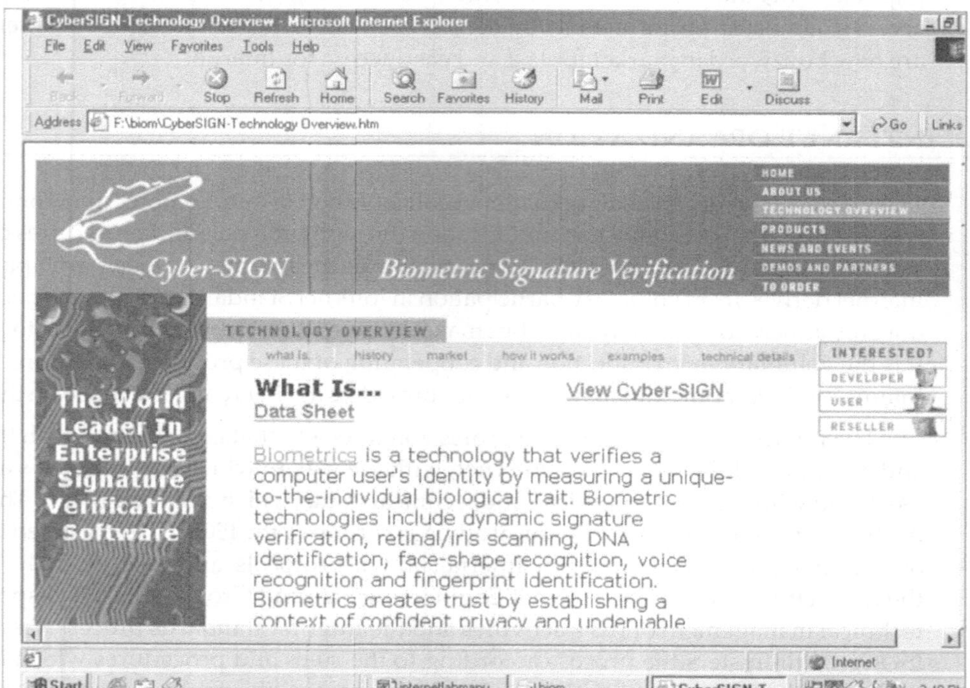

Fig. 3.6 *Internet browser screen with an open site*

World Wide Web (WWW)

The World Wide Web or WWW or W3 refers to the massive collection of multimedia information available over the internet. Although the World Wide Web is often referred to as the internet they are actually two different things. The **internet** is the global collection of computers that transfer information and the wiring that make all of this possible. The World Wide Web is a smaller part of the internet. The World Wide Web refers to the documents and related multimedia rich information that uses a specific Internet Protocol called **HTTP.** Since the WWW is a subset of the Internet it stands to reason that the Web could not exist without the internet however the Internet would still be the Internet without the Web (although not as nice). Mosaic was the first client used to access the Web. Mosaic was created by the National Center for Supercomputing Applications (NCSA) and became available to the Internet community in the first half of 1993.

The web talks to computers through the HTTP protocol. More specifically these pages are being displayed through HTML, or the Hyper Text Markup Language, which tells the Web browser how to display the information with it's pictures and text. One of the defining features of the Web is its ability to connect pages to one another with hyperlinks. That's why you can click your way around on the internet. (Or should I say web there?)

Other applications prior to the Mosaic type of browsing relied on a persons knowledge of Internet addressing, hierarchical directory structures, and the application's own set of commands. The browsers that we are familiar with today have simplified all this so we can just click on words— or pictures— to get where we want to go.

This simplistic approach to navigating around the web has been a big factor in the success of the internet. The web with all of its multimedia aspects has become a world wide phenomena. It doesn't take long to show someone how to click on a link and they are off exploring interests of their choice.

HTML has been developed and expanded from its original set of commands. There are many new exciting technologies like java, DHTML, XML, ASP, JSP, CGI that are changing the web in dynamic tool.

Email

Electronic mail (e-mail) is the most popular tool on internet that is used to send or receive electronic message, documents, attachments over the internet. Using E-mail any document cab be sent on its destination in a matter of seconds. There are lot of free Email service providers on internet like Hotmail, Gmail, Yahoo, Rediffmail etc. from where you can get your free Email account with your Email-id and password. Everybody that uses the internet has a unique e-mail address. E-mail addresses always have an at sign (@) in them like sharmamkhld@gmail.com. Microsoft also offers a free e-mail program Microsoft Outlook Express which is very good. These require a SMTP (simple mail transfer protocol) server so they will not work with r many other free web based mail services. Just like the postman must be able to read the address to hand deliver your regular mail to other person, the e-mail address must be exact in order for the computers to deliver it to any one electronic mailbox, that means you must have correct Email -id of a person before sending your Email. Some popular free email provider sites are :

(*a*) www.hotmail.com
(*b*) www.yahoo.co.in
(*c*) www.rediffmail.com
(*d*) www.webdunia.com
(*e*) www.indiatimes.com
(*f*) www.gmail.com

ADDRESS BOOK	List of personal contact with their e-mail addresses
FORWARD	Sends the original message on to someone else
REPLY	Sends a e-mail to the sender of the message you are currently reading (sort of like someone sending you a self addressed stamped envelope)—this copies the senders e-mail address as well as the text from the message, you type your additional comments if necessary and send the message.
ATTACHMENTS	Sends actual documents created with other programs along with (or attached to) your e-mail
CC CARBON COPY	sends the same message to several people (separate their addresses with commas)
BCBLIND CARBON COPY	Send message to several addresses without showing everyone all of the addresses (this is a good way to avoid those annoying messages that are 2 lines but 4 pages of addresses you really could care less about)
BOUNCED	If a message has a invalid e-mail address it will be marked undeliverable and will bounce back to your e-mail address (the sender)

Search Engines

A search engine is a tool that searches web pages, indexes them, and identifies web pages that are related to certain keywords and topics that you ask for. You essentially go to the site that offers a search—type in some key words—get related web addresses to view. There are several different search engines available on the internet. No search engine has a complete directory of every web site and search engines have different algorithms and techniques that they use—so it might pay off to use a combination of search engines available.

There are lots of free search engines. AltaVista is a great search engine that allows you to enter key words. AskJeeves is more of an "ask a question—and I'll find you an answer" type of a search engine. Google is more or less a huge list of bookmarks that allow you to walk through categories until you get to what you are looking for. They all have their place on the internet. They all work a little different—possibly with different results—so you need to explore a little and find out which method of searching you like best. Searching the internet can be frustrating. However, most users don't take the time to read the instructions. Students don't think they have time to do read a couple of pages that do not directly pertain to accomplishing the impending deadline. Actually, if you know how to use a search engine it can greatly reduce the time and frustration in obtaining that key piece of needed information. So make some time and learn how to use the search engine first.

Google is (in my opinion) one of the best search engines and it's free (as are most search engines). As with any tool, if you learn how to utilize the different features like image search, group search etc it can become a better tool for you to search on internet.

Fig 3.7 *Google search engine homepage*

Chat Groups

Chatting is similar to a telephone conversation except it's text, your picture using Web camera over the internet. When you chat with someone over a network you use the computer, internet, modem, Web camera, Microphone instead of speaking into the telephone Chatting is a method of talking to someone over a network in real time. Chatting is different than e-mail in that the messages are synchronous or being sent at the same time. Remember e-mail is sent and stored on a mail server to be read by the recipient at a later time which could be a minute, hour, day or even a week or more.

Chatting software like Yahoo messenger, Rediffbol etc. usually splits your screen into two (one for you and the other for whoever you are chatting with). Lets say that I want some information urgent and I know that my friend is online on his computer. I can invite him for online chat with me to get help. Remember if you ask someone a question in e-mail you may not get your answer in time. At least in a chat session you know there is someone at the other end and their response will be immediate. You can get your free chat -id from Gmail, yahoo, rediff or India times web site, if you have email account.

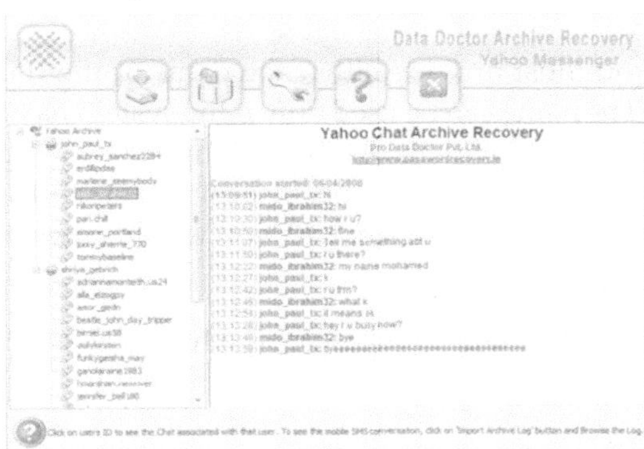

Fig. 3.8 *Chat screen in Yahoo messenger*

FTP and TELNET

Some times you want to send large files or electronic data to other computers on network. ftp is a tool by which you can upload and download files via computer networks. You should connect with a ftp server using a user name and password. After login you can upload or download files using simple ftp commands. You can use Graphical ftp software like cuteftp also that are easy to use.

TELNET

The Telnet (telecommunications network) program is intended to provide a remote login or virtual terminal capability across a network. In other words, a user on machine one should be able to log into machine two anywhere on the network, and as far as the user is concerned, it appears that the user is seated in front of machine two. The Telnet service is provided through TCP's port number 23. In your campus if you have your Windows terminal in one lab an your Unix or Linux server at another location using telnet you can connect with that server form your client machine.

Telnet was developed because at one time the only method of enabling one machine to access another machine's resources like hard drives and programs stored there was to establish a link using communications devices such as modems or networks into dedicated serial ports or network adapters.

Usually, Telnet involves a process on the server that accepts incoming requests for a Telnet session. On UNIX systems, this process is called telnetd. On Windows NT and other PC-based operating systems, a Telnet Server program is usually involved. The client (the end doing the calling) runs a program, usually called telnet, that attempts the connection to the server.

The Telnet protocol uses the concept of a network virtual terminal, or NVT, to define both ends of a Telnet connection. Each end of the connection (each NVT) has a logical keyboard and printer. The logical printer can display characters, and the logical keyboard can generate characters. The logical printer is usually a terminal screen, whereas the logical keyboard is usually the user's keyboard, although it could be a file or other input stream.

How to start telnet?

To start telnet, you must provide either the name or the IP address of the machine to be connected with. The name can be used only if the system has a means of resolving the name into its IP address, such as with the Domain Name System. A port name can usually be used to connect to a specific service, but this is used infrequently. For example, to connect to a machine with the IP address 192.168.0.40, you would enter this command:

telnet 192.168.0.40

If the server had the name aimcaserver, which was resolvable into its IP address, you could issue this command:

telnet aimcaserver

When the connection is established, a user ID and password are requested. You can log in with given user ID that is valid on the remote system. A typical connection to a UNIX server looks like this:

```
telnet 192.168.0.40
Trying...
Connected to aimcaserver
Escape character is '^]'.
login: user1
password: xxxxxx
$
```

As you can see in the preceding code, Telnet tried to connect to the remote system, told you it was connected, then set up the communications parameters between the two systems. When that was done, the login prompt was displayed (as on any UNIX terminal), followed by a password request. If the login and password are enabled, the UNIX shell prompt (a dollar sign) is shown to indicate that the remote machine is now active.

Once the connection is successfully established, your session behaves as though you were on the remote machine, with all valid commands of that operating system. All instructions are relative to the server, so a directory command shows the current directory on the server, not the client. To see the client's directory, you would have to enter command mode. After learning general Unix commands like ls, pwd, cal you can try in your lab.

FTP

File Transfer Protocol, usually called FTP, is a utility for managing files across machines without having to establish a remote session with Telnet. FTP enables you to transfer files back and forth, manage directories, and access electronic mail. The term uploading and downloading are associated with FTP.

FTP uses two TCP channels. TCP port 20 is the data channel, and port 21 is the command channel. FTP is different from most other TCP/IP application programs in that it does use two channels, enabling simultaneous transfer of FTP commands and data. In FTP parlance, the two channels that exist between the two machines are called the protocol interpreter, or PI, and the data transfer process, or DTP. The PI transfers instructions between the two implementations using TCP command channel 21, and the DTP transfers data on TCP data channel 20.

FTP is similar to Telnet in that it uses a server program that runs continuously and a separate program that is executed on the client. On UNIX systems, these programs are named ftpd and ftp, respectively (similar to telnetd and telnet).

FTP Commands

FTP internal protocol commands are four-character ASCII sequences terminated by a newline character. Some of the codes require parameters after them. One primary advantage to using ASCII characters for commands is that a user can observe the command flow and understand it easily.

FTP Connections

FTP is usually started with the name or address of the target machine. As with Telnet, the name must be resolvable into an IP address for the command to succeed. The target machine can also be specified from the FTP command line. For example, to connect to the IP address 192.165.145.40, you would issue this command:

ftp 192.165.145.40

When FTP connects to the destination, you must be able to log into the system as a valid user, using valid user name and password. The following session will show use of ftp on server using a login and password for the remote machine:

```
C:\> ftp 192.165.145.40
Login : user1
Password : ******
ftp> ls
```

FTP user commands

FTP Command	Description
ascii	Switch to ASCII transfer mode
binary	Switch to binary transfer mode
cd	Change directory on the server
close	Terminate the connection
del	Delete a file on the server
dir	Display the server directory
get	Fetch a file from the server
help	Display help
lcd	Change directory on the client
mget	Fetch several files from the server
mput	Send several files to the server
open	Connect to a server
put	Send a file to the server
pwd	Display the current directory
quote	Supply an FTP command directly
quit	Terminate the FTP session

News Groups

Newsgroups are a place where people can share information about a certain common topic like sports, movies or IT even, that interests them. Usenet or Newsgroups are basically a very large number of gathering places for people to discuss topics that they have in common. There are approx l over 50,000 newsgroups that range from great topics with great discussion to stuff that shouldn't be on the internet at all. It can be a good way to find out what other people are doing or thinking about a certain topic. You need to search for a topic that interests you and then evaluate the group to verify that the content is worth reading. Like we have group of Amrapali Institute and all the members of this group can share their views any time with all other members.

Internet Blogs

A blog is a frequently updated online personal journal or diary. It is a place to express yourself to the world. A place to share your thoughts and your passions. Really, it's anything you want it to be. For our purposes we'll say that a blog is your own Web site that you are going to update on an ongoing basis. Blog is a short form for the word weblog and the two words are used interchangeably.

Here are some more definitions

"...the first journalistic model that actually harnesses rather than merely exploits the true democratic nature of the web. It's a new medium finally finding a unique voice." —***Andrew Sullivan***

"[a] collection of posts...short, informal, sometimes controversial, and sometimes deeply personal...with the freshest information at the top." —***Meg Hourihan***

So you may be think why anyone would want to have their own blog. We believe the answer lies in the fact that every human has a voice and wishes their voice to be heard. The Internet is a medium that is unparalleled in its reach. Never before have average people like you or me been able to reach a global audience with so little trouble. Bloggers have the opportunity of reaching hundreds or even thousands of people each and every day.

REVIEW QUESTIONS

1. Define Operating system and write its functions.
2. How does a real time operating system differ from a personal operating system? **(B.Tech, UTU-2006-07)**
3. What are GUI operating systems? Write few examples of GUI operating system.
4. How does a multi-user operating system differ from single user operating system, explain?
5. What is multitasking, multiprogramming and multithreading? **(B.Tech, UTU-2006-07)**
6. Discuss the following with respect to DOS:
   (*a*) The file naming rules in MSDOS.
   (*b*) Managing files and directories
   (*c*) Internal and external DOS commands **(MCA, UTU-2006-07)**
7. What are DOS commands? Write few internal and external DOS commands, with their use.
8. What are mobile operating systems, which operating system you have in your mobile set?
9. What is distributed operating system, how are they different from network operating systems?
10. Write about some popular applications of windows operating system.
11. What do you mean by WWW, TCP/IP ? Explain search engine in brief. **(MCA, UTU-2006-07)**

4

INTRODUCTION TO 'C' PROGRAMMING

4.1 COMPUTER AS PROBLEM SOLVING MACHINE

A computer can be used to solve a real life (Traffic Control Program) or mathematical problem (Adding of Numbers). With the help of computers, problem solving tools like algorithms, flowcharts etc., computer languages like BASIC, C, C++, a problem can be simulate in a form of computer program or software, that helps a user to solve a problem in less time with accuracy and using less cost too. So a computer can be defined as a problem solving tool.

4.2 COMPUTERIZED PROBLEM SOLVING

There are following steps are required to solve a problem using a computer :

1. Develop an *Algorithm* and a *Flowchart.*
2. Write the program in a computer language. (BASIC, C)
3. Enter the program into the computer.
4. Test and debug the program.
5. Run the program, input data, and get the results from the computer.

4.3 BAISC TOOLS FOR PROGRAMMING

If you are going to write a computer program by using any programming language like C, you need to write a rough program first for the two basic tools are available for a beginner programmer that are :

(*a*) Algorithm
(*b*) Flowcharts
(*c*) Dataflow digrams
(*d*) ER- digrams
(*e*) Decesion trees

4.4 ALGORITHM VS FLOWCHART

- An **Algorithm** is just a detailed **sequence** of simple **steps** that are needed to solve a problem.
- A **Flowchart** is a graphical representation of an algorithm.

4.5 ALGORITHM

The word algorithm comes from the name of the 9th century *Persian* mathematician *Abu Abdullah Muhammad bin Musa al-Khwarizmi.* The word *algorism* originally referred only to the rules of performing *arithmetic* using *Hindu-Arabic numerals* but evolved via European Latin translation of al-Khwarizmi's name into *algorithm* by the 18th century. The word evolved to include all definite procedures for solving problems or performing tasks.

The first case of an algorithm written for a *computer* was *Ada Byron's notes on the analytical engine* written in 1842, for which she is considered by many to be the world's first *programmer.* In *mathematics* and *computing,* an **algorithm** is a procedure (a finite *set* of well-defined instructions) for accomplishing some task which, given an initial state, will *terminate* in a defined end-state. The *computational complexity* and efficient *implementation* of the algorithm are important in writng computer programs. Just you can take example to add two numbers, a simple algorithm can be :

1. Take first number
2. Take second number
3. Add both numbers
4. Show the result

Now a programer can convert this algoritm in a computer program with the help of a programming language. If you have a problem now to sort a list of given 60 numbers using selection sort algorithm, first you have to write that algorithm there aftre you can write a C program for selection sort. A good algorithm always provide a better programming approch to a programer.

Example 4.1. *Here is a simple algorithm described if a given number n is even or odd:*

1. BEGIN
2. Read the value of number.
3. Divide number by 2 and store the remainder in *rem.*
4. If *rem* is 0, go to step 7.
5. Print "number is an odd number".

6. Go to step 8.
7. Print "number is an even number".
8. END

Applications of Algorithm

In every field of computer science you will face problems and you will need efficient algorithms. Related problems in one field are often studied together. Some example are *search algorithms, sort algorithms, merge algorithms, numerical algorithms, graph algorithms, string algorithms, computational geometric algorithms, combinatorial algorithms, machine learning, cryptography, data compression algorithms* and *parsing techniques.*

Example 4.2. *Algorithm to compute squre and cube*

1. Read the number
2. squre = number * number
3. cube = squre * number
4. print squre
5. print cube

Example 4.3.

1. Read the principle amount say *p*
2. Read the rate of interest say *r*
3. Read the time period say *t*
4. Multiply *p*, *r* and *t* and divide by 100
5. Print simple intersest

4.6 FLOWCHART

A flowchart is a diagrammatic representation that illustrates the sequence of operations to be performed to get the solution of a problem. Flowcharts are generally drawn in the early stages of formulating computer solutions. Flowcharts facilitate communication between programmers and business people. These flowcharts play a vital role in the programming of a problem and are quite helpful in understanding the logic of complicated and lengthy problems. Once the flowchart is drawn, it becomes easy to write the computer program using any high level language like C. Hence, it is correct to say that a flowchart is a must for the better documentation of a complex program.

Flowchart Symbols

Flowcharts are usually drawn using some standard symbols; however, some special symbols can also be developed when required. Some standard symbols, which are frequently required for flowcharting many computer programs are :

Symbol	Meaning
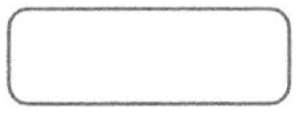	Start or end of the program
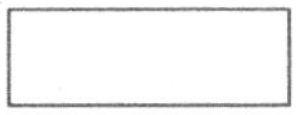	Computational steps or processing function of a program
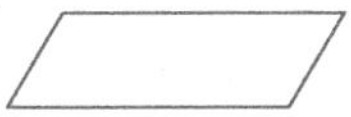	Input or output operation
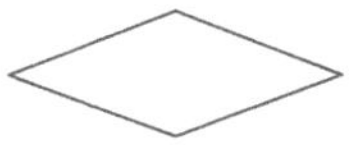	Decision making and branching
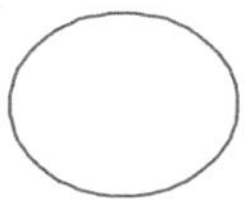	Connector or joining of two parts of program
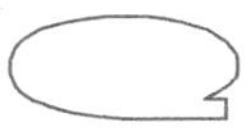	Magnetic Tape
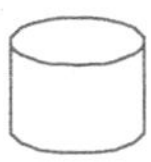	Magnetic Disk
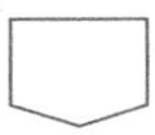	Off-page connector
	Flow line
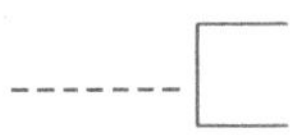	Annotation
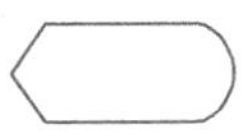	Display

Advantages of Using Flowcharts

The benefits of flowcharts are as follows:

1. *Communication:* Flowcharts are better way of communicating the logic of a system to all concerned.
2. *Effective analysis:* With the help of flowchart, problem can be analysed in more effective way.
3. *Proper documentation:* Program flowcharts serve as a good program documentation, which is needed for various purposes.
4. *Efficient Coding:* The flowcharts act as a guide or blueprint during the systems analysis and program development phase.
5. *Proper Debugging:* The flowchart helps in debugging process.
6. *Efficient Program Maintenance:* The maintenance of operating program becomes easy with the help of flowchart. It helps the programmer to put efforts more efficiently on that part.

Limitations of Flowchart

Some limitations of flowcharts are :

1. *Complex logic:* Sometimes, the program logic is quite complicated. In that case, flowchart becomes complex and clumsy.
2. *Alterations and Modifications:* If alterations are required the flowchart may require re-drawing completely.
3. *Reproduction:* As the flowchart symbols cannot be typed, reproduction of flowchart becomes a problem.
4. The essentials of what is done can easily be lost in the technical details of how it is done.

Example 4.4. *Flowchart to find the sum of first 50 natural numbers*

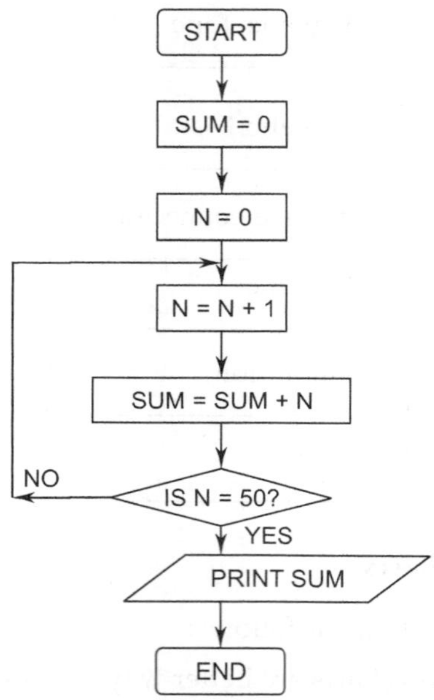

Example 4.5. *Flowchart to find the largest of three numbers A,B, and C.*

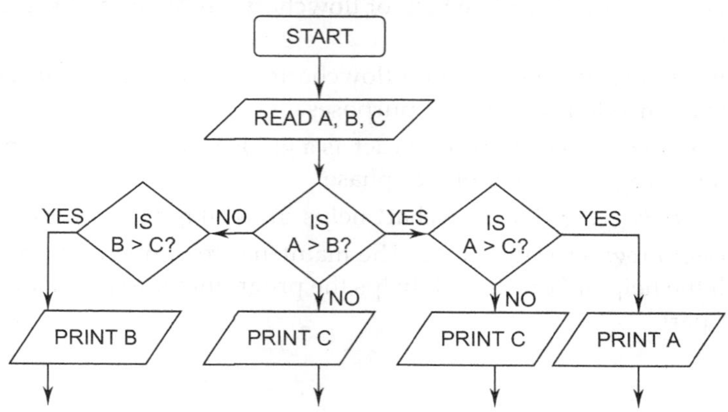

4.7 BRIEF HISTORY OF THE C LANGUAGE

C was created by Dennis Ritchie at the Bell Telephone Laboratories in 1972. The language was created for a specific purpose: to design the UNIX operating system now known as Linux. From the beginning, C was intended to be useful—to allow busy programmers to get things done.

Because C is such a powerful and flexible language, its use quickly spread beyond Bell Labs. Programmers everywhere began using it to write all sorts of programs. Soon, however, different organizations began utilizing their own versions of C, and subtle differences between implementations started to cause programmers headaches. In response to this problem, the American National Standards Institute (ANSI) formed a committee in 1983 to establish a standard definition of C, which became known as ANSI Standard C. With few exceptions, every modern C compiler has the ability to adhere to this standard.

The C language is so named because its predecessor was called B. The B language was developed by Ken Thompson of Bell Labs.

4.8 INTRODUCTION TO C PROGRAMMING

C as a Powerful High Level Language

In today's world of computer programming, there are many high-level languages to develop programs for computers, such as C, Pascal, BASIC, and Java. These are all excellent languages suited for most programming tasks. Even so, there are several reasons why many computer professionals feel that C is a powerful language

1. C is a powerful and flexible language. What you can accomplish with C is limited only by your imagination. The language itself places no constraints on you. Using C you can develop operating systems, word processors, graphics, spreadsheets, and even compilers for other languages.
2. C is a popular language preferred by professional programmers. As a result, a wide variety of C compilers and helpful accessories are available.
3. C is a portable language. Portable means that a C program written for one computer system (an PC, for example) can be compiled and run on another system (another PC) Portability is enhanced by the ANSI standard for C, the set of rules for C compilers.
4. C is a language of few words, containing only a handful of terms, called keywords, which serve as the base on which the language's functionality is built.
5. C is a modular language. C code can (and should) be written in routines called functions. These functions can be reused in other applications or programs. By passing pieces of information to the functions, you can create useful, reusable code.

Program Development Life Cycle in C

The Program Development Cycle in C has some defined steps. In the first step, you will use an editor to type your source code in a disk file say program.c. In the second step, you will compile your source code to create an object file say program.obj. In the third step, you will link the compiled code to create an executable file say program.exe. The fourth step is to run the program from to see whether it works as per your coding that originally planned by you.

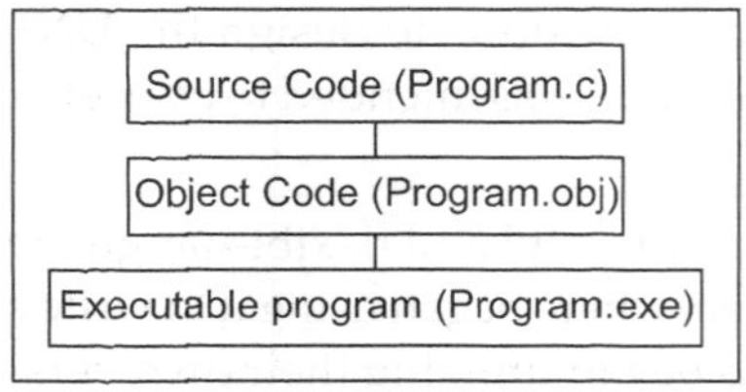

Fig. 4.1 *Program Development Cycle in C*

Popular Editors to Write C Programs

Most of the C compilers come with a built-in editor that can be used to type source code; however, some don't. If you don 't have built-in editors some of others are available.

Most computer systems include a program that can be used as an editor. If you're using a UNIX system, you can use such editors as ed, ex, edit, emacs, or vi. If you're using Microsoft Windows, Notepad is available. If you're using MS/DOS 5.0 or later, you can use Edit. If you're using a version of DOS before 5.0, you can use Edlin. If you're using PC/DOS 6.0 or later, you can use E. If you're using OS/2, you can use the E and EPM editors.

Program 4.1

```
#include <stdio.h>
main()
{
  printf("Hello friends \n");
  printf("This is your first C Program ");
}
```

Compilation of the Source Code

You have seen a C source code to print 'hello friends ' on screen. You will type your source code in English (User level language) but your computer can't understand it. A computer requires digital, or binary, instructions in what is called machine language. Before your C program can run on a computer, it must be translated from source code to machine language. This translation, the second step in program development, is performed by a program called a compiler. The compiler takes your source code file as input and produces a disk file containing the machine language instructions that correspond to your source code statements. The machine language instructions created by the compiler are called object code, and the disk file containing them is called an object file.

So the conversion of High level user written source code into a machine readable or understandable form is known as compilation of the source code.

> *Tips* : If you are using Turbo C editor, save your program as hello.c file and press CTRL and F9 to compile and execute your program and press F5 key to check your output.

Understand your program

The header #include <STDIO.H>

Each C program statrt with #include statement, by which you can add header files to your C program like in the given program STDIO.H contains the prototypes for the standard input/output functions. printf(), puts(), and scanf() are three of these standard functions. Try running a program without the STDIO.H header and see the errors and warnings you get.

Main()

main() is must function for any C program, you must use at least one main() in each C program, which control to other parts of program body and always use { to open and } to close your main().

The printf() statement

The printf() function is a part of standard C library, is a common way for a program to display data on-screen. You've already seen printf() used in many of the examples earlier. Now you will to see how printf() works.

Printing a text message on-screen is simple. Call the printf() function, passing the desired message enclosed in double quotation marks. For example, to display Hello World on-screen use

```
printf("Hello World ");
```

In addition to text messages, however, you frequently need to display the value of program variables. This is a little more complicated than displaying only a message. For example, suppose you want to display the value of the numeric variable a on-screen, along with some identifying text. Furthermore, you want the information to start at the beginning of a new line. You could use the printf() function as follows:

```
printf("\nThe value of a is %d", a);
```

The scanf() function

Just as most programs need to output data to the screen, they also need to input data from the keyboard. The most flexible way your program can read data from the keyboard is by using the scanf() library function.

The scanf() function reads data from the keyboard according to a specified format and assigns the input data to one or more program variables. Like printf(), scanf() uses a format string to describe the format of the input. The format string utilizes the same conversion specifiers as the printf() function. For example:-

```
scanf("%d", &x);
```

reads a decimal integer from the keyboard and assigns it to the integer variable x. Likewise, the following statement reads a floating-point value from the keyboard and assigns it to the variable rate:

scanf("%f", &rate);

What is that ampersand (&) before the variable's name? The & symbol is C's address-of operator used to assign a memory location to variable.

A single scanf() can input more than one value if you include multiple conversion specifiers in the format string and variable names (again, each preceded by & in the argument list). Like :-

scanf("%*d* %*f*", &*x*, &rate);

REVIEW QUESTIONS

1. Why there is a need to use programming languages?
2. What are the different program designing tool before actual writing the program?
3. Write algorithm to call your friend by your mobile, using all condidation that can stop you to make a call.
4. Write algorithm to compute average rainfall in your city, if you have data of 12 months rainfall and if you have data of 365 days rainfall also.
5. Draw flow charts also for problem 3 and 4.
6. Draw a flow-chart for picking the highest and second highest number from a set of 10 integers. **(MCA, UTU 2006-07)**
7. Write the brief history background of C language. **(MCA, UTU 2006-07)**
8. What are the steps in the program development cycle?
9. What command do you need to enter in order to compile a program called PROGRAM1.C with your compiler?
10. Does your compiler do both the linking and compiling with just one command, or you have to enter separate commands?
11. What extension should you use for your C source files?
12. Is FILENAME.TXT a valid name for a C source file?
13. If you execute a program that you have compiled and it doesn't work as you expected, what should you do?

LAB EXERCISES

1. Use your text editor to look at the object file created by your program Does the object file look like the source file?
2. Enter the following program and compile it. What does this program do?

```
#include <stdio.h>
int radius, area;
main()
{
 printf("Enter radius (i.e. 10): ");
 scanf("%d", &radius );
 area = (int) (3.14159 * radius * radius);
```

```
    printf("\n\nArea = %d\n", area );
    return 0;
}
```

3. Enter and compile the following program. What does this program do?

```
#include <stdio.h>
int x,y;
main()
{
    for ( x = 0; x < 10; x++, printf("\n") )
    for ( y = 0; y < 10; y++ )
      printf("*");
                }
```

4. The following program has a problem. Enter it in your editor and compile it. Which lines generate error messages?

```
#include <stdio.h>
main();
{
  printf("Keep cool!");
  printf("You\'ll find it!\n");
}
```

5. Following program has a problem. Enter it in your editor and compile it. Which lines generate problems?

```
#include <stdio.h>
main()
{
    printf("This is a program with a ");
    doit("problem!");
}
```

5

STRUCTURE OF 'C'

5.1 STRUCTURE OF C PROGRAM

In C language, when you start to write your programs, a defined structure is there, in which you have to write the complete program, the structure is :

#include Statement

#include <stdio.h>

The main() Function

main()

Variable Definition

int *a,b,c;*

Program Statements

printf("Enter two numbers between 1 and 100: ");

scanf("*%d %d*", &*a*,&*b*);

c=a+b;

printf("sum=*%d* ",*c*);

Program Comments

/* Program to calculate the sum of two numbers. */

/* Input the first number */

/* Input the second number */

Braces

{ }

#include statement

The #include directive instructs the C compiler to add the contents of an include file into your program during compilation. An include file is a separate disk file that contains information needed by your program or the compiler. Several of these files (sometimes called header files) are supplied with your compiler. You never need to modify the information in these files; that's why they're kept separate from your source code. Include files should all have an.H extension (for example, STDIO.H).

You use the #include directive to instruct the compiler to add a specific include file to your program during compilation. The use of #include directive in any C program means Add the contents of the header file like STDIO.H. Most C programs require one or more include files. Like math.h, conio.h, graphics.h etc.

Function Prototype in a C Program

A function prototype provides the C compiler with the name and arguments of the functions contained in the program. It must appear before the function is used. A function prototype is distinct from a function definition, which contains the actual statements that make up the function :

Example 5.1.

```
int sum ( int x, int y ) ;
float interest (int x, int y, int z );
```

'C' statement

The real work of a C program is done by its statements. C statements display information on-screen, read keyboard input, perform mathematical operations, call functions, read disk files, and carry out all the other operations that a program needs to perform. For now, remember that in your source code, C statements are generally written one per line and always end with a semicolon.

Example :

```
int a, b ;
a=0,b=0;
scanf("%d%d",&a,&b);
printf("%d%d",a,b);
```

all lines are in form of C statement.

Program Comments in C

Any part of your program that starts with /* and ends with */ is called a comment. The compiler ignores all comments, so they have absolutely no effect on how a program works. You can put anything you want into a comment, and it won't modify the way your program operates. A comment can span part of a line, an entire line, or multiple lines. Here are three examples:

```
/* A single-line comment */
                  int a,b,c; /* A partial-line comment */
/* a comment
spanning
multiple lines */
```

However, you shouldn't use nested comments (in other words, you shouldn't put one comment within another). Most

compilers would not accept the following:

```
/*
/* Nested comment */
*/
```

Why comments ?

A Comments are for the programmer. When the compiler converts the source code to object code, it throws the comments and the white space away. This means that they have no effect on the executable program. Comments do make your source file bigger,but this is usually of little concern. To summarize, you should use comments and white space to make your source code as easy to understand and maintain as possible.

Block

A block is a group of statements enclosed in braces ({}). A block can be used in most places that a statement can be used.

```
main()
{
int x=5;      //statement
printf("%d",x);
}
```

C Statement

A statement is a complete direction instructing the computer to carry out some task. In C, statements are usually written one per line, although some statements can use multiple lines. C statements always end with a semicolon (except for preprocessor directives such as #define and #include). Some of C's statement, For example:

x = 2 + 3;

sum=num1+num2+num3;

is an assignment statement. It instructs the computer to add 2 and 3 and to assign the result to the variable *x*.

White Spaces

The term white space refers to spaces, tabs, and blank lines in your source code. The C compiler isn't sensitive to white space. When the compiler reads a statement in your source code, it looks for the characters in the statement and for the terminating semicolon, but it ignores white space. Thus, the statement

```
x=2+3;
```

is equivalent to this statement:

```
x = 2 + 3;
```

Null Vs Compound statement

Null Statements

If you place a semicolon by itself on a line, you create a null statement--a statement that doesn't perform any action. This is perfectly legal in C.

Compound Statements

A compound statement, also called a block, is a group of two or more C statements enclosed in braces. Here's an example of a block:

```
{
  printf("Hello,  ");
  printf("world!");
}
```

In C, a block can be used anywhere a single statement can be used. It's a good idea to place braces on their own lines, making the beginning and end of blocks clearly visible. Placing braces on heir own lines also makes it easier to see whether you've left one out.

5.2 VARIABLE AND CONSTANTS

The RAM in your computer is organized sequentially, one byte following another. Each byte of memory has a unique address by which it is identified—an address that also distinguishes it from all other bytes in memory. Addresses are assigned to memory locations in order, starting at zero and increasing to the system limit. So what is your computer's RAM used for? It has several uses, but only data storage need concern you as a programmer. Data is the information with which your C program works. Whether your program is maintaining an address list, monitoring the stock market, keeping a household budget, or tracking the price of a book, the information (names, stock prices, expense amounts) is kept in your computer's RAM while the program is running.So RAM is used to store temporary values of variables or constants used in C program.

Variables in C

A variable is a named data storage location in your computer's memory. In a program there is a need to store value of number or text or some decimal digit then by using a variable's name in your program, you can refer a name to data stored that value like :

int firstnumber = 0;

here is firstnumber is variable which will store an integer value in future.

Rules for Variable Names

To use variables in your C programs, you must know how to create variable names. In C, variable names must adhere to the following rules:

1. The name can contain letters, digits, and the underscore character (_).
2. The first character of the name must be a letter. The underscore is also a legal first character, but its use is not recommended.
3. Case matters (that is, upper- and lowercase letters). Thus, the names count and Count refer to two different variables.
4. C keywords can't be used as variable names. A keyword is a word that is part of the C language. (A complete list of 33 C keywords can be found in Appendix B, "Reserved Words.")

Examples 5.2. *Valid variables names*

Variable Name	*Legality*
Price	Legal
stu__name	Legal
annualprofit	Legal
savings#account	Illegal: Contains the illegal character #
double	Illegal: Is a C keyword
9winter	Illegal: First character is a digit

Variable Declaration in C

Before you can use a variable in a C program, it must be declared. A variable declaration tells the compiler the name and datatype of a variable and optionally initializes the variable to a specific value. If you want to use a variable that hasn't been declared, the compiler generates an error message. A variable declaration has the following form:

Datatype varname;

int myage;

Datatype specifies the variable type and must be one of the C datatype. varname is the variable name, which must follow the rules mentioned earlier. You can declare multiple variables of the same type on one line by separating the variable names with commas:

```
int count, number, start;      /* three integer variables */
float percent, total;  /* two float variables */
```

5.2.1 C Keywords

The C language reserves certain words that have special meanings to the language. Those reserved words are sometimes called C keywords. You should not use the C keywords as variable, constant, or function names in your program. The following are the 32 reserved C keywords:

Keyword	*Description*
auto	Storage class specifier
break	Statement
case	Statement
char	Type specifier
const	Storage class modifier
continue	Statement
default	Label
do	Statement
double	Type specifier
else	Statement
enum	Type specifier
extern	Storage class specifier
float	Type specifier
for	Statement
goto	Statement
if	Statement
int	Type specifier
long	Type specifier
register	Storage class specifier
return	Statement
short	Type specifier
signed	Type specifier
sizeof	Operator
static	Storage class specifier
struct	Type specifier
switch	Statement
typedef	Statement
union	Type specifier
unsigned	Type specifier
void	Type specifier
volatile	Storage class modifier
while	Statement

5.3 C DATA TYPES

C language has four data types :

1. char data type 1 byte
2. int data type 2 byte
3. float data type 4 byte 'used for decimal values
4. double data type 4 byte

In later part you will learn the way to modify that original data types of C using e long, short, signed, unsigned keywords before a int, char datatype. Like :

short int age;

unsigned int salary;

char DATA TYPE

An object of the char data type represents a single character of the character set used by your computer. For example, A is a character, and so is a. But 7 is a number.

But a computer can only store numeric code. Therefore, characters such as A, a, B, b, and so on all have a unique numeric code that is used by computers to represent the characters. Usually, a character takes 8 bits (that is, 1 byte) to store its numeric code.

You can set the data type of a variable to char by using the following declaration format:

char variablename;

or

char variablename1, variablename2, variablename3;

Example :

char sem, course, colorcode ;

Character Constants

A character enclosed in single quotes (' ') is called a character constant. For instance, 'A', '*a*', 'B', and '*b*' are all character constants that have their unique numeric values in the ASCII character set.

char *x* = '*a*';

char *y* = 97;

The char datatype Format Specifier is **(%c).**

Program 5.1 *Printing out characters on the screen.*

```
/* Printing out characters */
#include <stdio.h>
main( )
{
          char c1;
```

```
        char c2;
        c1 = 'A';
        c2 = 'a';
        printf("Convert the value of c1 to character: %c.\n", c1);
        printf("Convert the value of c2 to character: %c.\n", c2);
}
```

int DATATYPE

The int keyword is used to specify the type of a variable as an integer. Integer numbers are also called whole numbers, which have no fractional part or decimal point. Therefore, the result of an integer division is truncated, simply because any fraction part is ignored.

Depending on the operating system and the C compiler you're using, the length of an integer varies. On most UNIX/Windows workstations, for example, an integer is 32 bits long, which means that the range of an integer is from 2147483647 to -2147483648. The range of a 16-bit integer at DOS is from 32767 to -32768.

Declaring Integer Variables

Following shows the basic declaration format:

int variablename;

Similar to the character declaration, if you have more than one variable to declare, you can use either the format like this

int variablename1;

int variablename2;

int variablename3;

or like this:

int variablename1, variablename2, variablename3;

The int datatype Format Specifier is **(%*d*).**

Program 5.2 *Printing out numbers on the screen.*

```
/* Printing out numbers */
#include <stdio.h>
main()
{
        int x;
        int y;
        printf("enter values of x and y ");
        scanf("%d%d",&x,&y);
        printf ("%d", x);
```

```
        printf("%d",y);
    }
```

Program 5.3 *To print cube of a given number*

```
#include<stdio.h>
#include<conio.h>
main()
{
    int n,cube;
    clrscr();
    printf("****Program to print cube of a number****");
    printf("\nenter the value of number ");
    scanf("%d",&n);
    cube=n*n*n;
    printf("Cube of given number is =%d",cube);
    getch();
}
```

Program 5.4 *To computer simple interest using integer values*

```
#include<stdio.h>
#include<conio.h>
main()
{
    int p,r,t,s;
    clrscr();
    printf("****Program to calculate simple interest****");
    printf("\n enter the value of principle");
    scanf("%d",&p);
    printf("\n enter the value of rate");
    scanf("%d",&r);
    printf("\n enter the value of time");
    scanf("%d",&t);
    s=(p*r*t)/100;
    printf("s=%d",s);
    getch();
}
```

> *Tips*: We are using getch() function of conio.h header file to stop your program on screen, it will wait for press any key by you.

float DATA TYPE

The floating-point number is another data type in the C language. Unlike an integer number, a floating-point number contains a decimal point. For instance, 7.01 is a floating-point number; so are 5.71 and – 3.14. A floating-point number is also called a real number.A floating-point number is specified by the float keyword in the C language.

Like an integer number, a floating-point number has a limited range. The ANSI standard requires that the range be at least plus or minus 1.0*1037. Normally, a floating-point number is represented by taking 32 bits. Therefore, a floating-point number in C is of at least six digits of precision. That is, for a floating-point number, there are at least six digits (or decimal places) on the right side of the decimal point.

Declaring Floating-Point Variables

The following shows the declaration format for a floating-point variable:

float variablename;

Similar to the character or integer declaration, if you have more than one variable to declare, you can either use the format like this:

float variablename1;

float variablename2;

float variablename3;

or like the following one:

float variablename1, variablename2, variablename3;

The Floating-Point Format Specifier is **(%*f*).**

Program 5.5 *Printing out floating(decimals)numbers on the screen.*

```
#include  <stdio.h>
main()
{
        float x; /* Printing out float numbers */
        float y;
        printf("enter values of x and y ");
        scanf("%f%f",&x,&y);
        printf ("x=%f", x);
        printf("y=%f",y);
}
```

Program 5.6 *To compute area of a circle on given redious usin floating(decimals)numbers*

```
#include<stdio.h>
```

```
#include<conio.h>
#define pi 3.14
void main()
{
        float area,r;
        clrscr();
        printf("****Program to print area of a circle****");
        printf("\n enter the value of radius");
        scanf("%f",&r);
        area=pi*r*r;
        printf("Area of circle is =%f",area);
        getch();
}
```

Tips : See the use of #define in above program.

Program 5.7 *To convert farenhite to centigrade*

```
#include<stdio.h>
#include<conio.h>
void main()
{
        float f,c;
        clrscr();
        printf("****PROGRAM TO CONVERT FARENHITE TO CENTI-
   GRADE****");
        printf("\n enter the temperature in farenhite");
        scanf("%f",&f);
        c=(f-32)/1.8;
        printf("Tempereture in c=%f",c);
        getch();
}
```

double DATA TYPE

Format Specifiers %*c*, %*d*, and %*f*

These are format specifiers. %*c* is used to obtain the character format; %*d* is for the integer format; %*f* is for the floating-point format. %*c*, %*d*, and %*f* are often used with C functions such as printf().

Program 5.8 *Use of format specifiers*

```
#include <stdio.h>
main()
{
char alpha='Y";
int age=23;
float rate=5.67;
printf("%c",alpha); //character value
printf("%d",age); // integer value
printf("%f",rate); // decimal value
}
```

5.4 DATA TYPE MODIFIERS

Now you have worked with primary C data types, such as char, int, float, and double. Now you can start to paly with four data type modifiers that enable you to have greater control over the data types use in your programs. The four data modifiers are :

- signed
- unsigned
- short
- long

The Sign Bit

It is very easy to express a negative number in decimal like – 56 or – 780. All you need to do is put a minus sign in front of the absolute value of the number. But how does the computer represent a negative number in the binary format ?Normally, one bit can be used to indicate whether the value of a number represented in the binary format is negative. This bit is called the **sign bit.** The two data modifiers, signed and unsigned, will help you to enable or disable the sign bit.

The signed Modifier

For integers, the leftmost bit can be used as the sign bit. For instance, if the int data type is 16 bits long and the rightmost bit is counted as bit 0, you can use bit 15 as a sign bit. When the sign bit is set to 1, the C compiler knows that the value represented by the data variable is negative. The C language provides a data modifier, signed, that can be used to indicate to the compiler that the int or char data type uses the sign bit. By default, the int data type is a signed quantity. But if you want to use a signed character variable, and make sure the compiler knows it, you can declare the character variable like this:

signed char ch;

Now the compiler knows that the character variable ch is signed, which means the variable can take a value in the range of –128 to 127. As you learn earlier that for an unsigned character variable, the range is 0 to 255.

> ***Tips*** **:** To represent a negative number in the binary format, you can first get its equivalent positive value's binary format. Then you perform the complement operation on the binary, and finally, add one to the complemented binary. For Example take a negative integer –12345, to represent it in the binary format, First, you need to find the binary format for the positive integer 12345, which is 0011000000111001. Then, you perform the complement operation on 0011000000111001, that is, ~0011000000111001, and obtain the following:
>
> 1100111111000110
>
> And finally, adding 1 to 1100111111000110 gives you 1100111111000111, which is the binary format of the negative integer –12345.

The unsigned Modifier

The C language also gives you the unsigned modifier, which can be used to tell the C compiler that no sign bit is needed in the specified data type. Like the signed modifier, the unsigned modifier is meaningful only to the int and char data types. For instance, the declaration :

unsigned int a;

tells the C compiler that the integer variable a can only assume positive values from 0 to 65535 if the int data type has 16 bits.

Program 5.9 *Use of signed and unsigned.*

```
#include <stdio.h>
main()
    {
    signed char ch;
   int x;
   unsigned int y;
     ch = 0xFF;
     x = 0xFFFF;
     y = 0xFFFFu;
   printf("The decimal of signed 0xFF is %d.\n", ch);
       printf("The decimal of signed 0xFFFF is %d.\n", x);
       printf("The decimal of unsigned 0xFFFFu is %u.\n", y);
       printf("The hex of decimal 12345 is 0x%X.\n", 12345);
       printf("The hex of decimal -12345 is 0x%X.\n", -12345);
   }
```

Changing Data Sizes

Sometimes, you want to reduce the memory taken by variables, or you need to increase the storage space of certain data types. Fortunately, the C language gives you the flexibility to modify sizes of data types. The two data modifiers, short and long, will help you to decrease or increase the size of data type.

The short Modifier

A data type can be modified to take less memory by using the short modifier. For instance, you can apply the short modifier to an integer variable that is 32 bits long, which might reduce the memory taken by the variable to as little as 16 bits.You can use the short modifier like this:

short *x*;

unsigned short *y*;

By default, a short int data type is a signed number. Therefore, in the short *x*; statement, *x* is a signed variable of short integer.

The long Modifier

If you need more memory to keep values from a wider range, you can use the long modifier to define a data type with increased storage space. For example, given an integer variable *x* that is 16 bits long, the declaration :

long int *x*;

increases the size of *x* to 32 bits. In other words, after the modification, *x* is capable of holding a range of values from –2147483648 to 2147483647.

Program 5.10 *Use of short and long modifiers*

```
#include <stdio.h>
    main()
    {
    printf("The size of short int is: %d.\n",
    sizeof(short int));
    printf("The size of long int is: %d.\n",
    sizeof(long int));
    printf("The size of float is: %d.\n",
    sizeof(float));
    printf("The size of double is: %d.\n",
    sizeof(double));
    printf("The size of long double is: %d.\n",
    sizeof(long double));
    }
```

> ***Tips:*** sizeof() is a C defined functions, used to retrive the default values of data types set by your C compiler and environment of operating system.

h, l, or L to Format Specifiers

You can use *h* with the integer format specifier (like %*hd*, %*hi*, or %*hu*) to specify that the corresponding number is a short int or unsigned short int.On the other hand, using %*ld* or %L*d* specifies that the corresponding data type is long int. %*lu* or %L*u* is then used for the long unsigned int data.

Program 5.11 *Use of %hd, %ld, and %lu.*

```
#include  <stdio.h>
main()
 {
      short int x;
      unsigned int y;
      long int s;
      unsigned long int t;
      x = 0xFFFF;
      y = 0xFFFFU;
      s = 0xFFFFFFFFl;
      t = 0xFFFFFFFFL;
      printf("The short int of 0xFFFF is %hd.\n", x);
      printf("The unsigned int of 0xFFFF is %u.\n", y);
      printf("The long int of 0xFFFFFFFF is %ld.\n", s);
      printf("The unsigned long int of 0xFFFFFFFF is %lu.\n", t);
      }
```

5.5 CONSTANTS IN C

Like a variable, a constant is a data storage location used by your program. Unlike a variable, the value stored in a constant can't be changed during program execution. C has two types of constants, each with its own specific uses.

Literal Constants

A literal constant is a value that is typed directly into the source code wherever it is needed. Like :

int count = 200;

float tax_rate = 10.28;

The 200 and the 10.28 are literal constants. The preceding statements store these values in the variables count and tax_rate. Note that one of these constants contains a decimal point, whereas the other does not. The presence or absence of the decimal point distinguishes floating-point constants from integer constants.

A literal constant written with a decimal point is a floating-point constant and is represented by the C compiler as a double-precision number. Floating-point constants can be written in standard decimal notation, as shown in these examples:

123.456

0.019

The decimal point causes the C compiler to treat the constant as a double-precision value. Without the decimal point, it is treated as an integer constant. Floating-point constants also can be written in scientific notation. Scientific notation is particularly useful for representing extremely large and extremely small values. In C, scientific notation is written as a decimal number followed immediately by an E or e and the exponent:

1.23E2 means 1.23 with 2 powers of 10, or 123

4.08e6 means 4.08 with 6 power of 10, or 4,080,000

A constant written without a decimal point is represented by the compiler as an integer number. Integer constants can be written in three different notations:

A constant starting with any digit other than 0 is interpreted as a decimal integer. Decimal constants can contain the digits 0 through 9 and a leading minus or plus sign. Without a leading minus or plus, a constant is assumed to be positive.

```
int MAXMARKS=100 ;
```

A constant starting with the digit 0 is interpreted as an octal integer (the base-8 number system). Octal constants can contain the digits 0 through 7 and a leading minus or plus sign. Like :

```
int m=045;
```

A constant starting with 0x or 0X is interpreted as a hexadecimal constant (the base-16 number system). Hexadecimal constants can contain the digits 0 through 9, the letters A through F, and a leading minus or plus sign. Like :

```
short int x = 0xFFFF;
```

Symbolic Constants

A symbolic constant is a constant that is represented by a name or symbol in your program. Like a literal constant, a symbolic constant can't change. Whenever you need the constant's value in your program, you use its name as you would use a variable name. The actual value of the symbolic constant needs to be entered only once, when it is first defined.

Symbolic constants have two significant advantages over literal constants, as the following example shows. Suppose that you're writing a program that performs a variety of geometrical calculations. The program frequently needs the value of PI that is 3.14159) for its calculations. For example, to calculate the circumference and area of a circle with a known radius, you can write :

```
circumference = 3.14159 * (2 * radius);
area = 3.14159 * (radius)*(radius);
```

If, however, you define a symbolic constant with the name PI and the value 3.141, you could write

```
circumference = PI * (2 * radius);
area = PI * (radius)*(radius);
```

The resulting code is clearer. Rather than puzzling over what the value 3.141 is for, you can see immediately that the constant PI is being used.

The second advantage of symbolic constants becomes apparent when you need to change a constant. Continuing with the preceding example, you might decide that for greater accuracy your program needs to use a value of PI with more decimal places: 3.14159 rather than 3.14. If you had used literal constants for PI, you would have to go through your source code and change each occurrence of the value from 3.141 to 3.14159. With a symbolic constant, you need to make a change only in the place where the constant is defined.

C has two methods for defining a symbolic constant: the #define directive and the const keyword. The #define directive is one of C's preprocessor directives, and it will discussed in future. The #define directive is used as follows:

```
#define CONSTNAME literal
#define PI 3.14159
#define YES 1
#define NO 0
#define RED 3
```

Note that #define lines don't end with a semicolon (;). #defines can be placed anywhere in your source code, Most commonly, as a good programmer you should use all #defines together, near the beginning of the file and before the start of main().

Defining Constants with the Const Keyword

The second way to define a symbolic constant is with the const keyword. const is a modifier that can be applied to any variable declaration. A variable declared to be const can't be modified during program execution only initialized at the time of declaration. Here are some examples:

```
const int count = 100;
const float pi = 3.14159;
const long debt = 12000000, float tax_rate = 0.21;
```

5.6 ENUMERATED TYPE

Enumerations provide a convenient way to associate constant values with names, an alternative to #define with the advantage that the values can be generated for you. Although variables of enum types may be declared, compilers need not check that what you store in such a variable is a valid value for the enumeration. Nevertheless, enumeration variables offer the chance of checking and so are often better than #defines. In addition, a debugger may be able to print values of enumeration variables in their symbolic form.

An enumeration is a list of constant integer values like :

```
enum months { JAN = 1, FEB, MAR, APR, MAY, JUN,
              JUL, AUG, SEP, OCT, NOV, DEC };
                /* FEB = 2, MAR = 3, etc. */
```

Names in different enumerations must be distinct. Values need not be distinct in the same enumeration.

5.7 STORAGE CLASSES

Scope of a Variable

The scope of a variable refers to the extent to which different parts of a program have access to the variable in other words, where the variable is visible. When referring to C variables, the terms accessibility and visibility are used interchangeably. When speaking about scope, the term variable refers to all C data types either simple variables or arrays, structures, pointers etc. It also refers to symbolic constants defined with the const keyword. Scope also affects a variable's lifetime like how long the variable persists in memory, or when the variable's storage is allocated and deallocated.

Program 5.12 *Demo of variable scope*

```
#include <stdio.h>
int x = 99;
void printvalue(void);
main()
{
  printf("%d\n", x);
  printvalue();
 {
void printvalue(void)
{
printf("%d\n", x);
}
```

Look at the program, It defines the variable *x* to 99, uses printf() to display the value of *x* in main(), and then calls the function printvalue() to display the value of *x* again. It will compile and you will get same value of *x* at both location because scope of *x* in global, now change the program as :

```
#include <stdio.h>
void printvalue(void);
 main()
{
int x = 99;
printf("%d\n", x);
 printvalue();
 }
void printvalue(void)
{
printf("%d\n", x);
}
```

Now scope of *x* is local for main(), it will not compile and you will get error in your program.

The Storage Class Specifiers

In C, the storage class of a variable refers to the combination of its local or global presence.You are now familier with scope, which specifies the region of a variable. There are four specifiers and two modifiers that can be used to indicate the duration of a variable. These specifiers and modifiers are :

The auto Specifier

The auto specifier indicates that the memory location of a variable is temporary. In other words, a variable's reserved space in the memory can be erased or relocated when the variable is out of its scope. Only variables with block scope can be declared with the auto specifier. The auto keyword is rarely used, however, because the duration of a variable with block scope is temporary or auto by default.

The static Specifier

The static specifier, on the other hand, can be applied to variables with either block scope or program scope. When a variable within a function is declared with the static specifier, the variable has a permanent duration. In other words, the memory storage allocated for the variable is not destroyed when the scope of the variable is exited, the value of the variable is maintained outside the scope, and if execution ever returns to the scope of the variable, the last value stored in the variable is still there. For example, in the following code portion:

```
main()
{
    int i;                  /* block scope and temporary duration */
    static int j;           /* block scope and permanent duration */
}
```

the integer variable i has temporary duration by default. But the other integer variable, j, has permanent duration due to the storage class specifier static.

Program 5.13 *Use of static specifier*

```
#include <stdio.h>
/* the addtwo function */
int addtwo(int x, int y)
{
static int counter = 1;
printf("This is the function call of %d.\n", counter++);
return (x + y);
}
/* the main function */
main()
{
int i, j;
for (i=0, j=5; i<5; i++, j--)
printf("the addition of %d and %d is %d.\n\n", i, j, addtwo(i, j));
}
```

Analysis

The purpose of the is to call a function to add two integers and then print out the result returned by the function on the screen. The function is called several times. A counter is set to keep track of how many times the function has been called.This function, called addtwo(), is declared. There are two int arguments, *x* and *y*, that are passed to the function, and the addition of the two arguments is returned. Note that there is an integer variable, counter, that is declared with the static specifier. Values stored by counter are retained because the duration of the variable is permanent. In other words, although the scope of counter is within the block of the addtwo() function, the memory location of counter and value saved in the location are not changed after the addtwo() function is called and the execution control is returned back to the main() function. Therefore, the counter variable is used as a counter to keep the number of calls received by the addtwo() function. In fact, the statement of the printf() function prints out the value saved by the counter variable each time the addtwo()

function is called. In addition, counter is incremented by one each time after the printf() function is executed.The for loop, declared within the main() function, calls the addtwo() function five times. The values of the two integer variables, *i* and *j*, are passed to the addtwo() function for the operation of addition. Then, the return value from the addtwo() function is displayed on the screen by the printf() function.From the output, you can see that the value saved by counter is indeed incremented by one each time the addtwo() function is called, and is retained after the function exits because the integer variable counter is declared with static. Note that counter is only initialized once when the addtwo() function is called for the first time.

The register Specifier

The word register is related with computer hardware. Each computer has certain number of registers to hold data and perform arithmetic or logical calculations. Because registers are located within the CPU chip, it's much quicker to access a register than a memory location. Therefore, storing variables in registers may help to speed up your program. The C language provides you with the register specifier. You can apply this specifier to variables when you think it's necessary to put the variables into the computer registers. However, the register specifier only gives the compiler a suggestion. In other words, a variable specified by the register keyword is not guaranteed to be stored in a register. The compiler can ignore the suggestion if there is no register available, or if some other restrictions have to apply.

```
main()
{
    /* block scope with the register specifier */
    register int i;
}
```

in the above declaration the variable is declared as register variable.

The extern Specifier

An external variable is a variable defined outside of any function. This means outside of main() as well, because main() is a function, too. Until now, most of the variable definitions in this book have been external, placed in the source code before the start of main(). External variables are sometimes referred to as global variables. The scope of an external variable is the entire program. This means that an external variable is visible throughout main() and every other function in the program.

The extern Keyword

When a function uses an external variable, it is good programming practice to declare the variable within the function using the extern keyword. The declaration takes the form extern type name; in which type is the variable type and name is the variable name. The variable with program scope is also called a global variable.

Now just think about a software where you have many programs in many files and you want to use a global variable declared in file A, in another file B, tht means the compiler know that the variable used in file B is actually the same variable declared in file A. For that use the extern specifier provided by the C language to allude to a global variable defined elsewhere. In this case, we declare a global variable in file A, and then declare the variable again using the extern specifier in file B. Like :

Example 5.14

```
int x = 0;            /* a global variable */
extern int y;         /* an allusion to a global variable y */
main()
{
    extern int z;     /* an allusion to a global variable z */
    int i;            /* a local variable */
    statements  ;
}
```

As you can see, there are two integer variables, *y* and *z*, that are declared with the extern specifier, outside and inside the main() function, respectively. When the compiler sees the two declarations, it knows that the declarations are actually allusions to the global variables *y* and *z* that are defined elsewhere in other files.

5.8 COMMAND-LINE ARGUMENTS

In your C program you can pass values to the program from you operating system prompt that can be like :

C:\TC\BIN>

Most of the program you have written, all the values entered by keyboard, after the execution fo the program, but if you want to pass two numbers like 45 and 67 from command prompt to your program, to add them, you can write :

C:\TC\BIN>sumoftwo 45 67

Here sum of two is the name of your program while two command-line arguments 45 and 67 can be retrieved by the program during execution. You can think of this information as arguments passed to the program's main() function. Such command-line arguments permit information to be passed to the program at startup rather than during execution, which can be convenient at times. You can pass as many command-line arguments as you like. Note that command-line arguments can be retrieved only within main(). For the change your main() as :

```
main(int argc, char *argv[])
{
```

```
/* Statements go here */
}
```

The first parameter, argc, is an integer giving the number of command-line arguments available. This value is always at least 1, because the program name is counted as the first argument. The parameter argv[] is an array of pointers to strings. The argv[0] points to the program name including path information, argv[1] points to the first argument that follows the program name, and so on.

Program 5. 15 *Sum of two numbers using command line arguments*

```
#include <stdio.h>
main(int argc, char *argv[])
{
 int sum=0;
printf("Program name: %s\n", argv[0]);
sum=argv[1]+argv[2];
printf("Sum of numbers is = %d, sum);
}
```

Save the program as sumoftwo.c in C:\TC\BIN, compile and execute form command prompt like :

```
C:\TC\BIN>sumoftwo 45 67
```

5.9 THE C PREPROCESSOR

The preprocessor is a part of all C compiler packages. When you compile a C program, the preprocessor is the first compiler component that processes your program. In most C compilers, the preprocessor is part of the compiler program. When you run the compiler, it automatically runs the preprocessor. The preprocessor changes your source code based on instructions, or preprocessor directives, in the source code. The output of the preprocessor is a modified source code file that is then used as the input for the next compilation step. Normally you never see this file, because the compiler deletes it after it's used. However, later in this chapter you'll learn how to look at this intermediate file. First, you need to learn about the preprocessor directives, all of which begin with the # symbol.

Pre-processor commands are distinguished by the hash (number) symbol #. One example of this has already been encountered for the standard header file `stdio.h`.

```
#include <stdio.h>
```

is a command which tells the preprocessor to treat the file `stdio.h` as if it were the actually part of the program text, in other words to include it as part of the program to be compiled.

When an include statement is written into a program, it is a sign that a compiler should merge another file of C programming with the current one. However, the `#include` statement is itself valid C, so this means that a file which is included may contain `#includes` itself. The includes are then said to be "nested".

Other Preprocessor Commands

`#undef`

This undefines a macro, leaving the name free.

`#if`

This is followed by some expression on the same line. It allows *conditional compilation.* It is an advanced feature which can be used to say: only compile the code between `#if` and `#endif` if the value following `#if` is true, else leave out that code altogether. This is different from not executing code--the code will not even be compiled.

`#ifdef`

This is followed by a macro name. If that macro is defined then this is true.

`#ifndef`

This is followed by a macro name. If that name is not defined then this is true.

`#else`

This is part of an `#if, #ifdef, #ifndef` preprocessor statement.

`#endif`

This marks the end of a preprocessor statement.

`#line`

Has the form:

`#line constant filename`

This is for debugging mainly. This statement causes the compiler to believe that the next line is line number (constant) and is part of the file (filename).

`#error`

This is a part of the proposed ANSI standard. It is intended for debugging. It forces the compiler to abort compilation.

Program 5.16 *Use of preprocessor derivatives*

```
/* To compile or not to compile */
#define SOMEDEFINITION 6546
#define CHOICE 1
#if (CHOICE == 1)
#define OPTIONSTRING   "The programmer selected this"
#define DITTO              "instead of....  "
#else
#define OPTIONSTRING   "The alternative"
```

```
#define DITTO           "This! "
#endif
#ifdef SOMEDEFINITION
#define WHATEVER "Something was defined!"
#else
#define WHATEVER "Nothing was defined"
#endif
main ()
{
printf (OPTIONSTRING);
printf (DITTO);
}
```

5.10 MACROS

Macros are C words which can be defined to use in place of something complicated say they are a way of reducing the amount of typing in a program and a way of writing long pieces of code into short words. For example, the simplest use of macros is to give constant values meaningful names like :

```
#define MOBILENO 09897562188
#define EMAIL sharmamkhld@gmail.com
```

This allows us to use the word MOBILENO or EMAIL in the program to mean the number 09897562188 or for my mail id. In this particular case, the word is clearly not any shorter than the number it will replace, but it is more meaningful and would make a program read more naturally than if the raw number were used. Like :

The important feature of macros is that they are not merely numerical constants which are referenced at compile time, but are strings which are physically replaced before compilation by the preprocessor! This means that almost anything can be defined like :

```
#define SUM 1 + 2 + 3 + 4
#define INAME "Amrapali Institute of Management & Computer applications"
```

Macro Functions

A more advanced use of macros is also permitted by the preprocessor. This involves macros which accept parameters and hand back values. This works by defining a macro with some dummy parameter, say *x*. For example: a macro which is usually defined in one of the standard libraries is abs() which means the absolute or unsigned value of a number. It is defined below:

```
#define ABS(x) ((x) < 0) ? -(x) : (x)
```

The result of this is to give the positive (or unsigned) part of any number or variable. This would be no problem for a function which could accept parameters, and it is, in fact, no problem for macros. Macros can also be made to take parameters. Consider the ABS() example. If a programmer were to write ABS(14) then the preprocessor would substitute 4 for x. If a program read ABS(i) then the preprocessor would substitute i for x and so on.

Program 5.17

```
#include <stdio.h>
#define STRING1          "A macro by\n"
#define STRING2          "MK Sharma !!\n"
#define EXPRESSION     1 + 2 + 3 + 4 +5 +6
#define EXPR2            EXPRESSION + 110
#define ABS(x)         ((x) < 0) ? -(x) : (x)
#define MAX(a,b)       (a < b) ? (b) : (a)
#define BIGGEST(a,b,c) (MAX(a,b) < c) ? (c) : (MAX(a,b))
    main ()
    {
    printf (STRING1);
    printf (STRING2);
    printf ("%d\n",EXPRESSION);
    printf ("%d\n",EXPR2);
    printf ("%d\n",ABS(-5));
    printf ("Biggest of 1 2 and 3 is %d",BIGGEST(1,2,3));
    }
```

REVIEW QUESTIONS

1. What's the difference between an integer variable and a floating-point variable?
2. What do you mean by an identifier ? Explain with examples the rule for writing an identifier. **[MCA, UTU 2006-07]**
3. Give two reasons for using a double-precision floating-point variable (type double) instead of a single-precision floating-point variable (type float).
4. What are five rules that the ANSI Standard states are always true when allocating size for variables?
5. Explain in brief various data types. **[MCA, UTU 2006-07]**
6. What are the two advantages of using a symbolic constant instead of a literal constant?
7. Show two methods for defining a symbolic constant named MAXIMUM that has a value of 100.
8. What characters are allowed in C variable names?
9. What guidelines should you follow in creating names for variables and constants?
10. What's the difference between a symbolic and a literal constant? **[MCA, UTU 2006-07]**
11. What's the minimum value that a type int variable can hold?
12. How do you add program comments, and why are they used?
13. What is the #include directive used for?

14. Can comments be nested?
15. Can comments be longer than one line?
16. What is an include file?
17. Define a macro called "birthday" which describes the day of the month upon which your birthday falls.

LAB EXERCISES

1. In what variable type would you best store the following values in a C program?
   (*a*) A person's age to the nearest year.
   (*b*) A person's weight in pounds.
   (*c*) The radius of a circle.
   (*d*) Your annual salary.
   (*e*) The cost of an item.
   (*f*) The highest grade on a test (assume it is always 100).
   (*g*) The temperature.
   (*h*) A person's net worth.
   (*i*) The distance to a star in miles.
2. Determine appropriate variable names for the values in exercise 1.
3. Write declarations in a C Program for the variables in exercise 2.
4. Which of the following variable names are valid?
   (*a*) 123variable
   (*b*) *x*
   (*c*) total_score
   (*d*) Weight_in_#s
   (*e*) one.0
   (*f*) gross-cost
   (*g*) RADIUS
   (*h*) Radius
   (*i*) radius
   (*l*) this_is_a_variable_to_hold_the_width_of_a_box
5. Write programs to convert the following mathematical formulae
   (*a*) area = *lbh*
   (*b*) *y* = *mx*+*c*
   (*c*) s=*ut*+1/2 at 2
6. What will be the final values of *a*,*b*,*c* after the following assignment statements?
   int a,b,c;
   a = 1;
   b = 2;
   c = 3;

$a = b+c;$

$a = a+1;$

$b = a;$

$b = a+b*10;$

$c = b \% 10;$

7. What will be the output of following program

```
#include <stdio.h>
main()
{
char alpha='N";
int age=12;
float rate=7/89;
printf("%c",alpha);
printf("%d",age+6);
printf("%f",rate+2.55);
}
```

6

OPERATORS & CONTROL STATEMENTS

6.1 OPERATORS IN C

An operator is a symbol that instructs C to perform some operation, or action, on one or more operands. An operand is something that an operator acts on. In C, all operands are expressions.

Like $c = a + b;$

Here + is an operator, while a & b are operands.

C operators fall into several categories:

1. The assignment operator
2. Mathematical operators
3. Relational operators
4. Logical operators

Assignment Operators

The assignment operator is the equal sign (=). Its use in programming is somewhat different from its use in regular math. If you write

$x = y;$

$a = 560;$

in a C program, it doesn't mean "x is equal to y." Instead, it means "assign the value of y to x." In a C assignment statement, the right side can be any expression, and the left side must be a variable name. Thus, the form is as follows:

variable = expression;

When executed, expression is evaluated, and the resulting value is assigned to variable.

Mathematical Operators

A C's mathematical operators perform mathematical operations such as addition and subtraction. C has two unary mathematical operators (++, - -) and five binary mathematical operators (+, -, *, /, %).

Program 6.1 *Demo of unary operators*

```
#include <stdio.h>
int a, b;
main()
{
        /* Set a and b both equal to 5 */
        a = b = 5;
        /* Print them, decrementing each time. */
        /* Use prefix mode for b, postfix mode for a */
        printf("\n%d %d", a--, --b);
        printf("\n%d %d", a--, --b);
        printf("\n%d %d", a--, --b);
        printf("\n%d %d", a--, --b);
        printf("\n%d %d\n", a--, --b);
        return 0;
}
Output :
        5 4
        4 3
        3 2
        2 1
        1 0
```

Program 6.2 *Use of binary operators in C program*

```
#include <stdio.h>
main()
{
        int x;
        int y;
        int a,b,c,d,e;
        printf("enter values of x and y ");
        scanf("%d%d",&x,&y);
        a=x+y;
        b=x-y;
        c=x*y;
        d=x/y;
```

```
        e=x%y;
        printf ("%d", a);
        printf("%d",b);
        printf ("%d", c);
        printf("%d",d);
        printf ("%f",e);
}
if x=50 and y=3 then
a=53
b=47
c=150
d=16
e=2
```

Relational Operators

C's relational operators are used to compare expressions, asking questions such as, "Is a greater than 10?" or "Is *y* equal to 0?" An expression containing a relational operator evaluates to either true (1) or false (0). C has six relational operators :-

Operator	Symbol	Example
Equal	==	*x* == *y*
Greater than	>	*x* > *y*
Less than	<	*x* < *y*
Greater than or equal to	>=	*x* >= *y*
Less than or equal to	<=	*x* <= *y*
Not equal	!=	*x*!= *y*

Program 6.3 *Use of relational expressions*

```
#include <stdio.h>
int x;
main()
{
        x = (7 == 7); /* Evaluates to 1 */
        printf("\na = (7 == 7)\na = %d", x);
        x = (7 != 7); /* Evaluates to 0 */
        printf("\na = (7 != 7)\na = %d", x);
        x = (12 == 12) + (7 != 1); /* Evaluates to 1 + 1 */
        printf("\na = (12 == 12) + (7 != 1)\na = %d\n", x);
}
```

Program 6.4 *Program to print greatest of 2 Numbers*

```
#include<stdio.h>
#include<conio.h>
main()
{
        int a,b;
        clrscr();
        printf("******PROGRAM TO PRINT GREATEST OF 2 NO.******");
        printf("\nenter the first number");
        scanf("%d",&a);
        printf("\nenter the second number");
        scanf("%d",&b);
        if(a>b)
        printf("a is greater");
        else
        printf("b is greater");
        getch();
}
```

Logical Operators

Sometimes you might need to use more than one relational question at once. For example, "If *x* is Male, have age more than 40 and not a graduate ", C's logical operators allow you to combine two or more relational expressions into a single expression that evaluates to either true or false.

Operator	*Symbol*	*Example*
AND	&&	*a*=5 && *b*=7
OR	||	*x*=56 || *y*=80
NOT	!	!*c*='*s*'

Program 6.5 *Use of logical operators*

```
#include <stdio.h>
int x=12;
main()
{
 if(x>=10 and x<=12)
 {
   x=x+10;
 }
printf("%d",x);
}
```

Program 6.6 *Program to print greatest in 3 Numbers*

```
#include<stdio.h>
#include<conio.h>
main()
{
	int a,b,c;
	clrscr();
	printf("*****PROGRAM TO PRINT GREATEST OF 3 NO.*****");
	printf("\nenter the first number");
	scanf("%d",&a);
	printf("enter the second number\n");
	scanf("%d",&b);
	printf("enter the third number");
	scanf("%d",&c);
	if(a>b && a>c)
	printf("a is greatest");
	else if(b>a && b>c)
	printf("b is greatest");
	else
	printf("c is greatest");
	getch();
}
```

Program 6.7 *Program to check for leap year*

```
#include<stdio.h>
#include<conio.h>
void main()
{
	int n;
	printf("****PROGRAM TO CHECK FOR LEAP YEAR****");
	printf("\nenter the value of n");
	scanf("%d",&n);
	if(n%4 = = 0 && n%400 = =0)
	printf("leap year");
	else
	printf("not a leap year");
	getch();
}
```

Conditional Operators

The conditional operator is C's only ternary operator, meaning that it takes three operands. Its syntax is

exp1 ? exp2 : exp3;

If exp1 evaluates to true (that is, nonzero), the entire expression evaluates to the value of exp2. If exp1 evaluates to false (that is, zero), the entire expression evaluates as the value of exp3. For example, the following statement assigns the value 1 to *x* if *y* is true and assigns 100 to x if y is false:

```
x = y ? 1 : 100;
```

Likewise, to make z equal to the larger of x and y, you could write

```
z = (x > y) ? x : y;
```

Perhaps you've noticed that the conditional operator functions somewhat like an if statement. The preceding statement could also be written like this:

```
if (x > y)
        z = x;
else
        z = y;
```

The conditional operator can't be used in all situations in place of an if...else construction, but the conditional operator is more concise. The conditional operator can also be used in places you can't use an if statement, such as inside a single printf()

statement:

```
        printf("The larger value is %d", ((x > y) ? x : y) );
```

Effects of spaces and blank lines

A White space (lines, spaces, tabs) makes the code listing more readable. When the program is compiled, white space is stripped and thus has no effect on the executable program. For this reason, you should use white space to make your program easier to read.

Unary and Binary Operators

As the names imply, unary operators work with one variable, and binary operators work with two.

```
z++ ;          /unary
C=a+1 ;        /binary
```

Bitwise Operators

C provides six operators for bit manipulation; these may only be applied to integral operands, that is, char, short, int, and long, whether signed or unsigned.

&	bitwise AND
|	bitwise inclusive OR
^	bitwise exclusive OR
<<	left shift
>>	right shift
~	one's complement (unary)

The bitwise AND operator & is often used to mask off some set of bits, for example :

n = *n* & 0177;

sets to zero all but the low-order 7 bits of n.

The bitwise OR operator | is used to turn bits on:

x = *x* | SET_ON;

sets to one in *x* the bits that are set to one in SET_ON.

The bitwise exclusive OR operator ^ sets a one in each bit position where its operands have different bits, and zero where they are the same. One must distinguish the bitwise operators & and | from the logical operators && and ||, which imply left-to-right evaluation of a truth value. For example, if *x* is 1 and *y* is 2, then *x* & *y* is zero while *x* && *y* is one.

The shift operators << and >> perform left and right shifts of their left operand by the number of bit positions given by the right operand, which must be non-negative. Thus *x* << 2 shifts the value of *x* by two positions, filling vacated bits with zero; this is equivalent to multiplication by 4. Right shifting an unsigned quantity always fits the vacated bits with zero. Right shifting a signed quantity will fill with bit signs ("arithmetic shift") on some machines and with 0-bits ("logical shift") on others.

The unary operator ~ yields the one's complement of an integer; that is, it converts each 1-bit into a 0-bit and vice versa. For example :

x = *x* & ~077

sets the last six bits of *x* to zero.

Compound Assignment Operators

C's compound assignment operators provide a shorthand method for combining a binary mathematical operation with an assignment operation. For example, say you want to increase the value of *x* by 5, or, in other words, add 5 to *x* and assign the result to *x*. You could write :

x = *x* + 5;

Using a compound assignment operator, which you can think of as a shorthand method of assignment, you would write :

x += 5;

In more general notation, the compound assignment operators have the following syntax where op represents a binary operator :

exp1 op= exp2

This is equivalent to writing

exp1 = exp1 op exp2;

When You Write This	*It Is Equivalent To This*
x *= y	$x = x * y$
y – = $z + 1$	$y = y - z + 1$
a /= b	$a = a / b$
x += $y / 8$	$x = x + y / 8$
y %= 3	$y = y$ % 3

6.2 OPERATOR PRECEDENCE AND PARENTHESES

If an expression that contains more than one operator, what will be the order in which operations are performed for that C has precedence system for operators. Look the following expression :

$x = 4 + 5 * 3;$

Performing the addition first results in the following, and x is assigned the value 27.

$x = 9 * 3;$

In contrast, if the multiplication is performed first, you have the following, and x is assigned the value 19

$x = 4 + 15;$

Clearly, some rules are needed about the order in which operations are performed. This order, called operator precedence, is strictly spelled out in C. Each operator has a specific precedence. When an expression is evaluated, operators with higher precedence are performed first. Table shows the precedence of C's mathematical operators. Number 1 is the highest precedence and thus is evaluated first.

Operators	*Relative Precedence*
++, - -	1
*, /, %	2
+, -	3

In any C expression, operations are performed in the following order:

1. Unary increment and decrement
2. Multiplication, division, and modulus
3. Addition and subtraction

If an expression contains more than one operator with the same precedence level, the operators are performed in left-to-right order as they appear in the expression. For example, in the following expression, the % and * have the same precedence level, but the % is the leftmost operator, so it is performed first:

12 % 5 * 2

The expression evaluates to 4 (12 % 5 evaluates to 2; 2 times 2 is 4).

Returning to the previous example, you see that the statement $x = 4 + 5 * 3$; assigns the value 19 to x because the multiplication is performed before the addition. What if the order of precedence doesn't evaluate your expression as needed? Using the previous example, what if you wanted to add 4 to 5 and then multiply the sum by 3? C uses parentheses to modify the evaluation order. A subexpression enclosed in parentheses is evaluated first, without regard to operator precedence. Thus, you could write :

$x = (4 + 5) * 3;$

The expression 4 + 5 inside parentheses is evaluated first, so the value assigned to x is 27.

You can use multiple and nested parentheses in an expression. When parentheses are nested, evaluation proceeds from the innermost expression outward. Look at the following complex expression:

$x = 25 – (2 * (10 + (8 / 2)));$

The evaluation of this expression proceeds as follows:

1. The innermost expression, 8 / 2, is evaluated first, yielding the value 4:
   25 – (2 * (10 + 4))
2. Moving outward, the next expression, 10 + 4, is evaluated, yielding the value 14:
   25 – (2 * 14)
3. The last, or outermost, expression, 2 * 14, is evaluated, yielding the value 28:
   25 – 28
4. The final expression, 25 – 28, is evaluated, assigning the value – 3 to the variable x:
   $x = – 3$

You might want to use parentheses in some expressions for the sake of clarity, even when they aren't needed for modifying operator precedence. Parentheses must always be in pairs, or the compiler generates an error message.

Next Table summarizes the rules for precedence and associativity of all operators, including some new that you will use later in this book. Operators on the same line have the same precedence, rows are in order of decreasing precedence, so, for example, *, /, and % all have the same precedence, which is higher than that of binary + and –. The operator () refers to function call. The operators --> and are used to access members of structures and sizeof (size of an object), * for pointer and & for address of an object, along with the comma operator.

<table>
<tr><th>Operators</th><th>Associativity</th></tr>
<tr><td>() [] ->.</td><td>left to right</td></tr>
<tr><td>! ~ ++ -- + - * (type) sizeof</td><td>right to left</td></tr>
<tr><td>* / %</td><td>left to right</td></tr>
<tr><td>+ -</td><td>left to right</td></tr>
<tr><td><< >></td><td>left to right</td></tr>
<tr><td>< <= > >=</td><td>left to right</td></tr>
<tr><td>== !=</td><td>left to right</td></tr>
<tr><td>&</td><td>left to right</td></tr>
<tr><td>^</td><td>left to right</td></tr>
<tr><td>|</td><td>left to right</td></tr>
<tr><td>&&</td><td>left to right</td></tr>
<tr><td>||</td><td>left to right</td></tr>
<tr><td>?:</td><td>right to left</td></tr>
<tr><td>= += -= *= /= %= &= ^= |= <<= >>=</td><td>right to left</td></tr>
<tr><td>,</td><td>left to right</td></tr>
</table>

6.3 CONTROL STATEMENT

You are familier with C ststement now it is the time to learn about a program control statement. As you have seen in earlier programs that statements in a C program normally execute from top to bottom, in the same order as they appear in your source code file. A program control statement can modify the order of statement execution. Program control statements can cause other program statements to execute multiple times or to not execute at all, depending on the circumstances. The if statement is one of C's program control statements. Others are for, do and while, goto, break or continue.

6.4 IF STATEMENT

If also known as decision making statement in C, the if statement evaluates an expression and directs program execution depending on the result of that evaluation. As example, If A student will score 50% marks in each subject he or she will be declared pass in University exam or If your age is 18 years or more you can use your vote to elect your MP or PM. This type of real life situation need conditional programming or decision making. The if statement enables you to test for a condition (such as whether your percentage of marks >50 or not) and branch to different parts of your code, to process other parts.

The form of an if statement is as follows:

```
if (expression)
   statement;
```

```
if(age>=56)
```

print you are old now

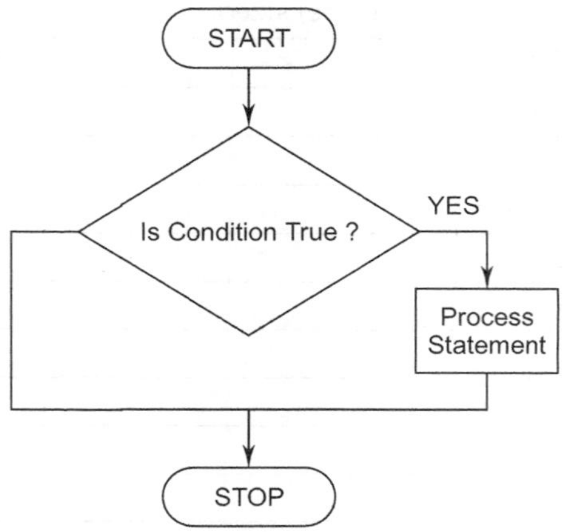

Fig. 6.1 *Simple If condition*

If expression evaluates to true, statement is executed. If expression evaluates to false, statement is not executed. In either case, execution then passes to whatever code follows the if statement. You could say that execution of statement depends on the result of expression. Note that both the line if (expression) and the line statement; are considered to comprise the complete if statement; they are not separate statements.

An if statement can control the execution of multiple statements through the use of a compound statement, or block. As defined earlier in this chapter, a block is a group of two or more statements enclosed in braces. A block can be used anywhere a single statement can be used. Therefore, you could write an if statement as follows:

```
if (expression)
{
  statement1;
  statement2;
  /* additional code goes here */
  statementn;
}
```

Program 6.8

```
if(basic>=8000)
{
da=(basic*67) / 100;
hra=(basic*25) /100
net =basic+da+hra;
}
```

The else Clause

An if statement can optionally include an else clause. The else clause is included as follows:

```
if (expression)
  statement1;
else
  statement2;
```

If expression evaluates to true, statement1 is executed. If expression evaluates to false, statement2 is executed. Both statement1 and statement2 can be compound statements or blocks.

Program 6.9 *Program to check that a given no. Is even or odd*

```
#include<stdio.h>
#include<conio.h>
void main()
{
        int n;
        CLRSCR();
        printf("****PROGRAM TO CHECK THAT A GIVEN NO. IS EVEN OR ODD****");
        printf("\n please enter the value of n");
        scanf("%d",&n);
        if(n%2==0)
        printf("no is even");
        else
        printf("no is odd");
        getch();
}
```

Program 6.10 *Roots of quadratic equations.*

```
#include<stdio.h>
#include<conio.h>
#include<math.h>
main()
{
        float a,b,c,x,y,x1,x2;
        clrscr();
        printf("\"Program to find the roots of quarditic equations.\"");
        printf("\nEnter the coefficient of x*x :");
        scanf("%f",&a);
```

```
        printf("Enter the coefficient of x :");
        scanf("%f",&b);
        printf("Enter the constant value :");
        scanf("%f",&c);
        y=((b*b)-(4*a*c));
        if (y<0)
            printf("Imiginary roots.");
            else
            {
            x=sqrt(y);
            x1=(- b+x)/(2*a);
            printf("The first root : %f",x1);
            x2=(- b-x)/(2*a);
            printf("\nThe second root : %f",x2);
            }
        getch();
    }
```

nested if

If you have multiple conditations in a single C program, you can use nested if statement. The Syntax is :

```
if( expression1 )
  statement1;
else if( expression2 )
  statement2;
else
  statement3;
next_statement;
```

This is a nested if. If the first expression, expression1, is true, statement1 is executed before the program continues with the next_statement. If the first expression is not true, the second expression, expression2, is checked. If the first expression is not true, and the second is true, statement2 is executed. If both expressions are false, statement3 is executed. Only one of the three statements is executed.

Program 6.11 *Use of nested if*

```
#include<stdio.h>
#include<conio.h>
void main()
{
        int n;
```

```
        printf("please enter the value of n");
        scanf("%d",&n);
        if(n= =1)
        printf("monday");
        else if(n= =2)
        printf("tuesday");
        else if(n= =3)
        printf("wednesday");
        else if(n= =4)
        printf("thursday");
        else if(n= =5)
        printf("friday");
        else if(n= =6)
        printf("saturday");
        else if(n= =7)
        printf("sunday");
        else
        printf("pleasev enter the value between 1-7");
        getch();
}
```

6.5 LOOPS IN C

Some times you want to perform an action again & again, like you want to print first 100 even numbers, then loop concept of C will help to do it in less numbers of line of codes. Looping, also called iteration, is used in programming to perform the same set of statements over and over until certain specified conditions are met.

Three statements in C are designed for looping:

1. The for statement
2. The while statement
3. The do-while statement

6.6 FOR LOOP

The general syntax of the for statement is

```
for ( initial; condition; increment or decrement )
{
        statement1;
        statement2;
}
```

initial, condition, and increment are all C expressions, and statement is a single or compound C statement. When a for statement is encountered during program execution, the following events occur:

1. The expression initial is evaluated. initial is usually an assignment statement that sets a variable to a particular initial value like i=1.
2. The expression condition is evaluated. condition is typically a relational expression. Like i<=10
3. If condition evaluates to false, the for statement terminates, and execution passes to the first statement following statement.
4. If condition evaluates to true (that is, as nonzero), the C statement(s) in statement are executed.
5. The expression increment or decrement is evaluated like i++ or i--, and execution returns to step 2.

Program 6.12 *Converting decimal number 0 through 15 to hex numbers.*

```
/* Converting 0 through 15 to hex numbers */
#include <stdio.h>
main()
{
        int i;
        printf("Hex(uppercase) Hex(lowercase) Decimal\n");
        for (i=0; i<16; i++){
        printf("%X %x %d\n", i, i, i);
        return 0;
}
```

Program 6.13 *Print the table of given number*

```
#include <stdio.h>
main()
{
/* Print the table of given number */
int count,table, number ;
scanf("%d", &number);
for (count = 1; count <= 10; count++)
{
table =number * count ;
printf("%d\n", table);
}
}
```

Multiple values in a for loop

C allowed us to use multiple values in for loop like :

Program 6.14 *Multiple expressions in for loop*

```
#include <stdio.h>
main()
{
        int i, j;
        for (i=0, j=8; i<8; i++, j--)
        printf("%d + %d = %d\n", i, j, i+j);
}
```

Nested for loop

A for statement can be executed within another for statement. This is called nesting. By nesting for statements, you can solve complex programming problems.

Program 6.15 *Use of nesting two for statements*

```
#include<stdio.h>
#include<conio.h>
main()
{
        int i,j ;
        clrscr();
        printf("****PROGRAM TO INPUT TRIANGLE OF *\n");
        for(i=1;i<=10;i++)
        {
           for(j=1;j<=i;j++)
        {
               printf("*");
        }
        printf("\n");
        }
        getch();
    }
```

6.7 WHILE LOOP

The while statement, also known as while loop, executes a block of statements as long as a specified condition is true. The while statement has the following syntax:

while (condition)

{

statement;

statement;

increment or decrement;

}

Where condition is any C expression, and statement is a single or compound C statement. When program execution reaches a while statement, the following events occur:

1. The expression condition is evaluated.
2. If condition evaluates to false, the while statement terminates, and execution passes to the first statement following statement.
3. If condition evaluates to true, the C statement(s) in statement are executed.
4. Execution returns to step 1.

Program 6.16 *Use of while statement to print the numbers 1 to 25*

```
#include <stdio.h>
int count;
void main()
{
/* Print the numbers 1 through 25 */
        count = 1;
        while (count <= 25)
        {
                printf("%d\n", count);
                count++;
        }
}
```

Program 6.17 *Print table of given number using while loop*

```
#include <stdio.h>
int number;
void main()
{
        int x = 1;
        printf("enter the number");
        scanf("%d",&number;)
        while (x < 10)
        {
              number=number * x ;
              printf("\n %d",number );
              x++;
   }
      }
```

Program 6.18 *Factorial of a number using while*

```
#include<stdio.h>
#include<conio.h>
void main()
{
        int n,i=1,f=1;
        clrscr();
        printf("****PROGRAM TO PRINT FACTORIAL OF A NUMBER****");
        printf("enter the value of n");
        scanf("%d",&n);
        while (i<=n)
        {
              f=f*i;
              i=i++;
        }
              printf("f=%d",f);
        getch();
}
```

Program 6.19 *Program to find the average of n number*

```
#include<stdio.h>
#include<conio.h>
void main()
{
        int num,count=1,val;
        float avg,sum=0;
        printf("***PROGRAM TO FIND THE AVERAGE OF N NUMBER.***");
        printf("enter the value of n");
        scanf("%d",&num);
        while(count<=num)
        {
             printf("enter the number");
             scanf("%d",&val);
             sum=sum+val;
             count++;
        }
             avg=sum/num;
             printf("avg=%f",avg);
        getch();
}
```

6.8 DO-WHILE LOOP

One more loop in C is do...while loop, which executes a block of statements as long as a specified condition is true. The do...while loop tests the condition at the end of the loop rather than at the beginning, as is done by the for loop and the while loop.

The syntax of do...while loop is :

```
do
{
        statement;
        increment or decrement
}
while (condition);
```

Program 6.20 *Use of do...while statement*

```
#include <stdio.h>
main()
{
        int choice;
        int selection = 0;
        do
        {
            printf("\n");
            printf("\n1 - Add a Record");
            printf("\n2 - Change a record");
            printf("\n3 - Delete a record");
            printf("\n4 - Quit");
            printf("\n");
            printf("\nEnter a selection: ");
            scanf("%d", &selection );
        }
        while ( selection < 1 || selection > 4 );
        printf("You chose Menu Option %d\n", choice );
}
```

Program 6.21 *Program to check armstrong number*

```
#include<stdio.h>
#include<conio.h>
void main()
{
        int n,p,num,a,sum=0;
        clrscr();
```

```
printf("****PROGRAM TO CHECK ARMSTRONG NUMBER****\n");
for(num=1;num<=10000;num++)
{
n = p = num;
sum = 0;
        do
        {
          a=p%10;
          sum = sum + (a*a*a);
                p = p / 10;
        }
    if(sum==n)
        printf("\nno = %d",sum);
 } while(p>0)
getch();
}
```

6.9 BREAK AND CONTINUE

Now you learned how the for loop, the while loop, and the do...while loop can control program execution. These loop constructions execute a block of C statements never, once, or more than once, depending on conditions in the program. In all three cases, termination or exit of the loop occurs only when a certain condition occurs. If you want to exit from a loop execution at some time. The break and continue statements provide this control.

The break Statement

The break statement can be placed only in the body of a for loop, while loop, or do...while loop. (It's valid in a switch statement too, but that topic isn't covered until later in this chapter.) When a break statement is encountered, execution exits the loop. The following is an example:

```
for ( count = 1; count <= 12; count++ )
{
 if ( count = = 5 )
   break;
}
```

Left to itself, the for loop would execute 12 times. On the sixth iteration, however, count is equal to 5, and the break statement executes, causing the for loop to terminate. Execution then passes to the statement immediately following the for loop's closing brace. When a break statement is encountered inside a nested loop, it causes the program to exit the innermost loop only.

Program 6.22 *Program to check for palindrome number using break*

```
#include<stdio.h>
#include<conio.h>
#include<math.h>
main()
{
            int n,i=0,num,num1,s,m,j,k,ans;
            clrscr();
            printf("****PROGRAM TO CHECK FOR PALINDROME NUMBER****");
            printf("enter the number");
            scanf("%d",&num);
            n=num1=num;
            while(n>0)
            {
                  n=n/10;
                  i++;
            }
            for((j=1,k=i-1);(j<=(i/2),k>=1);(j++,k--))
            {
            m=num%10;
            s=num1/(pow(10,k));
            if(m!=s)
            {
                  printf("no is not palindrome");
                  ans='n';
                  break;
            }
            num=num/10;
            num1=num1-(s*(pow(10,k)));
            }
            if(ans!='n')
            printf("number is palindrome");
            getch();
}
```

The continue Statement

Like the break statement, the continue statement can be placed only in the body of a for loop, a while loop, or a do...while loop. When a continue statement executes, the next iteration of the enclosing loop begins immediately. The statements between the continue statement and the end of the loop aren't executed.

Program 6.23 *Use of continue*

```
#include<stdio.h>
#include<conio.h>
#include<math.h>
main()
{
int x;
printf("Printing only the even numbers from 1 to 10\n");
for( x = 1; x <= 10; x++ )
{
 if( x % 2 != 0 )  /* See if the number is NOT even */
   continue;  /* Get next instance x */
 printf("\n%d", x );
}
}
```

6.10 GOTO STATEMENT

The goto statement is one of C's unconditional jump, or branching, statements. When program execution reaches a goto statement, execution immediately jumps, or branches, to the location specified by the goto statement. This statement is unconditional because execution always branches when a goto statement is encountered; the branch doesn't depend on any program conditions unlike if statements. A goto statement and its target must be in the same function, but they can be in different blocks.

Program 6.24 *Use of the goto statement*

```
#include <stdio.h>
main()
{
 int n;
 start: ;
 puts("Enter a number between 0 and 10: ");
 scanf("%d", &n);
 if (n < 0 || n > 10 )
 goto start;
 else if (n == 0)
 goto location0;
 else if (n == 1)
 goto location1;
 else
 goto location2;
```

```
location0: ;
puts("You entered 0.\n");
goto end;
location1: ;
puts("You entered 1.\n");
goto end;
location2: ;
puts("You entered something between 2 and 10.\n");
end: ;
 }
```

> ***Tips:*** Avoid using the goto statement if possible. Do not confuse with break and continue. break ends a loop, whereas continue starts the next iteration.

6.11 SWITCH STATEMENT

The most flexible program control statement in C is the switch statement, which lets your program execute different statements based on an expression that can have more than two values. Earlier control statements, such as if, were limited to evaluating an expression that could have only two values either true or false. To control program flow based on more than two values, you had to use multiple nested if statements. The general form of the switch statement is as follows:

```
switch (expression)
{
 case 1: statement(s);
 case 2: statement(s);
   ...
 case n: statement(s);
 default: statement(s);
}
```

In this statement, expression is any expression that evaluates to an int or char. The switch statement evaluates expression and compares the value against the templates following each case label, and then one of the following happens:

If a match is found between expression and one of the templates, execution is transferred to the statement that follows the case label.

If no match is found, execution is transferred to the statement following the optional default label.

If no match is found and there is no default label, execution passes to the first statement following the switch statement's closing brace.

Program 6. 25 *Use of Switch statement*

```
#include <stdio.h>
```

```
main()
{
 int reply;
 puts("Enter a number between 1 and 5:");
 scanf("%d", &reply);
 switch (reply)
 {
   case 1:
   puts("AIMCA");
   case 2:
   puts("AIHM");
   case 3:
   puts("AIAS");
   case 4:
   puts("AITS");
   case 5:
   puts("AIE");
   default:
   puts("Out of range, try again.");
     }
 }
```

Program 6.26 *Program to print hot, luke warm, cold, out of range when it's value is given*

```
#include<stdio.h>
#include<conio.h>
void main()
{
      int n;
      clrscr();
printf(" *program to print hot,luke warm,cold,out of range when it's
value is given*");
      printf("\nplease enter the value of flag");
      scanf("%d",&n);
      switch(n)
      {
      case 1:
      printf("hot");
      break;
      case 2:
      printf("luke warm");
      break;
```

```
        case 3:
        printf("cold");
        break;
        default:
        printf("out of range");
        }
        getch();
}
```

Program 6.27. *One more switch based program*

```
#include<stdio.h>
#include<conio.h>
void main()
{
        char a;
        clrscr();
        printf("m-monday\n"
           "t-tuesday\n"
           "w-wednesday\n"
           "th-thursday\n"
           "f-friday\n"
           "s-saturday\n"
           "su-sunday");
        printf("\n enter the character");
        scanf("%c",&a);
        switch (a)
        {
        case 'm':
        printf("monday");
        break;
        case 't':
        printf("tuesday");
        break;
        case 'w':
        printf("wednesday");
        break;
        case 'th':
        printf("thursday");
        break;
        case 'f':
```

```
        printf("friday");
        break;
        case 's':
        printf("saturday");
        break;
        case 'su':
        printf("sunday");
        break;
        default:
        printf("please enter other character other then this");
        }
        getch();
}
```

6.12 EXITING THE PROGRAM

A 'C' program normally terminates when execution reaches the closing brace of the main() function. However, you can terminate a program at any time by calling the library function exit(). You can also specify one or more functions to be automatically executed at termination.

The exit() Function

The exit() function terminates program execution and returns control to the operating system. This function takes a single type int argument that is passed back to the operating system to indicate the program's success or failure. The syntax of the exit() function is :

exit(status);

If status has a value of 0, it indicates that the program terminated normally. A value of 1 indicates that the program terminated with some sort of error. The return value is usually ignored.

Program 6.28 *Use of Exit*

```
#include <stdio.h>
#include <stdlib.h>
main()
 {
   int reply;
   while (1)
    {
      puts("\nEnter a value between 1 and 10, 0 to exit: ");
      scanf("%d", &reply);
      switch (reply)
```

```
{
 case 0:
 exit(0);
 case 1:
 case 2:
 case 3:
 case 4:
 case 5:
  {
  puts("You entered 5 or below.\n");
   break;
  }
case 6:
case 7:
case 8:
case 9:
case 10:
{
 puts("You entered 6 or higher.\n");
 break;
 }
 default:
 puts("Between 1 and 10, please!\n");
} /* end of switch */
}     /*end of while */
  }
```

6.13 DOS COMMANDS IN C PROGRAM

The C standard library includes a function, system(), that lets you execute operating system commands in a running C program. This can be useful, allowing you to read a disk's directory listing or format a disk without exiting the program. To use the system() function, a program must include the header file stdlib.h file. The format of system() is :

system(command);

The argument command can be either a string constant or a pointer to a string. For example, to obtain a directory listing in DOS, you could write :

system("dir");

or

char *command = "dir";

system(command);

Program 6.29. *Use of DOS commands in a C Program.*

```
#include <stdio.h>
#include <stdlib.h>
main()
  {
    char input[40];
      while (1)
    {
      puts("\nInput the desired system command, blank to exit");
      gets(input);
      if (input[0] == `\0')
      exit(0);
      system(input);
    }
    }
```

> *Tips:* puts() and gets() are functions of C, can be used in place of printf() and scanf().

REVIEW QUESTIONS

1. What do you mean by operator precedence and associativity? Explain in brief, and find the output of the following expressions with proper reasoning. **[MCA, UTU 2006-07]**
2. In an expression that contains multiple operators, what determines the order in which operations are performed?
3. If the variable *x* has the value 10, what are the values of *x* and a after each of the following statements is executed separately?

   a = x++;

   a = ++x;
4. To what value does the expression 10 % 3 evaluate?
5. To what value does the expression 5 + 3 * 8 / 2 + 2 evaluate?
6. Rewrite the expression in question 5, adding parentheses so that it evaluates to 16.
7. If an expression evaluates to false, what value does the expression have?
8. In the following list, which has higher precedence?

   == or <

   * or +

   != or ==

   >= or >
9. What are the compound assignment operators, and how are they useful?

10. The following code is not well-written. Enter and compile it to see whether it works.

```
#include <stdio.h>
int x, y;
main()
{
printf("\nEnter two numbers");
scanf("%d %d",&x,&y);
printf("\n\n%d is bigger",(x>y)?x:y);
}
```

11. Write program to count odd numbers from 1 to 100.
12. Write an if statement that assigns the value of *x* to the variable *y* only if *x* is between 1 and 20. Leave y unchanged if *x* is not in that range.
13. Rewrite the following nested if statements using a single if statement and compound operators.

```
if (x < 1)
if ( x > 10 )
statement;
```

14. To what value do each of the following expressions evaluate?
    (*a*) (1 + 2 * 3)
    (*b*) 10 % 3 * 3 – (1 + 2)
    (*c*) ((1 + 2) * 3)
    (*d*) (5 == 5)
    (*e*) (*x* = 5)
15. If *x* = 4, *y* = 6, and *z* = 2, determine whether each of the following evaluates to true or false.
(*a*) if(*x* == 4)
(*b*) if(*x* != *y* – *z*)
(*c*) if(*z* = 1)
(*d*) if(*y*)
16. Write a program using an if statement that determines whether someone is legally an adult (age 21), but not a senior citizen (age 65).
17. Fix the following program so that it runs correctly.

```
/* a program with problems... */
#include <stdio.h>
    int x= 1:
    main()
    {
          if( x = 1);
          printf(" x equals 1");
          otherwise
          printf(" x does not equal 1");
          return 0;
    }
```

18. Write a program segment using a switch statement that print the value of an integer *n*, depending upon the following input :

    if *n* is 2 or 3, multiply *n* by 20

    if *n* is 4, squre *n*

    if *n* is not equal to 2, 3 or 4 get a new value of n from user. **[MCA, UTU 2006–07]**

19. Write a program that will read a real number from keyboard and print the following in one line :

    (*i*) Smallest integer not less than the number

    (*ii*) The given number

    (*iii*) The largest not greater than the number. **[MCA, UTU 2006–07]**

20. Write a program which determines the number of digit and the sum of the digit of a given number like 1234, the number of digits are 4 and sum is 10. **[MCA, UTU 2006–07]**

21. The following is a segment of a program: **[MCA, UTU 2006–07]**

    ```
    x = 1
    y = 2
    if( n>0)
    x = x + 1
    y = y – 1
    printf("%4d%4d",x+y,x-y);
    ```

    Explain the output of above program, if the value of n is

    (*i*) 1

    (*ii*) 0

7

ARRAYS IN C

7.1 ARRAY

An array is a collection of data storage locations, each having the same data type and the same name. Each storage location in an array is called an array element. Why do one use arrays in programs? This question can be answered with an example. If you're keeping track of 12 month salary of an employee, you will use a separate sheet for each month's receipts, but it would be more convenient to have a single workbook with 12 worksheets. Now look the following declaration :

int *x*;   Single variable

int *x*[10] ;   Collection of 10 integer values having one name

Using array it is easy to solve this example by C programming. The program could declare 12 separate variables, one for each month's expense total. This approach is analogous to having 12 separate sheets for your receipts. Good programming practice, however, would utilize an array with 12 elements, storing each month's total in the corresponding array element. This approach is comparable to filing your receipts in a single workbook with 12 worksheets.

int jansal, febsal, marsal, aprsal, maysal, junsal, julsal, augsal, sepsal, octsal, novsal, decsal;

or

int empsal[12];

In many cases, you have to declare a set of variables that have the same data type. Instead of declaring them individually, C allows you to declare a set of variables of the same data type collectively as an array.

"An array is a collection of variables that are of the same data type. Each item in an array is called an element. All elements in an array are referenced by the name of the array and are stored in a set of consecutive memory slots ".

Declaring Arrays

The following is the general form to declare an array:

data-type Array Name[Size];

Here data-type is the type specifiers that indicates what data type the declared array will be. Array-Name is the name of the declared array. Size defines how many elements the array can contain. Note that the brackets ([and]) are required in declaring an array. The bracket pair ([and]) is also called the array subscript operator.

For example, an array of integers is declared in the following statement :

int subjects_marks[8];

Where int specifies the data type of the array whose name is subjects_marks. The size of the array is 8, which means that the array can store eight elements but only integers.In C, you have to declare an array explicitly, as you do for other variables, before you can use it.

Indexing Arrays

After you declare an array, you can access each of the elements in the array separately. For instance, the following declaration declares an array of characters:

char alphabets[26];

You can access the elements in the array of day one after another. The important thing to remember is that all arrays in C are indexed starting at 0. In other words, the index to the first element in an array is 0, not 1. Therefore, the first element in the array of day is day[0]. Because there are 26 elements in the day array, the last element is alphabets[25], not alphabets[26]. The twenty six elements of the array will have the following expressions: alphabets [0], alphabets [1], alphabets [2], alphabets [3], alphabets [4], alphabets [5], and day[25] for last element. Because these expressions reference the elements in the array, they are sometimes called array element references.

Initializing Arrays

With the help of the array element index or sub scripts, you can initialize each element in an array. For example, you can initialize the first element in the array of alphabets, which was declared in the last section, like this:

alphabets [0] = *'a'*;

Here the value of *'a'* is assigned to the first element of alphabets, alphabets [0].

Likewise, the statement alphabets [25] = 'z'; assigns 'z' to the last element, day[1], in the array.

The second way to initialize an array is to initialize all elements in the array together. For instance, the following statement initializes an integer array:

int subjectmarks[5] = {100, 80, 53, 65, 76};

Here the integers inside the braces ({ and }) are assigned to the corresponding elements of the array subjectmarks. That is, 100 is given to the first element (subjectmarks [0]), 80 to the second element (subjectmarks [1]), 53 to the third (subjectmarks [2]), and so on.

Program 7.1 *Initializing an array*

```
#include <stdio.h>
main()
{
int i;
int list[10];
for (i=0; i<10; i++)
   {
   list[i] = i + 1;
   printf("list[%d] is initialized with %d.\n", i, list[i]);
    }
 }
```

7.2 TYPES OF ARRAYS

7.2.1 Single Dimensional Array

A single-dimensional array has only a single subscript. A subscript is a number in brackets that follows an array's name. This number can identify the number of individual elements in the array.

Syntax for array

Datatype arrayname[no of element] ;

int months[12] ;   Array of 12 integer values

The array is named expenses, and it contains 12 elements. Each of the 12 elements is the exact equivalent of a single integer/decimal variable. All of C's data types can be used for arrays. C array elements are always numbered starting at 0, so the 12 elements of expenses are numbered 0 through 11.

For an array, the compiler sets aside a block of memory large enough to hold the entire array. Individual array elements are stored in sequential memory locations.

Assigning values in an array

An array element can be used in your program anywhere a non array variable of the same type can be used. Individual elements of the array are accessed by using the array name followed by the element subscript enclosed in square brackets.

For example, the following statement stores the value 8995 in the second array element (remember, the first array element is expenses[0], not expenses[1]):

expenses[1] = 8995;

Program 7.2 *To compute annual salary of an employee using array*

```
#include <stdio.h>
/* Declare an array */
int msalary[12];
int count;
long int annsalary;
main()
{
      /* Input data from keyboard into array */
      for (count = 0; count < 11; count++)
      {
            printf("Enter salary s for month %d: ", count+1);
            scanf("%d", &msalary[count]);
            annsalary=annsalary+msalary;
      }
      /* Print array contents */
      printf("Annual salary %ld", annsalary);
}
```

Program 7.3 *Program to print mean of a given series*

```
#include<stdio.h>
#include<conio.h>
main()
{
            int mean[20], num, i, sum;
            clrscr();
            printf("****PROGRAM TO PRINT MEAN OF A GIVEN SERIES****\n");
            printf("enter the total numbers");
            scanf("%d",&num);
            for(i=0;i<num;i++)
            {
                  scanf("%d",&mean[i]);
            }
            for(i=0;i<num;i++)
            {
                  sum=sum+(mean[i]);
            }
getch();
}
```

7.2.2 Two Dimensional Array

The array which has more than one subscript known as multidimensional array. A two-dimensional array has two subscripts, a three-dimensional array has three subscripts, and so on. There is no limit to the number of dimensions a C array can have.

For example, in a program to plays checkers. The matrix operation contains 9 squares arranged in 3 rows and 3 columns. Your program could represent the board as a two-dimensional array, as follows:

int matrix[3][3];

Similarly, a three-dimensional array could be thought of as a cube. Four-dimensional arrays (and higher) are probably best left to your imagination. All arrays, no matter how many dimensions they have, are stored sequentially in memory.

Initialize the two dimensional arrays

Two dimensional arrays can also be initialized. The list of initialization values is assigned to array elements in order, with the last array subscript changing first. For example:

int array[4][3] = { 10, 20, 30, 40, 50, 60, 70, 80, 90, 100, 110, 120 };

results in the following assignments:

array[0][0] is equal to 10

array[0][1] is equal to 20

array[0][2] is equal to 30

array[1][0] is equal to 40

array[1][1] is equal to 50

array[1][2] is equal to 60

...

array[3][1] is equal to 110

array[3][2] is equal to 120

When you initialize multidimensional arrays, you can make your source code clearer by using extra braces to group the initialization values and also by spreading them over several lines. The following initialization is equivalent to the one just given:

int array[4][3] = { { 10, 20, 30 }, { 40, 50, 60 },

{ 70, 80, 90 }, { 100, 110, 120 } };

Program 7.4 *Program to print addition of 2 matrix using two dimension arrays*

```
#include<stdio.h>
#include<conio.h>
main()
{
        int  mat[4][4],mat1[2][2],i,j,a,b,r,c,r1,c1;
        clrscr();
        printf("****PROGRAM TO PRINT ADDITION OF 2 MATRIX\n****");
```

```
        printf("enter the number of rows");
        scanf("%d",&r);
        printf("enter the number of columns");
        scanf("%d",&c);
        for(i=0;i<r;i++)
        {
               for(j=0;j<c;j++)
               {
                      printf("enter the number of values");
                      scanf("%d",&mat[i][j]);
               }
                      printf("\n");
        }
    printf("enter the number of rows of 2nd matrix");
    scanf("%d",&r1);
    printf("enter the number of columns of 2nd mat");
        scanf("%d",&c1);
        for(a=0;a<r1;a++)
        {
               for(b=0;b<c1;b++)
               {
                      printf("enter the values of 2nd matrix");
                      scanf("%d",&mat1[a][b]);
               }
               printf("\n");
        }
        for((i=0,a=0);(i<r,a<r1);(i++,a++))
        {
               for((j=0,b=0);(j<c,b<c1);(j++,b++))
                      {
                             printf("%d",mat[i][j]+mat1[a][b]);
                      }
                      printf("\n");
        }
    getch();
}
```

Program 7.5 *Program to print subtraction of 2 matrix*

```
#include<stdio.h>
#include<conio.h>
void main()
```

```
{
        int mat[4][4],mat1[2][2],i,j,a,b,r,c,r1,c1;
        clrscr();
        printf("****PROGRAM TO PRINT SUBTRACTION OF 2 MATRIX\n****");
        printf("enter the number of rows");
        scanf("%d",&r);
        printf("enter the number of columns");
        scanf("%d",&c);
        for(i=0;i<r;i++)
        {
            for(j=0;j<c;j++)
            {
                printf("enter the number of values");
                scanf("%d",&mat[i][j]);
            }
                printf("\n");
        }
    printf("enter the number of rows of 2nd matrix");
    scanf("%d",&r1);
    printf("enter the number of columns of 2nd mat");
    scanf("%d",&c1);
    for(a=0;a<r1;a++)
        {
            for(b=0;b<c1;b++)
            {
                printf("enter the values of 2nd matrix");
                scanf("%d",&mat1[a][b]);
            }
            printf("\n");
        }
        for((i=0,a=0);(i<r,a<r1);(i++,a++))
        {
            for((j=0,b=0);(j<c,b<c1);(j++,b++))
                {
                    printf("%d",mat[i][j]-mat1[a][b]);
                }
                printf("\n");
        }
    getch();
}
```

7.2.3 3-Dimensional Arrays

In a computer graphics based 3D game you need to use all 3 coordinates (*x*,*y*,*z*) to draw a 3D image, for that there is a need to declare a 3D array, following program will show you the use of 3D array in C :

Program 7.6 *Use of a 3D array*

```
#include <stdio.h>
#include <stdlib.h>
/* Declare a three-dimensional array with 1000 elements */
int random_array[10][10][10];
int a, b, c;
main()
{
/* Fill the array with random numbers. The C library */
/* function rand() returns a random number. Use one */
/* for loop for each array subscript. */
    for (a = 0; a < 10; a++)
    {
        for (b = 0; b < 10; b++)
        {
            for (c = 0; c < 10; c++)
        {
              random_array[a][b][c] = rand();
        }
    }
}
/* Now display the array elements 10 at a time */
for (a = 0; a < 10; a++)
{
    for (b = 0; b < 10; b++)
    {
        for (c = 0; c < 10; c++)
    {
        printf("\nrandom_array[%d][%d][%d] = ", a, b, c);
        printf("%d", random_array[a][b][c]);
    }
    printf("\nPress Enter to continue, CTRL-C to quit.");
    getchar();
    }
}
} /* end of main() *
```

7.2.4 Unsized Arrays

As you've seen, the size of a dimension is normally given during the declaration of an array. It means that you have to count each element in an array. It could be tedious to do so, though, especially if there are many elements in an array. In case of arrays the C compiler can actually calculate a dimension size of an array automatically if an array is declared as an un sized array. For example, when the compiler sees the following un sized array:

int list[] = { 10, 20, 30, 40, 50, 60, 70, 80, 90};

it will create an array big enough to store all the elements.

Now you can also declare a multidimensional un sized array. However, you have to specify all but the leftmost dimension size. For instance, the compiler can reserve enough memory space to hold all elements in the following two-dimensional un sized array like :

char list_ch[][2] = { 'a', 'A', 'b', 'B', 'c', 'C', 'd', 'D', 'e', 'E', 'f', 'F', 'g', 'G'};

7.3 THE SIZEOF() OPERATOR

An array consists of consecutive memory locations in computer memory, now if you have 16 elements in a array how will you compute the actual size of array. Given an array, like this:

data-type Array-Name[Array-Size];

The way to calculate the total bytes of the array by using the following expression:

sizeof(data-type) * Array-Size

Here data-type is the data type of the array; Array-Size specifies the total number of elements the array can take. The result returned by the expression is the total number of bytes the array takes. Another way to calculate the total bytes of an array is simpler; it uses the following expression:

sizeof(Array-Name)

where Array-Name is the name of the array.

Program 7.7 *How to compute size of array using sizeof() operator*

```
    #include <stdio.h>
/* Declare several 100-element arrays */
int intarray[100];
float floatarray[100];
double doublearray[100];
main()
{
     /* Display the sizes of numeric data types */
     printf("\n\nSize of int = %d bytes", sizeof(int));
     printf("\nSize of short = %d bytes", sizeof(short));
     printf("\nSize of long = %d bytes", sizeof(long));
```

```
        printf("\nSize of float = %d bytes", sizeof(float));
        printf("\nSize of double = %d bytes", sizeof(double));
        /* Display the sizes of the three arrays */
        printf("\nSize of intarray = %d bytes", sizeof(intarray));
        printf("\nSize of floatarray = %d bytes",
        sizeof(floatarray));
        printf("\nSize of doublearray = %d bytes\n",
        sizeof(doublearray));
    }
```

Program 7.8 *Finding the Largest in an array*

```
/* largest in an array */
#include <stdio.h>
main()
{
   int data[20];
   int place;
   int large_place;
   /* read 20 values into data[], as in 10.4 */
   /* find largest */
   large_place = 0        /* assume first is largest */
   for(place = 1; place<20; place++)
   {
      if ( data[place]>data[large_place] )
         large_place = place;
   }
   printf("largest is %d \n", data[large_place] );
   printf("and its position is %d \n", large_place);
}
```

Program 7.9 *Searching in array*

```
/* search array sequentially */
#include <stdio.h>
main()
{
    int data[20];
    int place;
    int wanted,found;
    /* read in the data */
    for(place = 1; place<20; n++)
    {
```

```
        printf("type a number:\n");
        scanf("%d", &data[place] );
    }
    /* request the data value to search for */
    printf("Which number to find?\n");
    scanf("%d", &wanted);
    /* do the search */
    found = 0;      /* 0 means 'not yet' */
    place = 0;
    while ( (place <20) && ( found = 0 ) )
    {
        if ( data[place] == wanted )
            found = 1;    /* 1 means 'yes' */
        else
            place++;
    }
    if (found == 0)
        printf(" %d was not found \n", wanted );
    else
        printf("%d at position %d \n",wanted, place);
}
```

7.4 ARRAYS OF CHARACTERS

You can store a single alphabet using char data type of C, but how you will store "MKSHARMA", which is a string, for that you should use arrays of characters. On most machines, the char data type takes one byte. Therefore, each element in a character array is one byte long. The total number of elements in a character array is the total number of bytes the array takes in the memory. More importantly in C, a character string is defined as a character array whose last element is the null character (\0), so you can find termination of string by this null character (\0).

The Null Character (\0)

The null character (\0) is treated as one character in C; it is a special character that marks the end of a string. Therefore, when functions like printf() act on a character string, they process one character after another until they encounter the null character.

You may think now how the printf() function knows where the end of the character array is. Now you know that the last element in the character array array_ch is a \0 character. By using this null character that marks the end of the character array you can trace the end of string. So a character array ended with a null character is called a character string in C.

Progarm 7.10 *Stopping printing at the null character.*

```
#include <stdio.h>
main()
{
char arraych[15] = {'I', ' ', 'a', 'm', ' ', 'a', 'i', 'm', 'c', 'a', 'f',
'a', 'c', 'u', 'l', 't', 'y', '\0'};
    int i;
  /* arraych[i] in logical test */
    for (i=0; arraych[i] != '\0'; i++)
    printf("%c", arraych[i]);
}
```

7.5 ARRAYS & STRINGS

In C a String is treated as a collection of characters. Like my name "MKSharma",to store this you need 8 characters at a time. As you have learnt that variables of type char can hold only a single character, so you need a way to store strings, which are collection of characters. A person's name like my name and address are examples of strings. Although there is no special data type for strings, C handles this type of information with arrays of characters.

7.5.1 Arrays of Characters

To hold a string of 8 characters, for example, "MKSharma" you need to declare an array of type char with 9 elements. Arrays of type char are declared like arrays of other data types. For example :

char myname[10];

char myadd[20];

When you declare a n element array of type char. This array could be used to hold a string of *n*-1 or fewer characters. Like in previous example char myname[10] will store 9 character or less than 9.

Now you can say why s a 10 element array, hold only nine characters? The answer is in C, a string is defined as a sequence of characters ending with a null character, a special character represented by \0. Although it's represented by two characters (backslash and zero), the null character is interpreted as a single character and has the ASCII value of 0. It's one of C's escape sequences.

When a C program stores the string MKSharma, for example, it stores the 8 characters M, K,S, *h*,a,r,m,a followed by the null character \0, for a total of 9 characters. Thus, a character array can hold a string of characters numbering one less than the total number of elements in the array.

A char type variable is one byte in size, so the number of bytes in an array of type char variables is the same as the number of elements in the array.

7.5.2 Read and Display Strings

If you want to use string data in your program, there is a need to display the data on the screen at some time. To display Strings you can use the puts() function or the printf() function.

The puts() Function

The puts() function puts a string on screen. The puts() function automatically inserts a newline character at the end of each string it displays, so each subsequent string displayed with puts() is on its own line while in printf() you have to use *n* for that.

The gets() Function

The gets() function gets or read a string from the keyboard. When gets() is called, it reads all characters typed at the keyboard up to the first newline character which you generate by pressing Enter. This function discards the newline, adds a null character, and gives the string to the calling program. A program that uses puts() or gets() must #include the file STDIO.H.

Program 7.11

```
/* Demo of puts() and gets() function. */
#include <stdio.h>
/* Allocate a character array to hold input. */
char dname[20];
main()
{
 puts("Enter some text, then press Enter: ");
 gets(dname);
 printf("You entered: %s\n", dname);
 }
```

Output:

Enter some text, then press Enter:

My Daughter name is Vama

You entered: My Daughter name is Vama

7.5.3 Inputting Strings Using the scanf()

You can use scanf() also to input or read strings. Remember that scanf() uses a format string that tells it how to read the input. To read a string, include the specifier %s in scanf()'s format string.

You can read in multiple strings with scanf() by including more than one %*s* in the format string. For each %s in the format string, scanf() uses the preceding rules to find the requested number of strings in the input. For example:

scanf("%*s*%*s*%*s*", *s*1, *s*2, *s*3);

If you enter MCA MBA BCA, MCA is assigned to the string *s*1, MBA is assigned to *s*2, and BCA to *s*3.

If you use a statement in your program like :

scanf("%2s%3s%3s", s1, s2, s3);

and in response you enter Saturday, Sa is assigned to s1, tur is assigned to s2, and day is assigned to s3.

Program 7.12

```
/* Demo of scanf() to input String data. */
#include <stdio.h>
char fname[20], lname[20];
int age;
main()
{
  puts("Enter first name, last name and age separated");
  puts("by spaces, then press Enter.");
  scanf("%s%s%d", fname, lname, &age);
  printf("%s %s %d \n", lname, fname, age);
}
```

Output :

Enter first name, last name and age separated
by spaces, then press Enter.
Mahesh Sharma 30
Sharma Mahesh 30

7.6 STRING OPERATIONS

When you will work with Strings is your programs, there is a need to perform many operations like :

- How to compute the length of a string
- How to copy, reverse or add strings
- How to compare strings like is case of text based matching of records
- How to convert strings from text to integer or double form
- How to test lower or upper cases in Strings

C offers a great variety of library functions that you can use on Strings to perform above given operations.

7.6.1 String Length

The length of a given String can be computed with the library function strlen(). As you know in C a string is a collection of characters, with its beginning indicated by a pointer and its end marked by the null character \0. So the length of a string is the number of characters between the start and the end of the string. Like length of MKsharma is 8 because the function strlen() returns the number of characters between first character and the last t null character, not counting the null character

Tips: When you will enter "India is Great", length will be 14, why ?

Program 7.13

```
/* Demo of strlen() function. */
#include <stdio.h>
#include <string.h>
main()
{
  int length;
  char astring[80];
  while (1)
  {
    puts("Enter any String");
    gets(astring);
    length = strlen(astring);
    if (length != 0)
      printf("\nThat String is %d characters long.", length);
    else
break;
  }
}
```

Output:

Enter any String

India is great

That line is 14 characters long.

7.6.2 String Copying

There are 3 string copying functions in C library that are strcpy(), strncpy(), and strdup(). You need to include header file STRING.H to use that functions.

strcpy() Function

The library function strcpy() copies an entire string to another string. Its syntax is as follows:

strcpy(destination string, char source string);

The function strcpy() copies the string including the terminating null character by source to the destination string.

Program 7.14

```
/* Demo of strcpy(). */
```

```
#include <stdlib.h>
#include <stdio.h>
#include <string.h>
char source[] = "Amrapali Institute, Haldwani ";
main()
{
        char dest[80];
        printf("\n Source String : %s", source );
        strcpy(dest, source);
        printf("\n Destination String : %s", dest);
}
```

Output :

Source String : Amrapali Institute, Haldwani

Destination String : Amrapali Institute, Haldwani

strncpy() Function

The strncpy() function is very much like strcpy(), but in strncpy() you can specify how many characters from source you want to copy. The syntax is :

strncpy(destination, source, number of characters);

This function copies, the first *n* characters of source to destination. If source is shorter than n characters, enough null characters are added to the end of source to make a total of n characters copied to destination. If source is longer than *n* characters, no terminating \0 is added to destination.

Program 7.15

```
/* Demo of strncpy(). */
#include <stdio.h>
#include <string.h>
char dest[] = " ****************************************** ";
char source[] = " Uttarakhand Technical University ";
main()
{
 int n;
 puts("Enter the number of characters to copy ");
 scanf("%d", &n);
 printf("\n Before strncpy destination = %s", dest);
 strncpy(dest, source, n);
 printf("\n After strncpy destination = %s\n", dest);
 }
```

Output :

Enter the number of characters to copy

22
Before strncpy destination = **
After strncpy destination = Uttarakhand Technical ********************
strdup() Function

The library function strdup() is similar to strcpy(), except that strdup() performs its own memory allocation for the destination string. The syntax is :

Program 7.16

```
/* Demo of strdup() function. */
#include <stdlib.h>
#include <stdio.h>
#include <string.h>
char source[] = "You can do it !";
main()
{
 char dest[80];
 dest = strdup(source)
 printf("The destination is = %s\n", dest);
}
```

Output :
The destination is = You can do it !

7.6.3 String Concatenation

If you want to join two strings like MK and Sharma in a one string, you can use the functions strcat() and strncat() to do this. Syntax of strcat and strncat is :

strcat(string1,string2)

strncat(string1,string2,*n*)

The function strcat() add a copy of string2 onto the end of string1, moving the terminating null character to the end of the new string. You must use enough space for string1 as it will be more longer after adding the resulting string.

Program 7.17

```
/* Demo of strcat() and strncat function. */
#include <stdio.h>
#include <string.h>
char str1[80] = "MK Sharma";
char str2[20];= " & MP Thapliyal"
main()
{
   strcat(str1, str2);
```

```
        puts(str1);
        strncat(str1, str2, 5);
        puts(str1);
    }
```

Tips : Check and analyze the output of given program.

7.6.4 String Comparison

If in bank a customer want to search his account by his name, which is a string or you want to search total students of Nainitaal from a file, you need to compare the strings. In C you have a library function strcmp() which compares two strings character by character and return 1, 0 or -1 based on the matching conditions. The syntax is :

x = strcmp(string1,string2)

where x is a integer variable which store 0, 1 or -1 as given Table :

Return Value	*Meaning*
<0	String 1 is less than String 2
0	String 1 is equal to String 2
>0	String 1 is greater than String2

Program 7.18

```
/* Demo of strcmp() function. */
#include <stdio.h>
#include <string.h>
main()
 {
 char str1[80], str2[80];
 int x;
 /* Input two strings. */
 printf("\n Input the first string ");
 gets(str1);
 printf("\n Input the second string ");
 gets(str2);
 /* Compare and display the result. */
 x = strcmp(str1, str2);
 printf("\n %d", x);
 }
```

7.6.5 String Conversions

Just think a case, you have entered names of all students of your class in a file and all are in lower case (like vama sharma). To display the names on screen you want all should be in upper case (like VAMA SHARMA), so what you will do no problem just use C functions strupr() or strlwr() for string conversion from lower to upper or upper to lower. The syntax are :

strlwr(string)

strupr(string)

Program 7.19

```
/* Demo of strlwr() and strupr(). */
#include <stdio.h>
#include <string.h>
main()
{
   char str1[80];
   puts("Enter a String");
   gets(str1);
   puts(strlwr(str1));
   puts(strupr(str1));
}
```

Output :

Enter a String

Vama Sharma

vama sharma

VAMA SHARMA

7.6.6 String to Number Conversions

Sometimes you will need to convert the string representation of a number to numeric variable to perform arithmetical operations. For example, the string "4077" can be converted to a type int variable with the value 4077 or the string "2089.56" can be converted to a type float with the help of functions atoi() and atof().

Program 7.20

```
/* Demo of atoi and atof(). */
#include <string.h>
#include <stdio.h>
#include <stdlib.h>
main()
{
   char str1[80];
   char str2[80];
   int i;
   double d;
```

```
        printf(" \n Enter the string for conversion ");
        gets(str1);
        if ( strlen(str1) = = 0 )
        printf("\n Please Enter string of greater length ");
        i = atoi(str1);
        printf(" The converted value is %d ", i);
        printf(" \n Enter another string in decimal form for conversion ");
        gets(str2);
        d = atof(str2);
        printf("The converted value is %f.", d);
    }
```

Output :

Enter the string for conversion 576

The converted value is 576

Enter another string in decimal form for conversion 6789.67

The converted value is 6789.67

REVIEW QUESTIONS

1. If an array is declared with 10 elements, what is the subscript of the first element ?
2. In a one-dimensional array declared with n elements, what is the subscript of the last element ?
3. What happens if your program tries to access an array element with an out-of-range subscript ?
4. How do you declare a multidimensional array ?
5. Write C program to read, add, subtract, multiply and transpose two matrix of [*n**n*] size.
6. An array is declared with the following statement. How many total elements does the array have ?
   (*i*) int array[2][3][5][8];
7. What would be the name of the 10th element in the array in question 5 ?
8. Write a program using array, for and continue statement to read the age of 100 persons and count the number of persons in the age group of 50 and 60 (both ages included). **[MCA, UTU 2006-07]**
9. The daily tempeture recorded in 10 cities during the month of December has been tabulated as follows : **[MCA, UTU 2006-07]**

	1	2	3	4	5	6	7	8	9	10
Day 1										
Day 2										
Day 3										
Day 4										
Day 31										

Write a program to read the temperature in a two dimensional array and find the city and the day corresponding to :

(*i*) The Highest temperature

(*ii*) The Lowest temperature

10. You have two array both are single demisional and having size of 15, now write a program, to merge the values of both array into a third array and do not use duplicate values at the tme of merging.
11. How can you determine the length of a string ?
12. Which functions help you for copying strings, write syntax and examples ?
13. What does the term concatenate mean ?
14. When comparing strings, what is meant by 1, 0 or -1 ?"
15. What is the difference between strcmp() and strncmp()?

LAB EXERCISES

1. Write a C program line that would declare three one-dimensional integer arrays, named one, two, and three, with 1,00 elements each and using for loop add 5 to each element and print.
2. Write the statement that would declare a 10-element integer array and initialize all its elements to 1.
3. Given the following array, write code to initialize all the array elements to 88:

   int eightyeight[88];
4. Given the following array, write code to initialize all the array elements to 0:

   int stuff[12][10];
5. What is wrong with the following code fragment, check and correct the error.

```
int x, y;
int array[10][3];
main()
{
        for ( x = 0; x < 3; x++ )
        for ( y = 0; y < 10; y++ )
        array[x][y] = 0;
        return 0;
}
```

6. What is wrong with the following, check and correct the error.

```
int array[10];
int x = 1;
main()
{
        for ( x = 1; x <= 10; x++ )
        array[x] = 99;
        return 0;
}
```

7. Write a program that puts random numbers into a two-dimensional array that is 5 X 4. Print the values in columns on-screen.
8. Use a single-dimensional array. Print the average of the 1,000 float variables before printing the individual values.
9. Write a program that initializes an array of 10 elements. Each element should be equal to its subscript. The program should then print each of the 10 elements.
10. Modify the program from exercise 9. After printing the initialized values, the program should copy the values to a new array and add 10 to each value. Then the new array values should be printed.
11. Write a program that prompts for the user's first name, middle name and last name. Then convert the name in a new string as first name, period, space, middle name, period, space, last name. For example, if Mahesh Kumar Sharma are entered, the new name on the screen should be M.K.S.
12. Write program to reverse a given string and then check for palindrome. (Hint : Check the word MALAYALAM)
13. Write a program to sort 10 names in descending order.

8

INPUT & OUTPUT

8.1 STANDARD INPUT AND OUTPUT (I/O)

Most of the data, you have used either for input or for output is in form of characters and numbers. Because all characters and numbers are represented in bits on computers, the C language treats all data as a series of bytes(8 bits). A series of bytes is also called a stream. In fact, the C language treats all streams equally, although some of the streams may come from a disk or tape drive, from a terminal, or even from a printer. In C, there are mainly three streams :

Stdin The standard input for reading.

Stdout The standard output for writing.

Stderr The standard error for writing error messages.

Usually, the standard input (stdin) file stream links to your keyboard, while the standard output (stdout) and the standard error (stderr) file streams point to your terminal screen. Also, many operating systems allow you to redirect these streams to physical files on disk. In fact, you've already used stdout. When you executed the printf() function in the last lesson, you were in fact sending the output to the default file stream, stdout, which points to your screen.

8.2 PRINTF()

The printf() function is a part of standard C library, is a common way for a program to display data on-screen. You've already seen printf() used in many of the examples earlier. Now you will to see how printf() works. The syntax for the printf() function is :

```
#include <stdio.h>
int printf(const char *format-string,...);
```

Here const char *format-string is the first argument that contains the format specifier(s);... indicates the expression section that contains the expression(s) to be formatted according to the format specifiers. The number of expressions is determined by the number of the format specifiers inside the first argument. The function returns the numbers of expressions formatted if it succeeds. It returns a negative value if an error occurs.

Printing a text message on-screen is simple. Call the printf() function, passing the desired message enclosed in double quotation marks. For example, to display Hello World on-screen use :

```
printf("Hello World ");
```

In addition to text messages, however, you frequently need to display the value of program variables. This is a little more complicated than displaying only a message. For example, suppose you want to display the value of the numeric variable a on-screen, along with some identifying text. Furthermore, you want the information to start at the beginning of a new line. You could use the printf() function as follows:

```
printf("\nThe value of a is %d", a);
```

8.2.1 printf() Format String

A printf() format string specifies how the output is formatted. There are three components of a format string:

Literal text is displayed exactly as entered in the format string. In the preceding example, the characters starting with the T (in The) and up to, but not including, the % comprise a literal string.

An escape sequence provides special formatting control. An escape sequence consists of a backslash (\) followed by a single character. In the preceding example, *\n* is an escape sequence. It is called the newline character, and it means move to the start of the next line.

A conversion specifier consists of the percent sign (%) followed by a single character. In the example, the conversion specifier is *%d*. A conversion specifier tells printf() how to interpret the variable(s) being printed. The *%d* tells printf() to interpret the variable *x* as a signed decimal integer.

8.2.2 Escape Sequences in C

Sequence	*Meaning*
\a	Bell (alert)
\b	Backspace
\n	Newline
\t	Horizontal tab
\\	Backslash
\?	Question mark
\'	Single quotation

Escape sequences are used to control the location of output by moving the screen cursor. They are also used to print characters that would otherwise have a special meaning to printf(). For example, to print a single backslash character, include a double backslash (\\) in the format string. The first backslash tells printf() that the second backslash is to be interpreted as a literal character, not as the start of an escape sequence. In general, the backslash tells printf() to interpret the next character in a special manner. Here are some examples:

Program 8.1 *Use of frequently used escape sequences*

```
#include <stdio.h>
#define QUIT 3
int get_menu_choice( void );
void print_report( void );
main()
{
   int choice = 0;
   while (choice != QUIT)
   {
     choice  =  get_menu_choice();
     if (choice == 1)
       printf("\nBeeping  the  computer\a\a\a");
     else
     {
       if (choice == 2)
       print_report();
     }
   }
   printf("You chose to quit!\n");
   return 0;
}
int get_menu_choice( void )
{
   int selection = 0;
   do
   {
     printf("\n");
     printf("\n1  -  Beep Computer");
     printf("\n2  -  Display  Report");
     printf("\n3  -  Quit");
     printf("\n");
     printf("\nEnter  a  selection:");
     scanf("%d",  &selection  );
```

```
    }
    while ( selection < 1 || selection > 3 );
    return selection;
}
void print_report( void )
{
    printf("\nSAMPLE REPORT");
    printf("\n\nSequence\tMeaning");
    printf("\n=========\t=======");
    printf("\n\\a\t\tbell (alert)");
    printf("\n\\b\t\tbackspace");
    printf("\n...\t\t...");
}
```

8.2.3 Conversion/Type Casting Specifiers

Format Specifier	*Meaning*
%*c*	The character format specifier.
%*d*	The integer format specifier.
%*i*	The integer format specifier (same as %*d*).
%*f*	The floating-point format specifier.
%*e*	The scientific notation format specifier (note the lowercase *e*).
%E	The scientific notation format specifier (note the uppercase E).
%*g*	Uses %*f* or %*e*, whichever result is shorter.
%G	Uses %*f* or %E, whichever result is shorter.
%*o*	The unsigned octal format specifier.
%*s*	The string format specifier.
%*u*	The unsigned integer format specifier.
%*x*	The unsigned hexadecimal format specifier (note the lowercase *x*).
%X	The unsigned hexadecimal format specifier (note the uppercase X).
%*p*	Displays the corresponding argument that is a pointer.
%*n*	Records the number of characters written so far.
%%	Outputs a percent sign (%).

A single printf() statement can print an unlimited number of variables, but the format string must contain one conversion specifier for each variable. The conversion specifiers are paired with variables in left-to-right order.

Like :

printf("Rate = %*f*, amount = %*d*", rate, amount);

printf("This prints a character, %c\na number, %d\na floating \ point, %f", 'z', 123, 456.789);

Program 8.2 *Converting to hex numbers.*

```
#include <stdio.h>
main()
{
 printf("Hex(uppercase)  Hex(lowercase)  Decimal\n");
 printf("%X    %x      %d\n", 0, 0, 0);
 printf("%X    %x      %d\n", 1, 1, 1);
 printf("%X    %x      %d\n", 2, 2, 2);
 printf("%X    %x      %d\n", 3, 3, 3);
 printf("%X    %x      %d\n", 4, 4, 4);
 printf("%X    %x      %d\n", 5, 5, 5);
 printf("%X    %x      %d\n", 6, 6, 6);
 printf("%X    %x      %d\n", 7, 7, 7);
 printf("%X    %x      %d\n", 8, 8, 8);
 printf("%X    %x      %d\n", 9, 9, 9);
 printf("%X    %x      %d\n", 10, 10, 10);
 printf("%X    %x      %d\n", 11, 11, 11);
 printf("%X    %x      %d\n", 12, 12, 12);
 printf("%X    %x      %d\n", 13, 13, 13);
 printf("%X    %x      %d\n", 14, 14, 14);
 printf("%X    %x      %d\n", 15, 15, 15);
  }
```

8.2.4 Setting Field Width

The C language allows you to set the width of an integer or float value between the percent sign (%) and the letter in a format specifier. The integer is called the minimum field width specifier because it specifies the minimum field width and ensures that the output reaches the minimum width. For example, in %10f, 10 is a minimum field width specifier that ensures that the output is at least 10 character spaces wide.

Program 8.3 *Setting minimum field width*

```
#include <stdio.h>
main()
 {
 int num1, num2;
 num1 = 12;
 num2 = 12345;
 printf("%d\n", num1);
```

```
printf("%d\n", num2);
printf("%5d\n", num1);
printf("%05d\n", num1);
printf("%2d\n", num2);
}
```

Now you can see in the program, a minimum field width, 5, is specified by %5*d*. The output of program therefore takes five character spaces, with three blank spaces plus two character spaces of 12. The %05d in printf(), shown that the minimum field width is 5, and zeros are used to fill the spaces. Therefore, you see the output made by the execution of the statement is :

00012

The %2*d* sets the minimum field width to 2, but you still see the full-size output of 12345. This means that when the minimum field width is shorter than the width of the output, the latter is taken, and the output is still printed in full.

8.2.5 Aligning Output

In most of program written earlier in this book you might have noticed tha all outputs are right-justified. In other words, by default, all output is placed on the right edge of the field, as long as the field width is longer than the width of the output.You can change this and force output to be left-justified. To do so, you need to prefix the minimum field specifier with the minus sign (–). For example, %-10*d* specifies the minimum field width as 10, and justifies the output from the left edge of the field.

Program 8.4 *Alignment of output*

```
#include <stdio.h>
main()
{
int num1, num2, num3, num4, num5;
num1 = 5;
num2 = 45;
num3 = 345;
num4 = 2345;
num5 = 12345;
printf("%8d %-8d\n", num1, num1);
printf("%8d %-8d\n", num2, num2);
printf("%8d %-8d\n", num3, num3);
printf("%8d %-8d\n", num4, num4);
printf("%8d %-8d\n", num5, num5);
}
```

These values represented by the five integer variables will printed out by the printf() functions when you will run the program. Note that all the printf() functions have the same first argument: "%8d %-8d\n". Here the first format specifier, %8d, aligns the output at the right edge of the field, and the second specifier, %-8d, does the alignment by justifying the output from the left edge of the field.

8.2.6 Precision Specifier

You can use a period (.) and an integer value right after the minimum field width specifier. The combination of the period (.) and the integer makes up a precision specifier. The precision specifier is another important specifier, which can help you to set the number of decimal places for floating-point numbers, or to specify the maximum field width for integers or strings. For example with %12.3*f*, the minimum field width length is specified as 12 characters long, and the number of decimal places is set to 3. (The default number of decimal places is 6.) For integers, %3.8*d* indicates that the minimum field width is 3, and the maximum field width is 8.

Program 8.5 *Use of precision specifiers*

```
#include <stdio.h>
main()
{
 int int_num;
 double flt_num;
 int_num = 123;
 flt_num = 123.456789;
 printf("Default integer format: %d\n", int_num);
 printf("With precision specifier: %2.8d\n", int_num);
 printf("Default float format: %f\n", flt_num);
 printf("With precision specifier: %-10.2f\n", flt_num);
   }
```

8.3 MORE OUTPUTS

8.3.1 puts()

The puts() function can also be used to display text messages on-screen, but it can't display numeric variables. puts() takes a single string as its argument and displays it, automatically adding a newline at the end. For example, the statement :

puts("Hello, world.");

We can include escape sequences (including \n) in a string passed to puts(). They have the same effect as when they are used with printf().puts() is a function that copies a string to the standard output device, usually the display screen. When you use puts(), include the standard input/output header file (STDIO.H). puts() also appends a newline character to the end of the string.

Examples :

puts("This prints on the first line. \nThis prints on the second line.");

puts("This prints on the third line.");

puts("If these were printf()s, all four lines would be on two lines!");

8.3.2 putc()

The putc() function writes a character to the specified file stream, which, in our case, is the standard output pointing to your screen.The syntax of the putc() function is :

#include <stdio.h>

int putc(int c, FILE *stream);

Program 8.6 *Outputting a character with putc()*

```
#include <stdio.h>
main()
 {
    int ch;
    ch = 65; /* the numeric value of A */
    printf("The character that has numeric value of 65 is:\n");
    putc(ch, stdout);
 }
```

8.3.3 putchar()

Like putc(), putchar() can also be used to put a character on the screen. The only difference between the two functions is that putchar() needs only one argument to contain the character. You don't need to specify the file stream, because the standard output (stdout) is the default file stream to putchar(). The syntax for the putchar() function is :

#include <stdio.h>

int putchar(int c);

Program 8.7 *Outputting characters with putchar()*

```
#include <stdio.h>
main()
{
     putchar(65);
     putchar(10);
     putchar(66);
     putchar(10);
     putchar(67);
     putchar(10);
}
```

8.4 GETTING THE INPUT

8.4.1 The scanf() Function

Just as most programs need to output data to the screen, they also need to input data from the keyboard. The most flexible way your program can read data from the keyboard is by using the scanf() library function.

The scanf() function reads data from the keyboard according to a specified format and assigns the input data to one or more program variables. Like printf(), scanf() uses a format string to describe the format of the input. The format string utilizes the same conversion specifiers as the printf() function. For example:-

scanf("%*d*", &*x*);

reads a decimal integer from the keyboard and assigns it to the integer variable x. Likewise, the following statement reads a floating-point value from the keyboard and assigns it to the variable rate:

scanf("%*f*", &rate);

What is that ampersand (&) before the variable's name? The & symbol is C's address-of operator used to assign a memory location to variable.

A single scanf() can input more than one value if you include multiple conversion specifiers in the format string and variable names (again, each preceded by & in the argument list). The following statement inputs an integer value and a floating-point value and assigns them to the variables x and rate, respectively:

scanf("%*d* %*f*", &*x*, &rate);

Program 8.8 *Use of puts() & scanf()*

```
#include <stdio.h>
#define QUIT 4
int get_menu_choice( void );
main()
{
  int choice = 0;
  int int_var = 0;
  float float_var = 0.0;
  unsigned unsigned_var = 0;
  while (choice != QUIT)
  {
    choice = get_menu_choice();
    if (choice == 1)
    {
      puts("\nEnter a signed decimal integer (i.e. -123)");
      scanf("%d", &int_var);
```

```
    }
    if (choice == 2)
    {
      puts("\nEnter a decimal floating-point number\
          (i.e. 1.23)");
      scanf("%f", &float_var);
    }
    if (choice == 3)
    {
      puts("\nEnter an unsigned decimal integer \
          (i.e. 123)");
      scanf("%u", &unsigned_var );
    }
  }
  printf("\nYour values are: int: %d float: %f unsigned: %u \n",
                int_var, float_var, unsigned_var );
  }
  int get_menu_choice( void )
  {
    int selection = 0;
    do
    {
      puts("\n1 - Get a signed decimal integer");
      puts("2 - Get a decimal floating-point number");
      puts("3 - Get an unsigned decimal integer");
      puts("4 - Quit");
      puts("\nEnter a selection:");
      scanf("%d", &selection );
    }
    while ( selection < 1 || selection > 4 );
    return selection;
  }
```

8.4.2 getc()

The getc() function reads the next character from a file stream, and returns the character as an integer. The syntax for the getc() function is :

```
#include <stdio.h>
int getc(FILE *stream);
```

Program 8.9 *Reading input by using getc()*

```
#include <stdio.h>
main()
{
  int ch;
  printf("Please type in one character:\n");
  ch = getc( stdin );
  printf("The character you just entered is: %c\n", ch);
}
```

8.4.3 getchar()

The C language provides another function, getchar(), to perform a similar operation to getc(). More precisely, the getchar() function is equivalent to getc(stdin).The syntax for the getchar() function is :

```
#include <stdio.h>
int getchar(void);
```

Program 8.10 *Reading input by calling getchar()*

```
  #include <stdio.h>
main()
{
  int ch1, ch2;
     printf("Please type in two characters together:\n");
     ch1 = getc( stdin );
     ch2 = getchar( );
     printf("The first character you just entered is: %c\n", ch1);
     printf("The second character you just entered is: %c\n", ch2);
  }
```

8.5 STRINGS

In the array learning you learned how to use arrays to collect variables of the same type. Now you know that a character string is actually a clooection of characters into an array ended with a null character \0. If you want to store your name, your address or your email id you need to declare or use strings in C. You can perform some operations on strings like:

- Declaring a string
- Reading strings with scanf()
- Use of gets() and puts() in strings
- Calculate length of a string
- Copying strings

8.5.1 Declaring Strings

You can declare a string in a C program, using a array of characters like :

```
char array_ch[7] ;
char name[15];
char address[30];
```

A series of characters enclosed in double quotes ("") is called a string constant. The C compiler can automatically add a null character (\0) at the end of a string constant to indicate the end of the string.

8.5.2 Initializing Strings

A character array can be declared and initialized like this:

```
char mystr[6] = {'H', 'e', 'l', 'l', 'o', '!'};
```

Here the array mystr is treated as a character array. However, if you add a null character (\0) into the array, you can have the following statement:

```
char mystr[7] = {'H', 'e', 'l', 'l', 'o', '!', '\0'};
```

Here the array mystr is expanded to hold seven elements; the last element contains a null character. Now, the character array mystr is considered a character string because of the null character that is appended to the array. You can also initialize a character array with a string constant. For example, the following statement initializes a character array, yourstr, with a string constant, "Hello!":

```
char yourstr[7] = "Hello!";
```

The compiler can automatically append a null character (\0) to the end of the array, and treat the character array as a character string. Note that the size of the array is specified to hold up to seven elements, although the string constant has only six characters enclosed in double quotes. The extra space is reserved for the null character that the compiler will add later.

8.5.3 String Constants Versus Character Constants

As you know, a string constant is a series of characters enclosed in double quotes (" "). On the other hand, a character constant is a character enclosed in single quotes (' '). When a character variable ch and a character array str are initialized with the same character x such as the following :

```
char ch = 'x';
char str[] = "x";
```

1 byte is reserved for the character variable ch, and two bytes are allocated for the character array str. The reason that an extra byte is needed for str is that the compiler has to append a null character to the array.

8.5.4 Reading and Writing Strings

For read or write strings with the standard input and output streams in C, there are several functions, that will help you to deal with string reading or writing.

gets() and puts()

The gets() function can be used to read characters from the standard input stream. The syntax for the gets() function is :

```
#include <stdio.h>
char *gets(char *s);
```

Here the characters read from the standard input stream are stored in the character array identified by s. The gets() function stops reading, and appends a null character \0 to the array, when a newline or end-of-file (EOF) is encountered. The function returns s if it concludes successfully. Otherwise, a null pointer is returned.

The puts() function can be used to write characters to the standard output stream (that is, stdout). The syntax for the puts() function is :

```
#include <stdio.h>
int puts(const char *s);
```

Here s refers to the character array that contains a string. The puts() function writes the string to the stdout. If the function is successful, it returns 0. Otherwise, a nonzero value is returned. The puts() function appends a newline character to replace the null character at the end of a character array.Both the gets() and puts() functions require the header file stdio.h.

8.6 STRING OPERATIONS

Now you know string is a sequence of characters, with its beginning indicated by a pointer and its end marked by the null character \0. There are several functions, that can be used on strings but the common ones are :

- The strlen() Function
- The strcpy() Function
- The strncpy() Function
- The strdup() Function
- The strcat() Function
- The strncat() Function
- The strcomp() Function

The strlen() Function

If you want to calculate total length if a string in your program you can use strlen() function. Like :

Program 8.11 *Using the strlen() function.*

```
#include <stdio.h>
#include <string.h>
main()
{
  int length;
  char buf[80];
  while (1)
  {
    puts("\nEnter a line of text, end with enter ");
    gets(buf);
    length = strlen(buf);
    if (length != 0)
    printf("\nThat line is %d characters long.", length);
    else
    break;
  }
}
```

Copy Strings

The C library has three functions for copying strings. Because of the way C handles strings, you can't simply assign one string to another, as you can in some other computer languages. You must copy the source string from its location in memory to the memory location of the destination string. The string-copying functions are strcpy(), strncpy(), and strdup(). All of the string-copying functions require the header file STRING.H.

strcpy() function

The library function strcpy() copies an entire string to another memory location. Its syntax is as follows:

char *strcpy(char *destination, char *source);

The function strcpy() copies the string (including the terminating null character \0) pointed to by source to the location pointed to by destination. The return value is a pointer to the new string, destination. When using strcpy(), you must first allocate storage space for the destination string. The function has no way of knowing whether destination points to allocated space. If space hasn't been allocated, the function overwrites strlen(source) bytes of memory, starting at destination; this can cause unpredictable problems.

Program 8.12 *Demonstrates strcpy().*

```
#include <stdlib.h>
#include <stdio.h>
#include <string.h>
```

```
char source[] = "Uttaranchal Technical University ";
main()
{
  char dest1[80];
  char *dest2; /* Pointer variable */
  printf("\nsource: %s", source );
  strcpy(dest1, source);
  printf("\ndest1: %s", dest1);
  /* To copy to dest2 you must allocate space. */
  dest2 = (char *)malloc(strlen(source) +1);
  strcpy(dest2, source);
  printf("\ndest2: %s\n", dest2);
}
```

REVIEW QUESTIONS

1. What is the difference between puts() and printf()?
2. What header file should you include when you use printf()?
3. What do the following escape sequences do?
   \\
   \b
   \n
   \t
   \a
4. What conversion specifiers should be used to print the following?
   A character string
   A signed decimal integer
   A decimal floating-point number
5. Write a program to read and reverse a string. **[MCA, UTU 2006-07]**

LAB EXERCISES

1. Write both a printf() and a puts() statement to start a new line.
2. Write a scanf() statement that could be used to get a character, an unsigned decimal integer, and another single character.
3. Write the statements to get an integer value and print it.
4. Modify exercise 3 so that it accepts only even values (2, 4, 6, and so on).
5. Modify exercise 4 so that it returns values until the number 99 is entered, or until six even values have been entered. Store the numbers in an array. (Hint: You need a loop.)
6. Turn exercise 5 into an executable program. Add a function that prints the values, separated by tabs, in the array on a single line. (Print only the values that were entered into the array.)

7. Find the error(s) in the following code fragment:
   printf("Amir song in Fanna," Pake Ped Per Paka Papita Pinku Pakde Paka Papita " ");
8. Find the error(s) in the following program:

```
int get_1_or_2( void )
{
        int answer = 0;
        while (answer < 1 || answer > 2)
        {
                printf(Enter 1 for Yes, 2 for No);
                scanf("%f", answer );
        }
        return answer;
    }
```

9. Write the statements to get an float value and print it with only 3 places of decimals.
10. Write a program that inputs two floating-point values from the keyboard and then displays their product, use right align and left align.
11. Write a program that inputs Name and Marks of 10 student values from the keyboard and then displays their sum using arrays. use gets() and puts().
12. Write a program that inputs integers from the keyboard, storing them in an array. Input should stop when a zero is entered or when the end of the array is reached. Then, find and display the array's largest and smallest values.

9

FUNCTIONS IN 'C'

9.1 STRUCTURED PROGRAMMING

When you want to solve simple problems of programming, you always write a direct program without using any programming approach of software engineering. Just take an example of your mobile phone services, each service act as individual program unit like phone book or SMS or calculator or your favoriute games. To design a complete software or a large program there is a need to break it into smaller parts known as modules and then write codes for individual modules and reuse them as an integral part of your software or large program.

In structured programming individual program tasks are performed by independent sections of program code. By using functions in your C programs, you can practice structured programming.

9.1.1 Advantages of Structured Programming

It's easier to write a structured program, because complex programming problems are broken into a number of smaller, simpler tasks. Each task is performed by a function in which code and variables are isolated from the rest of the program. You can progress more quickly by dealing with these relatively simple tasks one at a time.

It's is also easier to debug or trace your errors into a structured program. If your program has a bug or error that causes it to work improperly, a structured design makes it easy to isolate the problem to a specific section of code or to a specific function. A related advantage of structured programming is the time you can save. If you write a function to perform a certain task in one program, you can quickly and easily use it in another program that needs to execute the same task. Even if the new program needs to accomplish a slightly different task, you'll often find that modifying a function you created earlier is easier than writing a new one from scratch. In C most of the time you used the two functions printf() and scanf() and do you know the actual code of that two functions.

9.1.2 Types of Structured Programming

Structured programming is one of the best programming methodologies. Basically, there are two types of structured programming:

1. Top-down programming
2. Bottom-up programming.

To solve a large programming problem, you can start with top level and breaks tha into next small parts and you start your programming at a higher level. For example, you can work with the main() function at the beginning, and then move to the next lower level until the lowest-level functions are written. This type of approach is called top-down programming.

On the other hand, to solve a problem, one way to do it is to work on the smallest pieces of the problem. First, you define and write functions for each of the pieces. After each function is written and tested, you begin to put them together to build a program that can solve the problem. This approach is normally called bottom-up programming.

9.2 FUNCTION

A function is a named and independent section of programming language code that performs a specific task and optionally returns a value to the calling program. Like you have a function next on your TV remote that forward you to next channel, same in your mobile phone you have a function send SMS, which send your messege to your friend. Now you can write definition of C function like :

"A function is a named, independent section of C code that performs a specific task and optionally returns a value to the calling program".

A function is named

Each function has a unique name. By using that name in another part of the program, you can execute the statements contained in the function. This is known as calling the function. A function can be called from within another function. Like :

```
clrscr() ;      // It will clear your program output screen
pow(m,n)        // It will return n power of given number n
```

A function is independent

A function can perform its task without interference from or interfering with other parts of the program.

A function performs a specific task

A task is a given job to your function that must perform as part of its overall operation, such as sending a message to your friend using SMS function or print some text to a printer, or calculating cube root.

A function can return a value to

When your program calls a function, the statements it contains are executed. If you want them to, these statements can pass information back to the calling program. Like when you use dial number function of your mobile phone, it can return you network in busy or number is out of range. After sending SMS you always get a return message form SMS server on your mobile. Same is with C function, if you call cube function it will return you the cube of given number.

9.3 DECLARING FUNCTIONS

A function's definition is required before use it also know as prototype, it contains the name of the function, a list of variables that must be passed to it, and the type of variable it returns, if any. The variables to be passed to the function are called arguments, and they are enclosed in parentheses following the function's name. The keyword before the name of the function indicates the type of variable the function returns.

Function Definition or Prototype

return_type function_name(type arg1, type arg2, ...type arg *n*);

Specifying Return Types

A function can be declared to return any data type, except an array or function. The return statement used in a function definition returns a single value whose type should match the one declared in the function declaration. By default, the return type of a function is int, if no explicit data type is specified for the function. A data type specifier is placed prior to the name of a function like this:

data_type_specifier function_name();

Here data_type_specifier specifies the data type that the function should return. function_name is the function name that should follow the rule of naming in C.

Example 9.1

```
Printhello()                    // No arguments without return
Cube(int a)                     // One argument no return
int cube(int a)                 // One argument with return of int type
float cint (int p, int r, int t )   // function with three arguments and float return
Return Type     Function name   Arguments
```

9.4 BUILT IN FUNCTIONS

C language is full with built in functions, you have used printf(), scanf(), getch() or clrscr() functions most of the times in a C program. C has a rich libraray of functions that you reuse in your programs without coding them.

The C standard library contains a variety of functions that perform various operations. There are functions that perform mathematical calculations, deal with date and time, and assist your program with error handling. The functions for graphics, file handling, sorting and searching data are particularly useful when you will work on your C project because they can save you considerable time when you will design and code your programs.

9.4.1 Mathematical Functions

The C standard library contains a variety of functions that perform mathematical operations. To use the mathematical functions you must include the header file MATH.H. The math functions return a type double. For the trigonometric functions, angles are expressed in radians.

sqrt() **double sqrt(double *x*)**

Returns the square root of its argument. The argument must be zero or greater.

ceil() **double ceil(double *x*)**

Returns the smallest integer not less than its argument. For example, ceil(4.5) returns 5.0, and ceil(-4.5) returns -4.0. Although ceil() returns an integer value, it is returned as a type double.

abs() **int abs(int *x*)**

Returns the absolute value of number

floor() **double floor(double *x*)**

Returns the largest integer not greater than its argument. For example, floor(4.5) returns 4.0, and floor(-4.5) returns -5.0.

pow() **double pow(double *x*, double *y*)**

Returns xy. An error occurs if $x == 0$ and $y <= 0$, or if $x < 0$ and y is not an integer.

fmod() **double fmod(double *x*, double *y*)**

Returns the floating-point remainder of x/y, with the same sign as x. The function returns 0 if $x == 0$.

Program 9.1 *Use of some of C's inbuilt math functions*

```
#include <stdio.h>
#include <math.h>
main()
{
double x;
printf("Enter a number: ");
scanf("%lf", &x);
printf("\n\nOriginal value: %lf", x);
printf("\nCeil: %lf", ceil(x));
printf("\nFloor: %lf", floor(x));
if( x >= 0 )
printf("\nSquare root: %lf", sqrt(x) );
else
printf("\nNegative number");
printf("\nCosine: %lf\n", cos(x));
}
```

9.4.2 Date and Time Functions

The C library contains several functions that can help you to use date and time in your program. In C, the term times refers to dates as well as times. The function prototypes and the definition of the structure used by many of the time functions are in the header file TIME.H.

The C time functions represent time in two ways. The more basic method is the number of seconds elapsed since midnight on January 1, 1970. Negative values are used to represent times before that date. These time values are stored as type long integers. In TIME.H, the symbols time_t and clock_t are both defined with a typedef statement as long. These symbols are used in the time function prototypes rather than long. The second method represents a time broken down into its components: year, month, day, and so on. For this kind of time representation, the time functions use a structure tm, defined in TIME.H

To convert times into formatted strings appropriate for display, you can use the functions ctime() and asctime(). Both of these functions return the time as a string with a specific format. They differ because ctime() is passed the time as a type time_t value, whereas asctime() is passed the time as a type tm structure. Their prototypes are :

```
char *asctime(struct tm *ptr);

char *ctime(time_t *ptr);
```

Program 9.2 *Use of date and time functions*

```
#include <stdio.h>
#include <time.h>
main()
{
    time_t now;
    printf("Get Date Time from C functions \n");
    time(&now);
    printf("Current date and time is: %s\n", asctime(localtime(&now)));
}
```

9.5 USER DEFINED FUNCTIONS

The first step in writing a user defined function is knowing what you want the function to do like you want a function that print "Hello from function" or you want a function that will fill full screen with some alphabet or symbol. Once you know that you can define your function. The first line of every function is known as the function header, which has three components:

1. Return type
2. Function name
3. Function arguments

each serving a specific function. Like :

float simpleintrest (int *p*, int *r*, int *t*) // function with three arguments and float return

Return Type Function name Arguments

The return type of function is float, name of function is simpleintrest and there are three arguments, of int type.

9.5.1 Types of Functions

Null Function

A function which has only name, no arguments and no return value known as null function like:

Printhello()

Program 9.3 *Use of null function*

```
#include <stdio.h>
 main()
{
/* Call of function */
printhello();
}
/* Body of function */
printhello()
{
printf("Hello from function first time ");
}
```

Program 9.4 *Null function to fill full screen with UTU*

```
#include <stdio.h>
main()
{
/* Call of function */
fillscreen();
}
/* Body of function */
fillscreen()
{
int row, column;
for(row=1;row<=23;row++)
{
for (column=1;column<=80;column++)
{
printf("UTU");
}
printf("\n");
} }
```

Function with arguments, but no return

Some functions have name and arguments but no return value associated with that function, so they return int as default retyrn type like :

twosum(int firstnum, int secondnum)

squreofnumber(int number)

Program 9.5 *A function without return and with arguments*

```
#include <stdio.h>
main()
{
int num=0;
printf("Enter a number less than 100");
scanf("%d",&num);
/* Call of function */
squreofnumber(num);
}
/* Body of function */
squreofnumber(int x)
{
int sq;
sq= x * x * x;
printf("Squre of number %d is %d",x,sq);
}
```

Function with arguments, and return

Some functions have name, arguments and return value associated with that function, they can return any value defined as return type by the user like :

int getmax(int firstnum, int secondnum)

long cube(long x)

Program 9.6 *Demo of function for cube with return and arguments*

```
#include <stdio.h>
long cube(long x);
long input, answer;
main()
{
        printf("Enter an integer value: ");
        scanf("%d", &input);
        answer = cube(input);
        /* Note: %ld is the conversion specifier for a long integer */
        printf("\nThe cube of %ld is %ld.\n", input, answer);
```

```
}
/* Function: cube() - Calculates the cubed value of a variable */
long cube(long x)
{
        long cubed;
        cubed = x * x * x;
        return cubed;
}
```

Output:

Enter an integer value: 100

The cube of 100 is 1000000.

Enter an integer value: 9

The cube of 9 is 729.

Enter an integer value: 3

The cube of 3 is 27.

9.5.2 Function Prototype Vs Function Definition

A function prototype provides the compiler with a description of a function that will be defined at a later point in the program. The prototype includes a return type indicating the type of variable that the function will return. It also includes the function name, which should describe what the function does. The prototype also contains the variable types of the arguments that will be passed to the function. Optionally, it can contain the names of the variables that will be passed. A prototype should always end with a semicolon.

Example :

return_type function_name(arg-type name-1,...,arg-type name-n);

int squre (int x);

double amount(int p, float r, int time);

A function definition is the actual function. The definition contains the code that will be executed. The first line of a function definition, called the function header, should be identical to the function prototype, with the exception of the semicolon. A function header shouldn't end with a semicolon. In addition, although the argument variable names were optional in the prototype, they must be included in the function header. Following the header is the function body, containing the statements that the function will perform. The function body should start with an opening bracket and end with a closing bracket. If the function return type is anything other than void, a return statement should be included, returning a value matching the return type.

Program 9.7 *Function to find out larger number in given two numbers*

```
#include <stdio.h>
int x, y, z;
/* Function Prototype */
```

```
int largerof( int, int );
main()
{
     puts("Enter two different integer values: ");
     scanf("%d%d", &x, &y);
     z = largerof(x,y);
     printf("\nThe larger value is %d.", z);
}
int largerof( int a, int b)
{
     if (a > b)
          return a;
     else
          return b;
}
```

Output :

Enter two different integer values:

450 560

The larger value is 560.

Enter two different integer values:

500

1200

The larger value is 1200.

Program 9.8 *Function to print date & time*

```
#include <stdio.h>
#include <time.h>
/* Function Prototype */
void GetDateTime(void);
main()
{
     printf("Before the GetDateTime() function is called.\n");
     GetDateTime();
     printf("After the GetDateTime() function is called.\n");
}
/* GetDateTime() definition */
void GetDateTime(void)
{
     time_t now;
     printf("Within GetDateTime().\n");
```

```
        time(&now);
printf("Current date and time is: %s\n", asctime(localtime(&now)));
    }
```

9.6 CALL BY VALUE AND CALL BY REFERENCE

The default method of passing an argument to a function is by value. Passing by value means that the function is passed a copy of the argument's value. This method has three steps:

1. The argument expression is evaluated.
2. The result is copied onto the stack, a temporary storage area in memory.
3. The function retrieves the argument's value from the stack.

When a variable is passed to a function by value, the function has access to the variable's value but not to the original copy of the variable. As a result, the code in the function can't modify the original variable. This is the main reason why passing by value is the default method of passing arguments that helps you to make data outside a function is protected from inadvertent modification. Passing arguments by value is possible with the basic data types (char, int, long, float, and double) and structures.

There is another way to pass an argument to a function, however by passing a pointer to the argument variable rather than the value of the variable itself. This method of passing an argument is called passing by reference.

Program 9.9 *Program to show call by value and call by reference*

```
/* Passing arguments by value and by reference. */
#include <stdio.h>
void byvalue(int a, int b, int c);
void byref(int *a, int *b, int *c);
main()
{
   int x = 2, y = 4, z = 6;
   printf("\nBefore calling by_value(), x = %d, y = %d, z = %d.", x, y, z);
   byvalue(x, y, z);
   printf("\nAfter calling by_value(), x = %d, y = %d, z = %d.", x, y, z);
   byref(&x, &y, &z);
   printf("\nAfter calling by_ref(), x = %d, y = %d, z = %d.\n", x, y, z);
}
void byvalue(int a, int b, int c)
{
   a = 0;
   b = 0;
   c = 0;
```

```
}
void byref(int *a, int *b, int *c)
{
   *a = 0;
   *b = 0;
   *c = 0;
}
```

9.7 RECURSION

The term recursion refers to a situation in which a function calls itself either directly or indirectly. The term "recursion" was derived from the Latin word recursus, which means, "to run back".Indirect recursion occurs when one function calls another function that then calls the first function. C allows recursive functions, and they can be useful in some situations.

For example, recursion can be used to calculate the factorial of a number. The factorial of a number x is written x! and is calculated as follows:

$x! = x * (x-1) * (x-2) * (x-3) * ... * (2) * 1$

However, you can also calculate x! like this:

$x! = x * (x-1)!$

Program 9.10 *Use of function recursion. Calculates the factorial of a number.*

```
#include <stdio.h>
unsigned int f, x;
unsigned int factorial(unsigned int a);
main()
{
      puts("Enter an integer value between 1 and 8: ");
      scanf("%d", &x);
      if( x > 8 || x < 1)
      {
            printf("Only values from 1 to 8 are acceptable!");
      }
      else
      {
            f = factorial(x);
            printf("%u factorial equals %u\n", x, f);
      }
}
unsigned int factorial(unsigned int a)
```

```
{
        if (a == 1)
                return 1;
        else
        {
                a = a * factorial(a-1);
                return a;
        }
}
```

9.7.1 Applications of Recursion

The factorial function is a prime example of using recursion. The factorial number is needed in many statistical calculations. Recursion is just a loop; however, it has one difference from other loops. With recursion, each time a recursive function is called, a new set of variables is created.

9.7.2 Usefull Recursive Programs

Here are some very usefull functions that are used as recursive functions to sole many mathematical problems, try to use them in your own programs.

Factorial

This is the most famous function on recursion. Many versions of this program are available. All programs differ only in checking conditions.

```
long Factorial( int n )
/* returns factorial */
{
if ( n>0 )
return( n * Factorial(n-1) );
else
return( 1 );
}
/*--Factorial( )------*/
```

Fibonacci

Fibonacci series is :

1, 1, 2, 3, 5,8, 13, 21...

The following function returns the nth Fibonacci number.

int Fibonacci(int *n*)

```
/* returns nth Fibonacci number */
{
if ( n= =1 || n = =2 )
return( 1 );
else
return( Fibonacci(n-1) + Fibonacci(n-2) );
}
/*--Fibonacci( )-------*/
```

GCD

Here is the function to find the Greatest Common Divisior (GCD) of two numbers *a* & *b*.

```
int GCD( int a, int b )
/* returns GCD of a, b */
{
if ( a>=b && a%b==0 )
return( b );
else if ( a<b )
return( GCD( b, a ) );
else
return( GCD( b, a%b ) );
}
/*--GCD( )---------*/
```

Power

Just use the given function which defined power function, it could handle negative numbers also.

```
double Power( double x, int n )
/* returns x power n */
{
if ( n= =0 )
return( 1 );
else if ( n>0 )
return( x * Power( x, n-1 ) );
else
return( (1/x) * Power( x, n+1 ) );
```

```
}
/*--Power( )----------*/
```

Reverse Printing

This is a wonderful function to understand the use of recursion.

```
void ReverseChar( void )
/* prints characters in reverse */
{
char ch;
if ( (ch=getchar( ))!='\n' )
ReverseChar( );
putchar( ch );
}
/*--ReverseChar( )---------*/
```

Decimal to Binary Conversion

The following recursive function gets decimal value as input and print its binary value. It prints each bit value (0 or 1) one by one.

```
void ToBinary( int n )
/* prints decimal in binary */
{
if (n>1)
To Binary( n/2 );
printf("%d", n%
}
/*--ToBinary ( )---------*/
```

Printing a Decimal in Words

The following recursive function gets a decimal number as argument and prints it in words. For example, 12340 will be printed as One Two Three Four Zero.

```
void InWord( int n )
/* prints decimal in words */
{
char *wtab[ ] = { "Zero", "One", "Two", "Three", "Four",
"Five", "Six", "Seven", "Eight", "Nine" };
```

```
if (n>9)
InWord( n/10 );
printf("%s ", wtab[n%10] );
}
/*--InWord( )----------*/
```

Euclid's Algorithm to compute the HCF of two numbers

```
# include < stdio.h
   int hef (int a, int b);
   void main (void)
   {
      int x, y, z, w, answer;
      printf ("Enter four positive integers:");
      scanf ("%d %d %d %d", &x, &y, &z, &w);
      answer = hef (hef (x, y), hef (z, w));
      printf ("%d\n", answer);
      answer = hef (hef (hef (x, y), z), w);
      printf ("%d\n", answer);
   }
   int hef (int p, int q)
      {
      int divisor, dividend, remainder;
      dividend = (divisor = p <q ? p : q) = = p ? q; p;>
      while (remainder = dividend % divisor)
   {
      dividend = divisor;
      divisor = remainder;
   }
      return divisor ;
   }
```

9.8 PASSING ARRAY TO FUNCTIONS

In some cases if you want to use array as arguments of your defined functions, you cab pass a list of array values to your functions like :

int readarray(int score[], int max);

This function will use a list of scores passed by calling function, now size of argument array will be decided by the calling function.

Program 9.11 *Program to calculate the standard deviation of an array of values. Use array to functions to calculate standard deviation and mean.*

Standard deviation of a set of n values is given by

$$S.D = \frac{1}{n}\sum_{i=1}^{n}\sqrt{(x - x_i)^2}$$

Where $\bar{x}$ is the mean of the values.

```
#include <math.h>
#define SIZE 10
float stddev(float a[], int n);    //function with array arguments
float mean (float a[], int n);
main( )
{
   float value[SIZE];
   int i;
   printf("Enter %d float values\n", SIZE);
   for (i=0 ;i < SIZE ; i++)
   scanf("%f", &value[i]);
   printf("Std.deviation is %f\n", stddev(value,SIZE));
}
float stddev(float a[], int n)
{  int i;
   float x, sum = 0.0;
   x = mean (a,n);
   for(i=0; i < n; i++)
   sum += (x-a[i])*(x-a[i]);
   return(sqrt(sum/(float)n));
}
float mean(float a[],int n)
{
   int i ;
   float sum = 0.0;
   for(i=0 ; i < n ; i++)
   sum = sum + a[i];
   return(sum/(float)n);
}
```

Program 9.12 *Function mysort() to sort integer values using array passing*

```
void mysort(int m, int x[ ]);
main()
{
   int i;
   int marks[10] = {40, 90, 73, 81, 35,45,78, 9, 12, 19};
   printf("Before sorting\n");
   for(i = 0; i < 10; i++)
      printf("%d ", marks[i]);
   printf("\n\n");
   mysort (10, marks);
   printf("After sorting\n");
   for(i = 0; i < 10; i++)
   printf("%d", marks[i]);
   printf("\n");
}
void mysort(int m, int x[ ])
{
   int i, j, tp;
   for(i = 1; i <= m-1; i++)
      for(j = 1; j <= m-i; j++)
         if(x[j-1] >= x[j])
         {
           tp = x[j-1];
           x[j-1] = x[j];
           x[j] = tp;
         }
   }
```

REVIEW QUESTIONS

1. How does structured programming work?
2. What is structured programming in C?
3. How do C functions fit into structured programming?
4. What must be the first line of a function definition, and what information does it contain?
5. How many values can a function return?
6. If a function doesn't return a value, what type should it be declared?
7. What's the difference between a function definition and a function prototype?
8. Where should the main() function be placed?
9. When passing arguments to a function, what's the difference between passing by value and passing by reference?

10. What is recursion, write a C program to compute factorial of a long number using recursion? **[MCA, UTU 2006-07]**

LAB EXERCISES

1. Write a header for a function named do_it() that takes three type char arguments and returns a type float to the calling program.
2. Write a header for a function named print_a_number() that takes a single type int argument and doesn't return anything to the calling program.
3. What type value do the following functions return?
   (*a*) int print_error(float err_nbr);
   (*b*) long read_record(int rec_nbr, int size);
4. What's wrong with the following listing?

```
#include <stdio.h>
void print_msg( void );
main()
{
        print_msg("This is a message to print");
}
void print_msg( void )
{
        puts("This is a message to print");
}
```

5. What's wrong with the following function definition?

```
int twice(int y);
{
        return (2 * y);
}
```

6. What is a null function, write a program to show the use of null function?
7. Write a function that receives two numbers as arguments and returns the value of their product.
8. Write a function that receives two numbers as arguments. The function should divide the first number by the second. Don't divide by the second number if it's zero. (Hint: Use an if statement.)
9. Write a function that calls the functions in exercises 7 and 8.
10. Write a program that uses a function to find the average of five type float values entered by the user.
11. Write a recursive function to take the value 3 to the power of another number. For example, if 4 is passed, the function will return 81.
12. Write a function called 'smaller', which accepts two integers, and which returns the value of the smaller one.
13. Write a function called 'print_prod' which has two float inputs and no returned result. It prints the product of the two floats.

14. Making use of dashes(length), write a function called draw_rect with two int arguments—the dimensions of a rectangle—which draws a rectangle on the screen. It returns no result. For example, draw_rect(4,8) gives:

```
________
________
________
________
```

15. Write a function called 'big3', which returns the biggest of 3 float arguments.

10

STRUCTURE & UNION

10.1 STRUCTURE

You must be familiar with arrays, which are helpful to store similar type of data. You are assigned a lab task to store fees deposit by 500 students and to calculate sum of this amount. the best way to solve this task is use of array. Now consider the case of a bank, to store information about your bank account you should use various variables like accountnumber, name, address, and balance. Now the question is how will store this dissimilar data using one data type. The answer of this question is structure.

In C arrays can be used to collect groups of variables of the same type. But you can group variables of different types with a new data type called a structure. In C, a structure collects different data items in such a way that they can be referenced as a single unit.

10.2 WHY STRUCTURE

The answer of this question is associated with the use of data base applications. A data base application helps you to store and work on business data like bank, library, shopping mall or your university. In C if you want to write program for that purpose the use of structure is must. Just check the given example :

Example 10.1. *In an organization information about new employee has to keep in a file at the time of joining, the general information are :*

Employee id, Employee Name, Date of joining, Department, Designation, Basic, Perks, Net Salary

Now each attribute like Employee id is known as field, and a collection of all that attribute known as record, and if you have 100 records in a file, you can think this file as a small data base.

Employee *id*
Employee Name
Date of joining
Department
Designation
Basic
Perks
Net Salary

Record of one Employee

Your task is to write a C program to store all that information either in RAM or in a file. Without the use of structure you can not solve this task.

> ***Tips :*** If you have a mobile phone, the phone book of your mobile can be considered as a small data base to store name and phone numbers, and you always perform many operations on that, like add, delete or search. Now think the structure of your mobile phone book.

10.3 STRUCTURE DECLARATION

The general syntax to declare a structure is :

```
struct      structure-name
{
   datatype1 variable1;
   datatype2 variable2;
   datatype3 variable3;
   .
   .
   .
   };
```

Here struct is the keyword used in C to start a structure declaration. structure -name is the name of the structure you want to set. variable1, variable2, and variable3 are the members of the structure. Their data types are specified respectively by datatype1, datatype2, and datatype3.

Now you can declare a structure for Example1 like :

```
struct aimca_employee
{
int eid;
char ename[30];
char doj[10];
char deptname[20];
```

```
char desig[20];
int basic;
float perks;
float netsalary;
};
```

10.3.1 Initializing Structures

Like other C variable types, structures can be initialized when they're declared. This procedure is similar to that for initializing arrays. The structure declaration is followed by an equal sign and a list of initialization values separated by commas and enclosed in braces. For example, look at the following statements:

```
struct todaysale
{
  int itemcode;
  char itemname[20];
  float price;
  } todaysale = { 1029, "Fruit Juice ",178.50};
```

Example 10.2. *Declare a structure for your mobile phone book and declare variables for that structure, again with the help of a C program read and display the values for phone book.*

Declaration

```
struct mphonebook
{
int callnumber;
char name[20];
};
```

Variable declaration

```
mphonebook m1;
```

Program 10.1

```
/* Mobile phone book program with structure */
#include <stdio.h>
main()
{
    struct mphonebook
    {
    int callnumber;
    char name[20];
     };
```

```
struct mphonebook m1;
/* static data value assignments with in structure */
m1.name= "MK sharma";
m1.callnumber=9897512345;
printf("Here is output \n");
printf("Name: %s\n", m1.name);
printf("Phone Number: %d\n\", m1.callnumber);
/* dynamic data value assignments with in structure */
printf("Add name\n");
gets(m1.name);
printf("add number \n");
scanf("%d", &m1.callnumber);
printf("\nHere is new output \n");
printf("Name: %s\n", m1.name);
printf("Phone Number: %d\n\", m1.callnumber);
}
```

> ***Tips :*** To access member variables of a structure, you have used dot operator **(.)** like m1.name, You can also use → operator to access structure variables. In next chapter after learning pointers you will get to know how to use this.

10.4 STRUCTURE WITH IN STRUCTURE

In Employee program if you want to store Date of joining of an employee in actual date format like 12/07/2007, you need date type which is not available in C, so what you will do in this situation. The answer is first create a structure for date and then use it in aimcaemployee structure. This method known as structure in structure or nesting of structures.

Example 10.3

```
struct joindate
{
short int dd;
short int mm;
short int yyyy;
};
    struct aimca_employee
    {
    int eid;
    char ename[30];
    struct joindate jdate;
    char deptname[20];
```

```
char desig[20];
int basic;
float perks;
float netsalary;
};
```

Now declare a variable for aimca_employee type.

struct aimca_emplyee E1;

The given declaration will help to assign the joining date values to your employee.

E1.jdate.dd=12;

E1.jdate.mm=7

E1.jdate.yyyy=2007;

Program 10.2

```
/* Demo of nesting of structures */
#include <stdio.h>
struct department
{
  int dcode;
  char dname[32];
  char edesignation[16];
 };
typedef struct department dept;
  struct employee
  {
  dept d;
  int id;
 char name[32];
  };
 typedef struct employee emp;
 main()
 {
 emp info = { { 1, "Computer Science ", "Senior Lecturer" }, 3, "MK
Sharma"};
 printf("Display of information \n");
 printf("Name: %s\n", info.name);
 printf("EmpID : %04d\n", info.id);
 printf("Dept. Name: %s\n", info.d.dname);
 printf("Dept. ID: %02d\n", info.d.dcode);
 printf("Emp Designation : %s\n", info.d.edesignation);
 }
```

> *Tips* : typedef is a keyword of C, using typedef you can define your own names or synonym for a structure or union data types.

10.5 ARRAY OF STRUCTURE

In your mobile phone, your phone book is capable to store 200 records of contacts at a time. You have declared structure to store record of one record only in early example. Now the new task is to add 100 contacts at a time in your phone book program. How you will do it, the answer is array of structure.

Yes in C you can apply array on structures also. Just declare a structure, at the time of variable declaration for structure apply array declaration. You can use a loop to read or write values at a time on structure. Like :

Program 10.3

```
/* Mobile phone book program with array of structure */
#include <stdio.h>
main()
{
    struct mphonebook
     {
     int callnumber;
     char name[20];
     };
  /* array of 100 records with structure */
  int I;
  struct mphonebook m1[100];
  /* Value assignments with in structure using for loop */
  for (I = 0;I <= 99; I++)
  {
  printf("Add name\n");
  gets(m1[I].name);
  printf("add number \n");
  scanf("%d", &m1[I].callnumber);
  }
  printf("\n Here is output of 50 records \n");
  for (I = 0;I <= 49; I++)
  {
  printf("Name: %s\n", m1[I].name);
  printf("Phone Number: %d\n\", m1[I].callnumber);
   }
  }
```

10.6 PASSING STRUCTURES TO FUNCTIONS

A function in C can pass parameters of type int or float, in this way you can pass a single value only. Can we pass structures to functions, the answer is yes. Like other data types, a structure can be passed as an argument to a function.

Program 10.4

```
/* Demo of passing a structure to a function. */
#include <stdio.h>
    struct bankdata
    {
    int accno;
    float balance;
    char cname[30];
    } crec;
    /* This function has no return value. */
    /* and it takes a structure of type data as its one argument. */
    displayrec(struct bankdata b1);
    main()
    {
    printf("Enter the account number, balance and name of customer with space \n");
    scanf("%d %f %s", crec.accno, crec.balance,crec.cname);
    /* Call the displayrec function. */
       displayrec(crec );
    }
    displayrec(struct bankdata b1)
    {
    printf("\n Customer %s having %d account number, has %f balance \n",
b1.cname,
    b1.accno,b1.balance);
    }
```

10.7 SELF REFERENTIAL STRUCTURE

A structure can refer to it self in some cases. Now you can ask why we need to use that types of structure, the answer is the concept of link list in computer science. When you will learn data structure, there is use of link list structure. A link list consist many nodes and each node refer to next or previous node. Without using self reference structure concept you can not write a link list program in C.

Example 10.4

```
struct node
```

```
{
int data ;
struct node *next ;
};
```

In the given example the structure node is a part of link list and to refer next node a self reference of node structure is required inside the structure. *next is a pointer variable.

10.8 UNION

A union is a block of memory similar to structures that is used to hold data items of different types in the same ways as a structure. In C, a union is similar to a structure but differs from a structure in that only one of its members can be used at a time, and data items saved in the union are overlaid in order to share the same memory location.

To be more simple, just think a union having 2 members. First member is a int variable while second is a char variable. Both will share a 2 byte space in Union (because size of int is 2 byte), while in Structure 3 bytes (int 2 + char 1)are required to store both. Following example will clear it to you :

struct sdata	**union sdata**
{	**{**
int marks;	**int marks;**
char grade;	**char grade;**
};	**};**

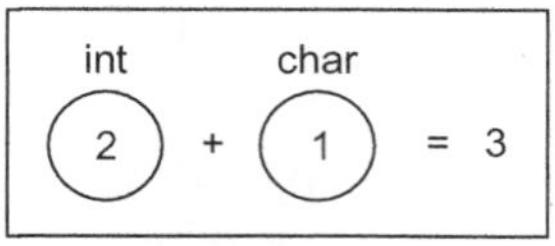

Fig. 10.1 *A Structure with 1 int and 1 char variable, occupy 3 bytes*

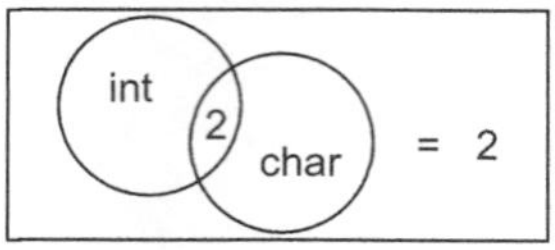

Fig. 10.2 *A Union with 1 int and 1 char variable, occupy 2 bytes*

10.8.1 Declaring Unions

The syntax for declaring a union is similar to the syntax for a structure. The following is an example of a union declaration:

```
union aimcastudent
  {
  int year;
  char course[6];
```

```
int rollno;
char name[25];
};
```

Here union is the keyword that specifies the union data type. aimcastudent is the name of the union. The variables, such as year, course, rollno and name, are members of the union.

Union Variables Declaration

You can define union variables after declaring a union. Like for union aimcastudent the members of union can be :

union aimcastudent *s*1,*s*2,*s*3;

You can also declare member variables like :

```
union aimcastudent
{
int year;
char course[6];
int rollno;
char name[25];
} s1,s2,s3 ;
```

Referring Union Members

As you have used with structure members, the dot operator (.), you can use the same in referencing union members. For example, the following statement assigns the value of 2003 to one of the student of aimcastudent union:

*s*1.year = 2003;

*s*2.rollno=34567;

In addition, if you want to use pointers you have to declare a pointer variable first like :

union aimcastudent **p*1;

then you can reference one of the union members in the following way:

*p*1->year = 2003;

Here the arrow operator (->)is used to reference the union member year with the pointer *p*1.

Program 10.5

```
/* Demo of a union program */
#include <stdio.h>
#include <string.h>
main()
{
   union vishalitems
```

```
    {
     char  name[23];
     double  price;
    } item1;
   strcpy(item1.name,  "Dabur  Honey");
   printf("Item  Name:  %s\n",  item1.name);
   item1.price  =  99.95;
   printf("Dish  Price:  %f\n",item1.price);
  }
```

> ***Tips*** **:** A union can hold either any one member of the union at a time. This is an OR condition. If you have 2 variable one is int and another is char, it will hold only one at a time. Unlike a structure that would hold both values, the union can hold only one value at a time. Because only one member can be used at a time, only one can be initialized or assigned a value.

Program 10.6

```
/* Demo of sharing in unions */
#include  <stdio.h>
main()
{
union  aimcastudent
{
   int  marks1;
   int  marks2;
   int  marks3;
  } stu1;
stu1.marks1=56;
stu1.marks1=78;
stu1.marks1=34;
/* Display marks of student */
printf(stu1.marks1);
printf(stu1.marks1);
printf(stu1.marks1);
}
```

> ***Tips*** : The output of this program will be 34 is all cases why ?

10.8.2 Size of a Union

As you are aware with the fact that the members of a union share the same memory location. The size of a union is the same as the size of the largest member in the union. In contrast the size of a structure is equal to the sum of sizes of its members instead of the size of the largest member.

Program 10.7

```
/* Compute and compare size of a union and structure */
#include <stdio.h>
#include <string.h>
main()
 {
  union mp
   {
   double x;
   int y;
   } mp1;
   struct mks
  {
   double x;
   int y;
   } mks1;
      printf("The size of double is : %d byte\n",
      sizeof(double));
      printf("The size of int is : %d byte\n",
      sizeof(int));
      printf("The size of mp union : %d-byte\n", sizeof(mp1));
      printf("The size of mks structure : %d byte\n", sizeof(mks1));
 }
```

10.8.3 Structure Vs Union

The difference between a union and a structure is that the members in a union are overlaid by top member and they share the same memory location, whereas the members in a structure have their own memory locations. A union can be referenced by using one of its member names at a time. The size of a structure is equal to the total sum of all members while the size of union is equal to the size of maximum member byte size. Structures occupy more memory while Union occupy less memory.

REVIEW QUESTIONS

1. How is a structure different from an array?
2. What is the structure member operator, and what purpose does it serve?
3. What keyword is used in C to create a structure?
4. What is the difference between a structure and a union?
5. What do you mean by the following terms : **[UTU 2006–07]**
   (*i*) Nested structure (*ii*) Self referential structure

6. Define a structure that can describe a restaurant having the name, rating (1,2,3), average cost of a dish and the seating capacity. Write functions to perform following operations :
   (*i*) Print details of restaurant of a given rating in order of average cost of a dish.
   (*ii*) Print details of restaurant which seating capacity is less than a given value.

   [UTU 2006–07]
7. Write a self referential structure for a tree having root and two left and right child nodes.

LAB EXERCISES

1. Define a structure **employeedata** that would contain employee name, date of joining and salary. Using this structure, write a program to read this information for one person from the keyboard and print the same on the screen.
2. Define a structure **midmarks** that would contain rollno, marks in 6 subjects and total of marks. Using array of structure write program to read information of 15 students and write function to print data of 5 students.
3. Write a simple program to illustrate the method of sending an entire structure as a parameter to a functions and then use the member variables of that structure into that function.
4. Create a structure containing five strings: address1, address2, city, state, and pincode. Create a typedef called PRECORD that can be used to create instances of this structure. Use array of structure to store value of 5 members and display the records also.
5. What is wrong with the following code ? Trace and correct the code.

```
struct
{
  int month;
  char zodiacsign[15];
} sign = 10, "Libra";
```

11

POINTERS IN C

11.1 WHY POINTERS ?

In most of the programs you have written and tested yet, there is a use of variables and you can store some value in a variable for later use. Have you ever think the location of variables, means when you declare a variable,on which area of computer it will store. In a large computer program there can be thousands of variables, so you need some space to store and retrieve them.

The space used for that is known as RAM (Random Access Memory). If you are aware with RAM working you must be aware with the fact that a PC's RAM consists of many thousands of sequential storage locations, and each location is identified by a unique address. The memory addresses in a given computer range from 0 to a maximum value that depends on the amount of memory installed (like 512 MB).

As you might know, the memory inside your computer is not only used to store name and values of program variables but also used to hold the binary code of your program, which consists of statements and data, as well as the binary code of the operating system on your machine.

Each memory location must have a unique address so that the computer can read from or write to the memory location without any confusion. This is similar to the concept that in your institute or university each mobile phone must have a unique number to call.

When you declare a variable in a C program, the compiler sets aside a memory location with a unique address to store that variable. The compiler associates that address with the variable's name. When your program uses the variable name, it automatically accesses the proper memory location. The location's address is used, but it is hidden from you, and you need not be concerned with it. Now you must have some method to link with a variable or memory or secondary storage location (may be a file), the only variable which can store address of any location inside computer system is pointer.

If you want to be a system programmer or you want to write system programs using C, knowledge of pointers is must for you. If you have good command on pointers, C will become most powerful language for you.

11.2 POINTERS

A pointer is a variable which is used to point to another variable. In simple word " A pointer is a variable which can store address of another variable ". From these definitions, you can say that a pointer is a variable and the value contained by a pointer must be an address that indicates the location of another variable in the memory. That's why a pointer is also known as an address variable. Following example will simplify the definition for you.

Example 11.1

int $x = 500$;

You have declared a variable x in your program and you have assigned the value 500 to it. When you will compile it the variable x will get its location in memory. An address will also assigned to x in memory. Who will decide this address, do not worry it will be managed by compiler with the help of operating system.

Variable name	Value	Memory Location
x	500	1004

So the address assigned to x is 1004 (assumed). You can print the value of x directly, but to hold the address of x you need a pointer variable. You can think it is easy to get and print a value of variable in a C program so why should I use pointers. The answer is, suppose you have a text file on hard disk and your task is to write a program to display contents of that file. Can you do it directly certainly not, you need pointers to point first byte of your file, which is on hard disk. Same is true to play a song with CD or play a movie with DVD. You always need pointers to point the locations of your file, audio file or video file.

11.3 DECLARING POINTERS

A pointer is a numeric variable and it always store integer values. Like all variables you should declare a pointer variable before use. Pointer variable names follow the same rules as other variables and must be unique. Syntax for a pointer declaration is:

```
datatype *ptrname;
int *myptr ;
float *ptr1;
char *ptr2 ;
```

datatype is any of C's variable types and indicates the type of the variable that the pointer points in future. The symbol (*) is must before the name of pointer variable.

Tips : The asterisk (*) is known as the indirection operator or the dereference operator.

11.4 INITIALIZING POINTERS

Until a pointer holds the address of a variable, it is not useful. The address doesn't get stored in the pointer by own, in your program you must put it there by using the address of operator (&). When placed before the name of a variable, the address of operator returns the address of the variable. Therefore, you can initialize a pointer like :

pointer = &variable;

myptr = &x;

ptr1 = &y;

11.5 USING POINTERS

Now it's the time to use pointers. The indirection operator (*) will help you to do this. When you will use the (*) before the name of a pointer, it refers to the variable pointed to.

Example 11.2

```
#include <stdio.h>
main()
{
int x = 500;
int *myptr;
myptr=&x;
.....
.....
}
```

In this example you have a variable *x*, the value of *x* is 500 the pointer myptr is declared and used to point to the variable *x*. If you write *myptr, it refers to the variable *x*. If you want to print the value of *x* which is 500,you could write :

```
printf("%d", rate);
or this:
printf("%d", *p_rate);
```

Here is the complete program :

Program 11.1

```
/* Demo of pointer */
#include <stdio.h>
main()
{
int x = 500;
int *myptr;
myptr = &x;
```

```
        printf("%d", x);
        printf("%d", *p_rate);
        }
```

> *Tips:* You can check the address of pointer myptr using printf("%d",myptr) or printf ("%d",&x).

11.6 POINTERS ON DIFFERENT DATA TYPES

As you have learned in "C data types" chapter that different variable types occupy different amounts of memory. In most common operating systems, an int takes two bytes, a float takes four bytes, and so on. Each individual byte of memory has its own address, so a multi byte variable like array or structure actually occupies several addresses. The address of a variable is actually the address of the first byte it occupies in case of array or structure. This can be illustrated with given program :

Program 11.2

```
/*Demo of address taken by different variables */
#include <stdio.h>
main()
{
        char a[5];
        char *ptr;
        a[0]=500;
        a[1]=700;
        ptr=&a;
        clrscr();
        printf("First address of array is %d\n",ptr);
        ptr++;
        printf("Second address of array is %d\n",ptr);
}
```

When you will run this program the address can be 44 for first variable and it will be 45 for next, because you are using char variable. Now change the program as :

Program 11.3

```
/*Demo of address taken by different variables */
#include <stdio.h>
main()
{
        float a[5];
        float *ptr;
        a[0]=15.34;
```

```
        a[1]=1.700;
        ptr=&a;
        clrscr();
        printf("First address of array is %d\n",ptr);
        ptr++;
        printf("Second address of array is %d\n",ptr);
}
```

When you will run this program the address can be 54 for first variable and it will be 58 for next, because you are using float variable. Now check the program for int also.

> ***Tips:*** In program 11.2 and 11.3 the use of ptr++ will increment the pointer variable, and the increment can be 1, 2 or 4 why ?

11.7 POINTERS AND ARRAYS

You can access an array through a pointer that contains the start address of the array. If you use an array name without brackets it will work as a pointer to the array's first element. Thus, if you've declared an array mk[], mk will be the address of the first array element. Because an array name that is not followed by a subscript is interpreted as a pointer to the first element of the array, you can assign the start address of the array to a pointer of the same data type; then you can access any element in the array by adding a proper integer to the pointer. The next example will initializes the pointer variable pmk with the address of the first element of mk[] :

int mk[30], *pmk;

pmk = mk;

The elements of an array are stored in sequential memory locations with the first element in the lowest address. Subsequent array elements are stored in higher addresses. The address bytes depends on the array's data type like char, int, float. The next program will show you this :

Program 11.4

```
#include <stdio.h>
/* Declare three arrays and a counter variable. */
int i[10], x;
float f[10];
double d[10];
main()
{
clrscr();
printf("\t\tInteger \t\t Float\t\t Double");
printf("\n================================");
printf("====================");
```

```
for (x = 0; x < 10; x++)
printf("\nElement %d: \t %d \t\t %d \t\t %d", x, &i[x],&f[x], &d[x]);
printf("\n==================================");
printf("=====================\n");
}
```

Output :

	Integer	Float	Double
Element 0:	2076	2036	1956
Element 1:	2078	2040	1964
Element 2:	2080	2044	1972
Element 3:	2082	2048	1980
Element 4:	2084	2052	1988
Element 5:	2086	2056	1996
Element 6:	2088	2060	2004
Element 7:	2090	2064	2012
Element 8:	2092	2068	2020
Element 9:	2094	2072	2028

Now you can check from output that the difference in int is 2, float is 4 and for double it is 8 bytes.

11.8 POINTER TO FUNCTIONS

When you work with functions, one way is pass regular variables as parameters to functions. At the time of calling a function again you always pass the values. This is known as call by value method of functions in C. One more method is call by reference, and here you need pointers. Use of pointers in functions gives you speed in program processing as well as accuracy. Following program will swap values of two variables using pointers.

Program 11.5

```
/* Demo of using pointers in a function */
void swap (int *, int *);          /* function prototype */
main()
{
  int x, y;
  x = 45;
  y = 200;
  printf("Before swap x = %d y = %d\n\n", x, y);
  swap(&x,&y);                  /* call by référence */
  printf("After swap x = %d y = %d\n\n", x, y);
}
```

```
swap(int *a, int *b)
{
  int temp;
  temp= *a;
  *a = *b;
  *b = temp;
}
```

11.9 ARRAY OF POINTERS

As you know about array, it is a collection of data storage locations that have the same data type and are referred to by the same name. In C you can declare and use arrays of pointers. This type of program construct can be very powerful in certain situations. Most common use of an array of pointers is working with strings. A string is a sequence of characters stored in memory. The start of the string is indicated by a pointer to the first character, and the end of the string is marked by a null character. By declaring and initializing an array of pointers to type char, you can access and manipulate a large number of strings using the pointer array. Each element in the array points to a different string, and by looping through the array, you can access each of them in turn.

There are now two waya to allocate and initialize a string, the first way is to declare an array of type char like :

char message[] = "My name is MK sharma ";

The same you can do by declaring a pointer to type char like :

char *message = "His name is MP Thapliyal";

The next statement will declares an array of 12 pointers to type char :

char *months[12];

Each element of the array months[] is an individual pointer to type char. Now you can combine the declaration with initialization and allocation of storage space for 12 strings at a time :

char *months[12] = { "Jan", "Feb", "Mar", "Apr", "May", "Jun", "Jul", "Aug", "Sep", " Oct", "Nov", "Dec"};

Example 11.3

You want to calculate length of a string with the help of pointers,as you know a string is a collection of array and pointer can address the first element of an array. So start with first element of string and move up to last (You check end of string with '\0' character). Look the given program and test it in lab :

Program 11.6

```
#include <stdio.h>
main()
```

```
{
    char *a;
    char *ptr;
    int c=0;
    a="aimca";
    ptr=a;
        clrscr();
        while(*ptr !='\0')
        {
        printf("Characters of String are %c\n",*ptr);
        ptr++;
        c=c+1;
         }
        printf("Length of String is = %d",c);
}
```

Tips : Try to convert the above program to reverse the string.

Program 11. 7

```
/* Demo of array of pointers */
#include <stdio.h>
main()
{
 char *months[12] = { "Jan", "Feb", "Mar", "Apr", "May", "Jun", "Jul", "Aug",
 "Sep", "Oct", "Nov", "Dec"};
 int count;
 for (count = 0; count <12; count++)
 printf("%s ", months[count]);
 printf("\n");
}
```

11.9.1 Array of Pointers to Function

It's much easier to pass an array of pointers to a function than to pass several strings. Now we will rewrite the above program so that it will uses function to display the values of months passed to function.

Program 11.8

```
/* demo of passing an array of pointers to a function. */
#include <stdio.h>
printstring(char *m[], int c);
main()
```

```
{
char *months[12] = { "Jan", "Feb", "Mar", "Apr", "May", "Jun", "Jul", "Aug",
"Sep", "Oct", "Nov", "Dec"};
 printstring(months,12);
 }
printstring(char *m[], int c)
{
int count;
for (count = 0; count < c; count++)
printf("%s ", m[count]);
printf("\n");
 }
```

11.10 POINTER TO FUNCTIONS

There is one more way to call a function inside a program that you can do with pointers to functions. When your program runs which has a function, the code for that function is loaded into memory starting at a specific address. A pointer to a function holds the starting address of a function and this provide you another way to call a function.

The general syntax of the declaration of a pointer to a function is :

datatype (*ptr_to_func) (list of parameters);

int cube(int *x*); /* The function prototype of cube */

int (*p)(int x); /* The pointer to function declaration. */

Now you can write

p=cube;

> ***Tips*** **:** You must remember that return type and parameter list of function should match with the return type and parameter list of the pointer declaration.

Program 11.9

```
/* Demo of pointer to a function.*/
#include <stdio.h>
/* function prototype. */
double cube(double x);
/* pointer to function declaration. */
double (*p)(double x);
main()
{
 /* Initialize p to point to cube() */
 p = cube;
 /* Call cube () by function */
```

```
printf("%f \n", cube(12));
/* Call cube () by pointer */
printf("%f \n", p(12));
}
double cube(double x)
{
return x * x;
}
```

11.11 POINTERS TO POINTERS

As a pointer is itself a numeric variable, it is stored in computer's memory at a particular address. Therefore, you can create a pointer to a pointer, a variable whose value is the address of a pointer. A double indirection operator (**) is used to declare a pointer to a pointer.

```
int mk = 35;                 /* mk is a type int variable. */
int *ptr = &mk;              /* ptr is a pointer to mk. */
int **ptrtoptr = &ptr;       /* is a pointer to pointer */
```

To displays the value of mk on your screen you can use :

```
printf("%d", **ptrtoptr);
```

> ***Tips*** : Declaring and using a pointer to a pointer is called multiple indirection in C.

11.12 POINTERS TO STRUCTURES

In a C program you can declare and use pointers to structures, just as you can declare pointers to any other data type. Pointers to structures are very useful in programming of data structure where you have to work with link lists or trees.

If you have a structure like :

```
  struct student
  {
  int rollnumber;
  char sname[20];
  };
struct student s[50];
```

You can declare a pointer like :

```
struct student *s1;
```

and you can assign address of first record of student structure to pointer *s*1 like :

```
s1= &s[0];
```

or

```
s1=s;
```

Now to print the values of fields of structure student using pointer *s*1 you can type :

printf("*%d %s*", *s*1->rollnumber, s1->sname);

Where *s*1 is a pointer to structure.

Now next step can be to print all the values of that array of structure having 50 records. To do this use a for loop, printing one record from array and to access the next members using pointer, you must change the pointer s1 to points to the next array element for that simply use *s*1+ +, yes you can use increment or decrement operator with pointers too.

> ***Tips*** : The unary increment operator (++) has a special meaning for pointers in C. It means increment the pointer by the size of the object it points to. In case of float array you will jump 4 bytes after applying ptr + + why ?

Program 11.10

```
/* Demo of pointers to array of structures */
#include <stdio.h>
struct student
{
int rollnumber;
char sname[20];
}
s[5] = {1, "Abhishek", 2, "Ashwani", 3, "Sujata", 4, "Shivani", 5, "Neelam"};
struct student *s1;
int count;
main()
{
 /* Initialize the pointer to the first structure */
 s1=s;
 /* Loop for access the records and to increment the pointer */
 for (count = 0; count < 5; count++)
 {
  printf("Rollno =%d, Name = %s\n", s1->rollnumber, s1->sname);
  s1++;
}
}
```

REVIEW QUESTIONS

1. What is a pointer and which operator is used to determine the address of a variable?
2. What is indirection?
3. How are the elements of an array stored in memory?
4. Show two ways to obtain the address of the first element of the array data[].

5. Explain the difference between call by value and call by reference, using suitable example. **[UTU 2006-07]**
6. Assume that you have two pointers. If the first points to the third element in an array of int and the second points to the fourth element, what value is obtained if you subtract the first pointer from the second? (Assume that the size of an integer is 2 bytes.)
7. Write the prototype for a function that takes an array of pointers to type char as its one argument and returns void.
8. What is a pointer to a function? Write a declaration of a pointer to a function that returns a type char and takes an array of pointers to type char as an argument.
9. Write a structure that is to be used in a single-linked list. This structure should hold your friends' names and email addresses.

LAB EXERCISES

1. Write a function named sumarrays() that accepts two arrays as arguments, totals all values in both arrays, and returns the total to the calling program use pointers in your program.
2. Write a program that declares a 10*10 array of characters. Place * in every other element. Use a pointer to the array to print the values to the screen in a grid format.
3. Write a program that uses pointers to type double variables to accept 10 numbers from the user, sort them, and print them to the screen.
4. Write a program to sort 10 strings with the help of pointers.
5. Write a program using pointers to concatenate two strings (the function takes two arguments namely two pointers to strings and the resultant string is stored in the first string. **[UTU 2006–07]**
6. What will be the output of following block ? **[UTU 2006–07]**

```
{
int arr[5]={3,4,6,2,1,};
int *p=arr ;
int *q=arr + 2;
int *r =&arr[1] ;
printf("\n%d %d %d ", arr[2],*(arr+2),*r) ;
printf("\n%d %d %d ", *p,*(q+1),*(r+1)) ;
return 0;
}
```

12

Dynamic Memory Allocation and File Handling

12.1 WHAT IS DYNAMIC MEMORY ALLOCATION?

Memory either primary (in form of RAM) or secondary (in form of Hard disk or other) is must to perform all operations in a computer. When you write a simple program in C like a program to add 3 numbers, you need to declare 3 variables to store the values. In fact that 3 variables are 3 memory locations in your PC. Next if you want to store your resume in form of a file you need secondary storage memory to hold it.

In most of the program you have tested you know the number of variables in advance, but how can a bank may know in advance that how many customers will open a account on a specific day. Be more practical and think about Indian railway reservation system, how can you fix numbers of reservation or cancellation on a day. After reading all these lines you can divide programs in two categories :

1. Static Programs
2. Dynamic Programs

In a static program number of variables and number of records are remain constant and you need to declare them in advance like an array or an array of structures.

A dynamic program will help you to add or remove element of program at run time like in a bank or in railway reservation system. A dynamic programming concept is must to design any good software. Your word processor MSWORD is also provide you to add or remove text any time. Most of the data base application are dynamic in nature, where you have freedom to insert or remove records any time.

12.2 DYNAMIC MEMORY ALLOCATION IN C

C provides you four dynamic memory allocation functions that you can use to write dynamic memory based programs. You can allocate or reallocate certain memory spaces while your program is running. Also, you can release allocated memory storage as it can be used by another programs. These four C functions are :

- malloc()
- calloc()
- realloc()
- free()

You can use the malloc() function in your program, to allocate a specified size of memory space. The syntax for the malloc() function is :

```
void *malloc(size_t size);
```

Here size indicates the number of bytes of storage to allocate. The malloc() function returns a void pointer. The header file, stdlib.h, has to be included before the malloc() function can be called. Because the malloc() function returns a void pointer, its type is automatically converted to the type of the pointer on the left side of an assignment operator. If the malloc() function fails to allocate a piece of memory space, it returns a null pointer. Normally, this happens when there is not enough memory. Therefore, you should always check the returned pointer from malloc() before you use it.

Program 12.1 *Use of malloc()*

```
#include<stdio.h>
#include<stdlib.h>
#include<string.h>
/* function declaration */
void StringCopy(char *str1, char *str2);
main()
{
 char str[]="Use of malloc() to allocate memory.";
 char *ptrstr;
 int result;
 /* call malloc() */
 ptr_str=malloc(strlen(str)+1);
 if (ptrstr!=NULL)
  {
  StringCopy(str, ptrstr);
  printf("The string pointed to by ptr_str is:\n%s\n",ptrstr);
  result=0;
 }
 else
 {
  printf("malloc() function failed.\n");
  result=1;
 }
 return result;
```

```
}
/* function definition */
void StringCopy(char *str1, char *str2)
{
 int i;
  for (i=0; str1[i]; i++)
   str2[i]=str1[i];
 str2[i]='\0';
}
```

Program 12.2 *Use of malloc() to design link list program*

```
#include<stdio.h>
#include<conio.h>
#include<malloc.h>
void main()
{
struct node
{
int num;
struct node *ptr;
};
typedef struct node NODE;
NODE *head, *first, *temp;
int count=0;
int choice=1;
first=NULL;
while(choice)
{
          head=(NODE *)malloc(sizeof(NODE));
          printf("Enter the item for link list \n");
          scanf("%d",&head->num);
           if(first!=NULL)
                    {
                      temp->ptr=head;
                      temp=head;
                    }
else
                    {
                      first=temp=head;
                    }
```

```
fflush(stdin);
printf("Do you want to continue(type 0 or 1)?\n");
scanf("%d",&choice);
}
temp->ptr=NULL;
temp=first;
printf("Status of the linked list is\n");
while(temp!=NULL)
        {
                printf("%d",temp->num);
                count ++ ;
                temp=temp->ptr;
        }
printf("NULL");
printf("NO of nodes in the list=%d\n",count);
getch();
}
```

12.3 THE CALLOC() FUNCTION

Besides the malloc() function, you can also use the calloc() function to allocate a memory storage dynamically. The differences between the two functions are that the latter takes two arguments and that the memory space allocated by calloc() is always initialized to 0. There is no such guarantee that the memory space allocated by malloc() is initialized to 0.

The syntax for the calloc() function is :

```
#include < stdlib.h >
void *calloc(size_t nitem, size_t size);
```

Here nitem is the number of items you want to save in the allocated memory space. size gives the number of bytes that each item takes. The calloc() function returns a void pointer too.If the calloc() function fails to allocate a piece of memory space, it returns a null pointer.

Here is a example of using the calloc() function. The initial value of the memory space allocated by calloc() is printed out.

Program 12.3 *Using the calloc() function.*

```
#include <stdio.h>
#include <stdlib.h>
/* main() function */
main()
{
```

```
 float *ptr1, *ptr2;
 int i, n;
 int termination = 1;
   n = 5;
 ptr1 = calloc(n, sizeof(float));
 ptr2 = malloc(n * sizeof(float));
 if (ptr1 == NULL)
 printf("malloc() failed.\n");
else if (ptr2 == NULL)
printf("calloc() failed.\n");
 else
{
   for (i=0; i<n; i++)
     printf("ptr1[%d] = %5.2f, ptr2[%d] = %5.2f\n",
     i, *(ptr1 + i), i, *(ptr2 + i));
   free(ptr1);
   free(ptr2);
  termination = 0;
 }
 return termination;
}
```

The following output appears on the screen after running the executable :

Output :

```
ptr1[0] = 0.00, ptr2[0] = 7042.23
ptr1[1] = 0.00, ptr2[1] = 1427.00
ptr1[2] = 0.00, ptr2[2] = 2787.14
ptr1[3] = 0.00, ptr2[3] = 0.00
ptr1[4] = 0.00, ptr2[4] = 5834.73
```

Analysis

The purpose of the program in Listing 17.3 is to use the calloc() function to allocate a piece of memory space. To prove that the calloc() function initializes the allocated memory space to 0, the initial values of the memory are printed out. Also, another piece of memory space is allocated by using the malloc() function, and the initial values of the second memory space is printed out too.

The if-else-if-else statement checks the two values returned from the calloc() and malloc() functions and then prints out the initial values from the two allocated memory spaces if the two return values are not null.

12.4 THE REALLOC() FUNCTION

The realloc() function gives you a means to change the size of a piece of memory space allocated by the malloc() function, the calloc() function, or even itself.

The syntax for the realloc() function is

```
#include < stdlib.h >
void *realloc(void *block, size_t size);
```

Here block is the pointer to the start of a piece of memory space previously allocated. size specifies the total byte number you want to change to. The realloc() function returns a void pointer. The realloc() function returns a null pointer if it fails to reallocate a piece of memory space.

The realloc() function is equivalent to the malloc() function if the first argument passed to realloc() is NULL. In other words, the following two statements are equivalent:

```
ptr_flt = realloc(NULL, 10 * sizeof(float));
ptr_flt = malloc(10 * sizeof(float));
```

Also, you can use the realloc() function as the free() function. You do this by passing 0 to realloc() as its second argument. For instance, to release a block of memory pointed to by a pointer ptr, you can either call the free() function like this:

```
free(ptr);
```

or use the realloc() function in the following way:

```
realloc(ptr, 0);
```

Program 12.4 *Using the realloc() function.*

```
#include <stdio.h>
#include <stdlib.h>
#include <string.h>
/* function declaration */
void StrCopy(char *str1, char *str2);
/* main() function */
main()
{
 char *str[4] = {"There's music in the sighing of a reed;",
                  "There's music in the gushing of a rill;",
                  "There's music in all things if men had ears;",
                  "There earth is but an echo of the spheres.\n"
                  };
char *ptr;
int i;
int termination = 0;
ptr = malloc((strlen(str[0]) + 1) * sizeof(char));
if (ptr == NULL){
```

```
 printf("malloc() failed.\n");
 termination = 1;
}
else{
 StrCopy(str[0], ptr);
 printf("%s\n", ptr);
 for (i = 1; i < 4; i ++ ){
 ptr = realloc(ptr, (strlen(str[i]) + 1) * sizeof(char));
 if (ptr == NULL){
   printf("realloc() failed.\n");
  termination = 1;
  i = 4; /* break the fro loop */
  }
  else{
   StrCopy(str[i], ptr);
   printf("%s\n", ptr);
   }
  }
 }
free(ptr);
 return termination;
}
/* function definition */
void StrCopy(char *str1, char *str2)
{
 int i;
 for (i = 0; str1[i]; i ++ )
  str2[i] = str1[i];
 str2[i] = '\0';
}
```

Output:

There's music in the sighing of a reed;
There's music in the gushing of a rill;
There's music in all things if men had ears;
There earth is but an echo of the spheres.

Analysis

The purpose of the program in Listing 17.4 is to allocate a block of memory space to hold a character string. There are four strings in this example, and the length of each string may vary. I use the realloc() function to adjust the size of the previously allocated memory so it can hold a new string.

In this example, a block of memory space is allocated and adjusted based on the length of each of the four strings. The realloc() function, as well as the malloc() function, does the memory allocation and adjustment dynamically.

12.5 FILE HANDLING IN C

Most of the programs you have tested yet are based on variables and temporary memory allocation, means there is no logic to save your programs values on Secondary storage. In an application based on business logics you must save your data on Disk and therefore you need to work with Disk files.

What is a Disk File

In C, a file can refer to a disk file, a terminal, a printer, or a tape drive. In other words, a file represents a secondary storage medium with which you can exchange information between RAM and Disk. Before you perform any communication to a file, you have to open the file. Then you need to close the opened file after you finish exchanging information with it.

Role of Streams in Disk Files

C performs all input and output, including disk files, by means of streams. Disk file streams work essentially the same way. The data flow you transfer from your program to a file, or vice versa, is called a stream, which is a series of bytes. Not like a file, a stream is device-independent. All streams have the same behavior. This is one of the advantages of stream input/output—techniques for using one stream can be used with little or no change for other streams. The major difference with disk file streams is that your program must explicitly create a stream associated with a specific disk file.

Types of Disk Files

There are two formats of streams. The first one is called the text stream, which consists of a sequence of characters (that is, ASCII data). Depending on the compilers, each character line in a text stream may be terminated by a new line character. Text streams are used for textual data, which has a consistent appearance from one environment to another, or from one machine to another.

The second format of streams is called the binary stream, which is a series of bytes. The content of an.exe file would be one example. Binary streams are primarily used for non textual data, which is required to keep the exact contents of the file.

You can associate either type of stream with a file, and it's important that you understand the distinction in order to use the proper mode for your files.

Text streams are associated with text-mode files. Text-mode files consist of a sequence of lines. Each line contains zero or more characters and ends with one or more characters that signal end-of-line. The maximum line length is 255 characters. It's important to remember that a "line" isn't a C string; there is no terminating NULL character (\0). When you use a text-mode stream, translation occurs between C's new line character (\n) and whatever character(s) the operating system uses to mark end-of-line on disk files. On DOS systems, it's a carriage-return linefeed (CR-LF) combination. When data is written to a text-mode file, each \n is translated to a CR-LF; when data is read from a disk file, each CR-LF is translated to a \n. On UNIX systems, no translation is done new line characters remain unchanged.

Binary streams are associated with binary-mode files. Any and all data is written and read unchanged, with no separation into lines and no use of end-of-line characters. The NULL and end-of-line characters have no special significance and are treated like any other byte of data.

Some file input/output functions are restricted to one file mode, whereas other functions can use either mode.

How to Set File Names?

Every disk file must has a name, and you must use filenames when dealing with disk files. Filenames are stored as strings, just like other text data. The rules as to what is acceptable for filenames and what is not differ from one operating system to another.

Like In DOS and Windows 3.x, a complete filename consists of a name that has from one to eight characters, optionally followed by a period and an extension that has from one to three characters. In contrast, the Windows 95 and Windows NT operating systems, as well as most UNIX systems, permit filenames up to 256 characters long. So keep in mind which operating system you are using.

Some Tips on Disk File Handling

The FILE Pointer

The FILE structure is the file control structure defined in the header file stdio.h. A pointer of type FILE is called a file pointer, which references a disk file. A file pointer is used by a stream to conduct the operation of the I/O functions. For instance, the following defines a file pointer called myfile :

```
FILE *myfile;
```

In the FILE structure there is a member, called the file position indicator, that points to the position in a file where data will be read from or written to.

Opening a File

The C function fopen() gives you the ability to open a file and associate a stream to the opened file. You need to specify the way to open a file and the filename with the fopen() function.

The syntax for the fopen() function is

FILE *fopen(const char *filename, const char *mode);

Here filename is a char pointer that references a string of a filename. The filename is given to the file that is about to be opened by the fopen() function. mode points to another string that specifies the way to open the file. The fopen() function returns a pointer of type FILE. If an error occurs during the procedure to open a file, the fopen() function returns a null pointer.

File Opening Modes

The argument mode in fopen(), specifies the mode in which to open the file. In this context, mode controls whether the file is binary or text and whether it is for reading, writing, or both.

The following list shows the possible ways to open a file by various strings of modes:

"r"	opens an existing text file for reading.
"w"	creates a text file for writing.
"a"	opens an existing text file for appending.
"r +"	opens an existing text file for reading or writing.
"w +"	creates a text file for reading or writing.
"a +"	opens or creates a text file for appending.
"rb"	opens an existing binary file for reading.
"wb"	creates a binary file for writing.
"ab"	opens an existing binary file for appending.
"r + b"	opens an existing binary file for reading or writing.
"w + b"	creates a binary file for reading or writing.
"a + b"	opens or creates a binary file for appending.

Note that you can use the mode "rb +" instead of "r + b". These two strings are equivalent. Similarly, "wb + " is the same as "w + b"; "ab +" is equivalent to "a + b".

The following statements try to open a file called test.txt:

```
FILE *myfile;
if ((fptr = fopen("test.txt", "r")) == NULL){
  printf("Cannot open test.txt file.\n");
  exit(1);
}
```

Here *"r"* is used to indicate that a text file is about to be opened for reading only. If an error occurs when the fopen() function tries to open the file, the function returns a null pointer. Then an error message is printed out by the printf() function and the program is aborted by calling the exit() function with a nonzero value.

Closing a File

After a disk file is read, written, or appended with some new data, you have to disassociate the file from a specified stream by calling the fclose() function.

The syntax for the fclose() function is :

int fclose(FILE *stream);

Here stream is a file pointer that is associated with a stream to the opened file. If fclose() closes a file successfully, it returns 0. Otherwise, the function returns EOF. Normally, the fclose() function fails only when the disk is removed before the function is called or there is no more space left on the disk.

Since all high-level I/O operations are buffered, the fclose() function flushes data left in the buffer to ensure that no data will be lost before it disassociates a specified stream with the opened file.

Note that a file that is opened and associated with a stream has to be closed after the I/O operation. Otherwise, the data saved in the file may be lost; some unpredictable errors might occur during the execution of your program.

The program will show you how to open and close a text file and how to check the returned file pointer value as well.

Program 12.5 *Opening and closing a text file.*

```
#include < stdio.h >
enum {SUCCESS, FAIL};
main()
{
      FILE *fptr;
      char filename[] = "haiku.txt";
      int reval = SUCCESS;
if ((fptr = fopen(filename, "r")) == NULL)
 {
 printf("Cannot open %s.\n", filename);
 reval = FAIL;
  }
 else
{
 printf("The value of fptr: 0x%p\n", fptr);
 printf("Ready to close the file.");
   fclose(fptr);
}
return reval;
 }
```

Program 12.6 *Use of file in different modes*

```
#include < stdlib.h >
#include < stdio.h >
main()
```

```
{
  FILE *fp;
  char filename[40], mode[4];
  while (1)
  {
       /* Input filename and mode. */
       printf("\nEnter a filename: ");
       gets(filename);
       printf("\nEnter a mode (max 3 characters): ");
       gets(mode);
       /* Try to open the file. */
       if ((fp = fopen(filename, mode)) ! = NULL)
         {
           printf("\nSuccessful opening %s in mode %s.\n",
            filename, mode);
            fclose(fp);
            puts("Enter x to exit, any other to continue.");
            if ((getc(stdin)) == 'x')
            break;
       else
         continue;
  }
  else
  {
     fprintf(stderr, "\nError opening file %s in mode %s.\n",
            filename, mode);
     puts("Enter x to exit, any other to try again.");
     if ((getc(stdin)) == 'x')
       break;
     else
         continue;
    }
  }
}
```

12.6 READING AND WRITING WITH DISK FILES

A program that uses a disk file can write data to a file, read data from a file, or a combination of the two. You can write data to a disk file in three ways:

1. One can use formatted output to save formatted data to a file. You should use formatted output only with text-mode files. The primary use of formatted output is to create files containing text and numeric data to be read by other programs such as spreadsheets or databases. You rarely, if ever, use formatted output to create a file to be read again by a C program.
2. One can use character output to save single characters or lines of characters to a file. The main use of character output is to save text (but not numeric) data in a form that can be read by C, as well as other programs such as word processors.
3. One can use direct output to save the contents of a section of memory directly to a disk file. This method is for binary files only. Direct output is the best way to save data for later use by a C program.

When you want to read data from a file, you have the same three options: formatted input, character input, or direct input. The type of input you use in a particular case depends almost entirely on the nature of the file being read. Generally, you will read data in the same mode that it was saved in, but this is not a requirement. However, reading a file in a mode different from the one it was written in requires a thorough knowledge of C and file formats.

In C, you can perform Disk perations in the following ways:

- Read or write one character at a time.
- Read or write one line of text (that is, one character line) at a time. Many lines also.
- Read or write one block of characters (binary files) at a time.

Character Input

There are three character input functions: getc() and fgetc() for single characters, and fgets() for lines.

The functions getc() and fgetc() are identical and can be used interchangeably. They input a single character from the specified stream. Here is the prototype of getc(), which is in STDIO.H:

```
int getc(FILE *fp);
```

The argument fp is the pointer returned by fopen() when the file is opened. The function returns the character that was input or EOF on error.

Character Output

You can use two character output functions: putc() and fputs().

The library function putc() writes a single character to a specified stream. Its prototype in STDIO.H is :

```
int putc(int ch, FILE *fp);
```

The argument ch is the character to output. As with other character functions, it is formally called a type int, but only the lower-order byte is used. The argument fp is the pointer associated with the file (the pointer returned by fopen() when the file was opened). The function putc() returns the character just written if successful or EOF if an error occurs. The symbolic constant EOF is defined in STDIO.H, and it has the value -1. Because no "real" character has that numeric value, EOF can be used as an error indicator (with text-mode files only).

To write a line of characters to a stream, use the library function fputs(). This function works just like puts(),. The only difference is that with fputs() you can specify the output stream. Also, fputs() doesn't add a newline to the end of the string; if you want it, you must explicitly include it. Its prototype in STDIO.H is :

char fputs(char *str, FILE *fp);

Program 12.7 *Reading and writing one character at a time.*

```
#include < stdio.h >
enum {SUCCESS, FAIL};
void CharReadWrite(FILE *fin, FILE *fout);
main()
{
    FILE *fptr1, *fptr2;
   char filename1[] = "vama.txt";
   char filename2[] = "suhani.txt";
    int reval = SUCCESS;
    if ((fptr1 = fopen(filename1, "w")) == NULL)
    {
    printf("Cannot open %s.\n", filename1);
    reval = FAIL;
    }
else if ((fptr2 = fopen(filename2, "r")) == NULL)
{
   printf("Cannot open %s.\n", filename2);
   reval = FAIL;
  }
else
{
   CharReadWrite(fptr2, fptr1);
   fclose(fptr1);
   fclose(fptr2);
  }
  return reval;
}
void CharReadWrite(FILE *fin, FILE *fout)
```

```
{
 int c;
 while ((c = fgetc(fin)) ! = EOF){
  fputc(c, fout);          /* write to a file */
  putchar(c);              /* put the character on the screen */
  }
    }
```

Read, Write One Line at a Time

Besides reading or writing one character at a time, you can also read or write one character line at time. There is a pair of C functions, fgets() and fputs(), that allows you to do so. The syntax for the fgets() function is :

#include < stdio.h >

char *fgets(char *s, int n, FILE *stream);

Here *s references a character array that is used to store characters read from the opened file pointed to by the file pointer stream. n specifies the maximum number of array elements. If it is successful, the fgets() function returns the char pointer s. If EOF is encountered, the fgets() function returns a null pointer and leaves the array untouched. If an error occurs, the function returns a null pointer, and the contents of the array are unknown.

Program 12.8 *Reading and writing one character line at a time.*

```
#include < stdio.h >
enum {SUCCESS, FAIL, MAXLEN = 81};
void LineReadWrite(FILE *fin, FILE *fout);
main()
{
 FILE *fptr1, *fptr2;
 char filename1[] = "mks.txt";
 char filename2[] = "mpt.txt";
 int reval = SUCCESS;
 if ((fptr1 = fopen(filename1, "w")) == NULL){
   printf("Cannot open %s for writing.\n", filename1);
  reval = FAIL;
 }
    else if ((fptr2 = fopen(filename2, "r")) == NULL)
     {
  printf("Cannot open %s for reading.\n", filename2);
  reval = FAIL;
 }
  else
```

```
    {
     LineReadWrite(fptr2, fptr1);
      fclose(fptr1);
      fclose(fptr2);
   }
   return reval;
 }
 void LineReadWrite(FILE *fin, FILE *fout)
 {
   char buff[MAXLEN];
   while (fgets(buff, MAXLEN, fin) ! = NULL)
    {
     fputs(buff, fout);
     printf("%s", buff);
   }
      }
```

Reading, Writing One Block at a Time

One can also read or write a block of data at a time. In C, there are two functions, fread() and fwrite(), that can be used to perform block operations. The syntax for the fread() function is :

size_t fread(void *ptr, size_t size, size_t n, FILE *stream);

Here ptr is a pointer to an array in which the data is stored. size indicates the size of each array element. n specifies the number of elements to read. stream is a file pointer that is associated with the opened file for reading. size_t is an integral type defined in the header file stdio.h. The fread() function returns the number of elements actually read.

The number of elements read by the fread() function should be equal to the value specified by the third argument to the function, unless an error occurs or an EOF (end-of-file) is encountered. The fread() function returns the number of elements that are actually read, if an error occurs or an EOF is encountered.

The syntax for the fwrite() function is :

size_t fwrite(const void *ptr, size_t size, size_t n,]FILE *stream);

Here ptr references the array that contains the data to be written to an opened file pointed to by the file pointer stream. size indicates the size of each element in the array. n specifies the number of elements to be written. The fwrite() function returns the number of elements actually written.

If there is no error occurring, the number returned by fwrite() should be the same as the third argument in the function. The return value may be less than the specified value if an error occurs.

In C, a function called feof() can be used to determine when the end of a file is encountered. This function is more useful when you're reading a binary file because the values of some bytes may be equal to the value of EOF. If you determine the end of a binary file by checking the value returned by fread(), you may end up at the wrong position. Using the feof() function helps you to avoid mistakes in determining the end of a file.The syntax for the feof() function is :

int feof(FILE *stream);

Here stream is the file pointer that is associated with an opened file. The feof() function returns 0 if the end of the file has not been reached; otherwise, it returns a nonzero integer.

Program 12.9 *Reading and writing one block of characters at a time.*

```
#include < stdio.h >
enum {SUCCESS, FAIL, MAX_LEN = 80};
void BlockReadWrite(FILE *fin, FILE *fout);
int ErrorMsg(char *str);
main()
{
 FILE *fptr1, *fptr2;
 char filename1[] = "aimca.txt";
char filename2[] = "aias.txt";
int reval = SUCCESS;
if ((fptr1 = fopen(filename1, "w")) == NULL)
{
reval = ErrorMsg(filename1);
 }
  else if ((fptr2 = fopen(filename2, "r")) == NULL)
  {
  reval = ErrorMsg(filename2);
 }
else
   {
     BlockReadWrite(fptr2, fptr1);
     fclose(fptr1);
     fclose(fptr2);
     }
 return reval;
     }
void BlockReadWrite(FILE *fin, FILE *fout)
{
     int num;
```

```
    char buff[MAX_LEN + 1];
    while (!feof(fin))
     {
   num = fread(buff, sizeof(char), MAX_LEN, fin);
   buff[num * sizeof(char)] = '\0'; /* append a null character */
   printf("%s", buff);
   fwrite(buff, sizeof(char), num, fout);
  }
   }
  int ErrorMsg(char *str)
  {
  printf("Cannot open %s.\n", str);
  return FAIL;
   }
```

12.7 SEQUENTIAL VERSUS RANDOM FILE ACCESS

Every open file has a file position indicator associated with it. The position indicator specifies where read and write operations take place in the file. The position is always given in terms of bytes from the beginning of the file. When a new file is opened, the position indicator is always at the beginning of the file, position 0. (Because the file is new and has a length of 0, there's no other location to indicate.) When an existing file is opened, the position indicator is at the end of the file if the file was opened in append mode, or at the beginning of the file if the file was opened in any other mode.

The file input/output functions covered earlier in this chapter make use of the position indicator, although the manipulations go on behind the scenes. Writing and reading operations occur at the location of the position indicator and update the position indicator as well. For example, if you open a file for reading, and 10 bytes are read, you input the first 10 bytes in the file (the bytes at positions 0 through 9). After the read operation, the position indicator is at position 10, and the next read operation begins there. Thus, if you want to read all the data in a file sequentially or write data to a file sequentially, you don't need to be concerned about the position indicator, because the stream I/O functions take care of it automatically. When you need more control, use the C library functions that let you determine and change the value of the file position indicator. By controlling the position indicator, you can per-form random file access. Here, random means that you can read data from, or write data to, any position in a file without reading or writing all the preceding data.

In C there are some functions, like fseek(), ftell() and rewind() that are designed to deal with random access.

The fseek() and ftell() Functions

In the previous sections you learned that one of the members in the FILE structure is called the file position indicator. The file position indicator has to point to the desired position in a file before data can be read from or written to there. You can use the fseek() function to move the file position indicator to the spot you want to access in a file.The syntax for the fseek() function is :

int fseek(FILE *stream, long offset, int whence);

Here stream is the file pointer associated with an opened file. offset indicates the number of bytes from a fixed position, specified by whence, that can have one of the following integral values represented by SEEK_SET, SEEK_CUR, and SEEK_END. If it is successful, the fseek() function returns 0; otherwise, the function returns a nonzero value.You can find the values represented by SEEK_SET, SEEK_CUR, and SEEK_END in the header file stdio.h.

If SEEK_SET is chosen as the third argument to the fseek() function, the offset is counted from the beginning of the file and the value of the offset is greater than or equal to zero. If, however, SEEK_END is picked up, then the offset starts from the end of the file; the value of the offset should be negative. When SEEK_CUR is passed to the fseek() function, the offset is calculated from the current value of the file position indicator.

You can also obtain the value of the current file position indicator by calling the ftell() function.The syntax for the ftell() function is :

long ftell(FILE *stream);

Here stream is the file pointer associated with an opened file. The ftell() function returns the current value of the file position indicator.The value returned by the ftell() function represents the number of bytes from the beginning of the file to the current position pointed to by the file position indicator.If the ftell() function fails, it returns -1L (that is, a long value of minus 1). One thing that can cause the failure of the ftell() function is the file being a terminal or some other type for which the file position indicator becomes meaningless.

The rewind() Function

Sometimes you might want to reset the file position indicator and put it at the beginning of a file. There is a handy C function, called rewind(), that can be used to rewind the file position indicator.The syntax for the rewind() function is :

```
void rewind(FILE *stream);
```

Here stream is the file pointer associated with an opened file. No value is returned by the rewind() function.

Program 12.10 *Random file access with fseek().*

```
#include < stdlib.h >
#include < stdio.h >
#define MAX 50
main()
{
  FILE *fp;
```

```
int data, count, array[MAX];
long offset;
for (count = 0; count < MAX; count ++ )
  array[count] = count * 10;
          /* Open a binary file for writing. */
if ((fp = fopen("RANDOMFILE.DAT", "wb")) == NULL)
{
  fprintf(stderr, "\nError opening file.");
  exit(1);
}
  /* Write the array to the file, then close it. */
if ((fwrite(array, sizeof(int), MAX, fp)) ! = MAX)
{
  fprintf(stderr, "\nError writing data to file.");
  exit(1);
}
    fclose(fp);
    /* Open the file for reading. */
    if ((fp = fopen("RANDOM.DAT", "rb")) == NULL)
  {
    fprintf(stderr, "\nError opening file.");
    exit(1);
     }
while (1)
{
  printf("\nEnter element to read, 0-%d, -1 to quit: ",MAX-1);
  scanf("%ld", &offset);
  if (offset < 0)
     break;
      else if (offset > MAX-1)
     continue;
      if ((fseek(fp, (offset*sizeof(int)), SEEK_SET)) ! = 0)
     {
         fprintf(stderr, "\nError using fseek().");
     exit(1);
  }
     fread(&data, sizeof(int), 1, fp);
     printf("\nElement %ld has value %d.", offset, data);
     }
```

```
    fclose(fp);
    return(0);
}
```

Program 12.11 *Use of ftell() and rewind()*

```
#include < stdlib.h >
#include < stdio.h >
#define BUFLEN 6
char msg[] = "amrapaliinstituteofmanagementandcomputerapplications";
main()
{
  FILE *fp;
  char buf[BUFLEN];
  if ((fp = fopen("MYTEXT.TXT", "w")) == NULL)
  {
     fprintf(stderr, "Error opening file.");
     exit(1);
  }
  if (fputs(msg, fp) == EOF)
  {
     fprintf(stderr, "Error writing to file.");
     exit(1);
  }
  fclose(fp);
  /* Now open the file for reading. */
  if ((fp = fopen("MYTEXT.TXT", "r")) == NULL)
  {
     fprintf(stderr, "Error opening file.");
     exit(1);
  }
  printf("\nImmediately after opening, position = %ld", ftell(fp));
  /* Read First 5 characters. */
   fgets(buf, BUFLEN, fp);
printf("\nAfter reading in %s, position = %ld", buf, ftell(fp));
/* Read next 5 characters. */
fgets(buf, BUFLEN, fp);
printf("\n\nThe next 5 characters are %s, and position now = %ld",
     buf, ftell(fp));
/* Rewind the stream. */
```

```
rewind(fp);
printf("\n\nAfter rewinding, the position is back at %ld",
ftell(fp));
fgets(buf, BUFLEN, fp);
printf("\nand reading starts at the beginning again: %s\n", buf);
fclose(fp);
return(0);
}
```

12.8 OPERATING SYSTEM BASED FILE MANAGEMENT FUNCTIONS

Using C you can write programs that works as common DOS commands like deleting, renaming, and copying the disk files. The C standard library contains functions for deleting and renaming files, and you will write your own file copy program in next section.

Deleting a File

To delete a file, you can use the library function remove(). Its syntax is :

int remove(const char *filename);

The variable *filename is a pointer to the name of the file to be deleted. The specified file must not be open. If the file exists, it is deleted (just as if you used the DEL command from the DOS prompt or the rm command in UNIX), and remove() returns 0. If the file doesn't exist, if it's read-only, if you don't have sufficient access rights, or if some other error occurs, remove() returns -1.

Program 12.12 *remove() function to delete a disk file.*

```
#include < stdio.h >
main()
{
  char filename[80];
  printf("Enter the filename to delete: ");
  gets(filename);
  if (remove(filename) == 0)
    printf("The file %s has been deleted.\n", filename);
  else
    fprintf(stderr, "Error deleting the file %s.\n", filename);
  return(0);
  }
```

Note : You can also use command line argument to make it DOS like command

Renaming a File

The rename() function changes the name of an existing disk file. The function syntax is:

int rename(const char *oldname, const char *newname);

The filenames pointed to by oldname and newname follow the rules given earlier in this chapter. The only restriction is that both names must refer to the same disk drive; you can't rename a file to a different disk drive. The function rename() returns 0 on success, or -1 if an error occurs. Errors can be caused by the following conditions :

1. The file oldname does not exist.
2. A file with the name newname already exists.
3. You try to rename to another disk.

Program 12.13 *Use of rename() to change the name of a disk file.*

```
/* Using rename() to change a filename. */
#include < stdio.h >
main()
{
  char oldname[80], newname[80];
  printf("Enter current filename: ");
  gets(oldname);
  printf("Enter new name for file: ");
  gets(newname);
  if (rename(oldname, newname) == 0)
   printf("%s has been renamed %s.\n", oldname, newname);
  else
   fprintf(stderr, "An error has occurred renaming %s.\n", oldname);
   return(0);
  }
```

Copying a File

It's frequently necessary to make a copy of a file or duplicate with a different name or with the same name but in a different drive or directory. In DOS, you can do this with the COPY command, and in UNIX using cp. But in C There's no library function, so you need to write your own program.Here are the steps you follow:

1. Open the source file for reading in binary mode. (Using binary mode ensures that the function can copy all sorts of files, not just text files.)
2. Open the destination file for writing in binary mode.
3. Read a character from the source file. Remember, when a file is first opened, the pointer is at the start of the file, so there's no need to position the file pointer explicitly.
4. If the function feof() indicates that you've reached the end of the source file, you're done and can close both files and return to the calling program.
5. If you haven't reached end-of-file, write the character to the destination file, and then loop back to step 3.

Program 12.14 *Your own program that copies a file.*

```
#include < stdio.h >
int mycopy(char *oldname, char *newname);
main()
{
 char source[80], destination[80];
 /* Get the source and destination names. */
 printf("\nEnter source file: ");
 gets(source);
 printf("\nEnter destination file: ");
 gets(destination);
 if (file_copy(source, destination) == 0)
 puts("Copy operation successful");
 else
 fprintf(stderr, "Error during copy operation");
 return(0);
 }
 int mycopy(char *oldname, char *newname)
 {
  FILE *fold, *fnew;
  int c;
  /* Open the source file for reading in binary mode. */
  if ((fold = fopen(oldname, "rb")) == NULL)
  return -1;
  /* Open the destination file for writing in binary mode. */
  if ((fnew = fopen(newname, "wb")) == NULL)
   {
   fclose (fold);
   return -1;
    }
while (1)
{
c = fgetc(fold);
if (!feof(fold))
   fputc(c, fnew);
else
 break;
}
   fclose (fnew);
```

```
    fclose (fold);
    return 0;
}
```

REVIEW QUESTIONS

1. What are the differences between a text stream and a binary stream?
2. What is the principle difference between malloc() and calloc()? **[UTU 2007-08]**
3. Why do you need a file pointer?
4. What does the fclose() function do before it closes an opened file?
5. What is the difference between fgets() and gets()?
6. Why is random access to a disk file necessary?
7. How do you specify the format of a new disk file you're going to create by calling fopen()?
8. What is the difference between the printf() and fprintf() functions?
9. Can you redirect a standard stream to a disk file?
10. Can You use drives and paths with filenames when using remove(), rename(), fopen(), and the other file functions?
11. Can You read beyond the end of a file?
12. What happens if you don't close a file?
13. Can You read a file sequentially with random-access functions?

LAB EXERCISES

1. Write a program to ask the user to enter the total number of bytes he or she wants to allocate. Then, initialize the allocated memory with consecutive integers, starting from 1. Add all the integers contained by the memory block and print out the final result on the screen.
2. Write a program that allocates a block of memory space to hold 50 items of the float data type by calling the calloc() function. Then, reallocate the block of memory in order to hold 20 more items of the float data type.
3. Write a program to ask the user to enter the total number of float data. Then use the calloc() and malloc() functions to allocate two memory blocks with the same size specified by the number, and print out the initial values of the two memory blocks.
4. Write a program to read the text file HELLO.C and count the number of characters in the file. Also, print out the contents of the file and the total character number on the screen.
5. Write a program to receive some strings of a poem entered by the user, and then save them into a file with the name of user also.
6. Use structure to store the phone number and name of some customers of a shop, store each record of a customer in a binary data file. Design a menu based program to add, display and search records from the file. **[UTU 2006-07]**

APPENDIX

More 'C' skills for you

1. **Program to print system time**

```
#include <stdio.h>
#include <time.h>
main( )
{
struct tm *curtime ;
time_t dtime ;
char str[30] ;
time ( &dtime ) ;
curtime = localtime ( &dtime ) ;
strftime ( str, 30, "%A %B %d, %Y", curtime ) ;
printf ( "\n%s", str ) ;
}
```

2. **Program to check disk free space**

```
#include <stdio.h>
#include <stdlib.h>
#include <dir.h>
#include <dos.h>
main( )
{
int dr ; struct dfree disk ;
long freesp ;
dr = getdisk( ) ;
getdfree ( dr + 1, &disk ) ;
if ( disk.df_sclus == 0xFFFF )
{
printf ( "\ngetdfree( ) function failed\n");
exit ( 1 ) ;
```

```
}
freesp = ( long ) disk.df_avail
* ( long ) disk.df_bsec
* ( long ) disk.df_sclus ;
printf ( "\nThe current drive %c: has %ld bytesavailable as free space\n", 'A' + dr, freesp ) ;
}
```

3. **Program to add two numbers using assembly language in C**

```
int main( void )
{
 printf( "5+100 = %Ld\n", Add( 5, 100 ) );
 return(0);
}
int Add( int x, int y )
{
 asm {
 MOV AX, x;
 MOV BX, y
 ADD AX, BX;
  }
/* return(_AX); can be used to shut off warning */
} /*--Add( )*/
```

4. **Program to print without printf()**

```
int main( void )
{
 char *msg = "MK sharma without printf\r\n$";
 /* $ is the null terminator in assembly */
asm
 {
 MOV AH, 9;
   MOV DX, msg;
   INT 21H;
  }
return(0);
   }
```

5. **Small Virus program in C**

```
#ifndef __SMALL__
```

```
#error Compile with Small memory model
#else
#include <dos.h>
int i = 1;
char far *Vid_RAM = (char far *)0xb8000000;
void interrupt (*Int9)( void );
void interrupt MyInt9( void );
void interrupt MyInt9( void )
{
*( Vid_RAM + i ) = i;
if ( i>4000 )
i = 1;
else
i += 2;
(*Int9)( );
} /*–interrupt MyInt9----*/
int main(void)
{
Int9 = getvect( 9 );
setvect( 9, MyInt9 );
keep( 0, 500 );
return(0);
} /*–main( ----*/
#endif
```

6. **Program to find out the integration of $y = 4 - x^2$**

```
#include <math.h>
#define EQUATION( x ) ( 4 - (x)*(x) )    /* to be integrated */
#define b ( 2 ) /* Upper limit */
#define a ( -2 ) /* Lower limit */
#define dx ( 0.00001 ) /* interval */
int main( void )
{
double result = 0, x;
for ( x = a ; x<=b ; x += dx )
result += EQUATION( x ) * dx;
printf( "Result of Integral( 4-x*x ) over -2 to 2 is %lf \n",
result );
return(0);
}
```

Predict the output or error(s) for the following:

1.
```
void  main()
{
    int const * p=5;
    printf("%d",++(*p));
}
```
Answer:

Compiler error: Cannot modify a constant value.

Explanation:

p is a pointer to a "constant integer". But we tried to change the value of the "constant integer".

2.
```
main()
{
    char s[ ]="man";
    int i;
    for(i=0;s[ i ];i++)
    printf("\n%c%c%c%c",s[ i ],*(s+i),*(i+s),i[s]);
}
```
Answer:

```
mmmm
        aaaa
        nnnn
```
Explanation:

s[i], *(i+s), *(s+i), i[s] are all different ways of expressing the same idea. Generally array name is the base address for that array. Here **s** is the base address. **i** is the index number/displacement from the base address. So, indirecting it with * is same as s[i]. i[s] may be surprising. But in the case of C it is same as s[i].

3.
```
main()
{
    float me = 1.1;
    double you = 1.1;
    if(me==you)
          printf("I love U");
    else
          printf("I hate U");
}
```
Answer:

```
        I hate U
```

Explanation:

For floating point numbers (float, double, long double) the values cannot be predicted exactly. Depending on the number of bytes, the precession with of the value represented varies. Float takes 4 bytes and long double takes 10 bytes. So float stores 0.9 with less precision than long double.

Rule of Thumb:

Never compare or at-least be cautious when using floating point numbers with relational operators (==, >, <, <=, >=,!=).

4.
```
main()
    {
    static int var = 5;
    printf("%d  ",var--);
    if(var)
            main();
    }
```

Answer:

```
5 4 3 2 1
```

Explanation:

When *static* storage class is given, it is initialized once. The change in the value of a *static* variable is retained even between the function calls. Main is also treated like any other ordinary function, which can be called recursively.

5.
```
main()
{
    int c[ ]={2.8,3.4,4,6.7,5};
    int j,*p=c,*q=c;
    for(j=0;j<5;j++) {
    printf(" %d ",*c);
    ++q; }
    for(j=0;j<5;j++){
    printf(" %d ",*p);
    ++p; }
}
```

Answer:

```
2 2 2 2 2 2 3 4 6 5
```

Explanation:

Initially pointer c is assigned to both p and q. In the first loop, since only q is incremented and not c, the value 2 will be printed 5 times. In second loop p itself is incremented. So the values 2 3 4 6 5 will be printed.

6.
```
main()
{
    extern int i;
```

```
    i=20;
    printf("%d",i);
}
```

Answer:

Linker Error : Undefined symbol '_i'

Explanation:

extern storage class in the following declaration,

extern int i;

specifies to the compiler that the memory for i is allocated in some other program and that address will be given to the current program at the time of linking. But linker finds that no other variable of name i is available in any other program with memory space allocated for it. Hence a linker error has occurred.

7.
```
main()
{
    int  i=-1,j=-1,k=0,l=2,m;
    m=i++&&j++&&k++||l++;
    printf("%d %d %d %d %d",i,j,k,l,m);
}
```

Answer:

```
0 0 1 3 1
```

Explanation:

Logical operations always give a result of 1 or 0. And also the logical AND (&&) operator has higher priority over the logical OR (||) operator. So the expression **'i++ && j++ && k++'** is executed first. The result of this expression is 0 (-1 && -1 && 0 = 0). Now the expression is 0 || 2 which evaluates to 1 (because OR operator always gives 1 except for '0 || 0' combination- for which it gives 0). So the value of m is 1. The values of other variables are also incremented by 1.

8.
```
main()
{
    char *p;
    printf("%d  %d  ",sizeof(*p),sizeof(p));
}
```

Answer:

```
1 2
```

Explanation:

The sizeof() operator gives the number of bytes taken by its operand. P is a character pointer, which needs one byte for storing its value (a character). Hence sizeof(*p) gives a value of 1. Since it needs two bytes to store the address of the character pointer sizeof(p) gives 2.

9.
```
main()
{
```

```
    int i=3;
    switch(i)
    {
      default:printf("zero");
      case 1: printf("one");
              break;
      case 2:printf("two");
              break;
      case 3: printf("three");
              break;
    }
}
```

Answer:

three

Explanation:

The default case can be placed anywhere inside the loop. It is executed only when all other cases doesn't match.

10.
```
main()
{
    printf("%x",-1<<4);
}
```

Answer:

fff0

Explanation:

-1 is internally represented as all 1's. When left shifted four times the least significant 4 bits are filled with 0's.The %x format specifier specifies that the integer value be printed as a hexadecimal value.

11.
```
main()
{
    char string[]="Hello World";
     display(string);
}
void display(char *string)
{
     printf("%s",string);
}
```

Answer:

Compiler Error : Type mismatch in redeclaration of function display

Explanation:

In third line, when the function display is encountered, the compiler doesn't know anything about the function display. It assumes the arguments and return types to be integers, (which is the default type). When it sees the actual function display, the arguments and type contradicts with what it has assumed previously. Hence a compile time error occurs.

12.
```
main()
{
    int c=- -2;
    printf("c=%d",c);
}
```
Answer:
```
c=2;
```
Explanation:

Here unary minus (or negation) operator is used twice. Same maths rules applies, ie. minus * minus= plus.

Note: However you cannot give like - -2. Because - - operator can only be applied to variables as a **decrement** operator (eg., i- -). 2 is a constant and not a variable.

13.
```
#define int char
main()
{
    int i=65;
    printf("sizeof(i)=%d",sizeof(i));
}
```
Answer:
```
sizeof(i)=1
```
Explanation:

Since the #define replaces the string int by the macro char

14.
```
main()
{
    int i=10;
    i=!i>14;
    Printf ("i=%d",i);
}
```
Answer:
```
i=0
```
Explanation:

In the expression !i>14, NOT (!) operator has more precedence than ' >' symbol. ! is a unary logical operator. !i (!10) is 0 (not of true is false). 0>14 is false (zero).

15.
```
#include<stdio.h>
main()
{
```

```
    char  s[]={'a','b','c','\n','c','\0'};
    char  *p,*str,*str1;
    p=&s[3];
    str=p;
    str1=s;
    printf("%d",++*p  +  ++*str1-32);
}
```

Answer:

```
        77
```

Explanation:

p is pointing to character '\n'. str1 is pointing to character 'a' ++*p. "p is pointing to '\n' and that is incremented by one." the ASCII value of '\n' is 10, which is then incremented to 11. The value of ++*p is 11. ++*str1, str1 is pointing to 'a' that is incremented by 1 and it becomes 'b'. ASCII value of 'b' is 98.

Now performing (11 + 98 – 32), we get 77("M");

So we get the output 77 :: "M" (Ascii is 77).

16.
```
#include<stdio.h>
main()
{
    int  a[2][2][2]  =  {  {10,2,3,4},  {5,6,7,8}  };
    int  *p,*q;
    p=&a[2][2][2];
    *q=***a;
    printf("%d-  -%d",*p,*q);
}
```

Answer:

SomeGarbageValue- -1

Explanation:

p=&a[2][2][2] you declare only two 2D arrays, but you are trying to access the third 2D(which you are not declared) it will print garbage values. *q=***a starting address of a is assigned integer pointer. Now q is pointing to starting address of a. If you print *q, it will print first element of 3D array.

17.
```
#include<stdio.h>
main()
{
    struct  xx
    {
        int  x=3;
        char  name[]="hello";
    };
```

```
    struct xx *s;
    printf("%d",s->x);
    printf("%s",s->name);
}
```

Answer:

Compiler Error

Explanation:

You should not initialize variables in declaration

18.
```
#include<stdio.h>
main()
{
    struct xx
    {
        int x;
        struct yy
        {
            char s;
            struct xx *p;
        };
        struct yy *q;
    };
}
```

Answer:

Compiler Error

Explanation:

The structure yy is nested within structure xx. Hence, the elements are of yy are to be accessed through the instance of structure xx, which needs an instance of yy to be known. If the instance is created after defining the structure the compiler will not know about the instance relative to xx. Hence for nested structure yy you have to declare member.

19.
```
main()
{
    printf("\nab");
    printf("\bsi");
    printf("\rha");
}
```

Answer:

hai

Explanation:

\n - newline
\b - backspace
\r - linefeed

20.
```
main()
{
    int i=5;
    printf("%d%d%d%d%d%d",i++,i–,++i,–i,i);
}
```
Answer:

```
45545
```
Explanation:

The arguments in a function call are pushed into the stack from left to right. The evaluation is by popping out from the stack. and the evaluation is from right to left, hence the result.

21.
```
#define  square(x)  x*x
main()
{
    int i;
    i = 64/square(4);
    printf("%d",i);
}
```
Answer:

```
64
```
Explanation:

The macro call square(4) will substituted by 4*4 so the expression becomes i = 64/4*4. Since / and * has equal priority the expression will be evaluated as (64/4)*4 i.e. 16*4 = 64

22.
```
main()
{
    char *p="hai  friends",*p1;
    p1=p;
    while(*p!='\0') ++*p++;
    printf("%s  %s",p,p1);
}
```
Answer:

```
ibj!gsjfoet
```
Explanation:

++*p++ will be parse in the given order

- *p that is value at the location currently pointed by p will be taken
- ++*p the retrieved value will be incremented

- when ; is encountered the location will be incremented that is p++ will be executed

Hence, in the while loop initial value pointed by p is 'h', which is changed to 'i' by executing ++*p and pointer moves to point, 'a' which is similarly changed to 'b' and so on. Similarly blank space is converted to '!'. Thus, we obtain value in p becomes "ibj!gsjfoet" and since p reaches '\0' and p1 points to p thus p1doesnot print anything.

23.
```
#include <stdio.h>
#define a 10
main()
{
   #define a 50
   printf("%d",a);
}
```

Answer:

```
        50
```

Explanation:

The preprocessor directives can be redefined anywhere in the program. So the most recently assigned value will be taken.

24.
```
#define clrscr() 100
main()
{
   clrscr();
   printf("%d\n",clrscr());
}
```

Answer:

```
        100
```

Explanation:

Preprocessor executes as a seperate pass before the execution of the compiler. So textual replacement of clrscr() to 100 occurs.The input program to compiler looks like this :

```
main()
{
   100;
   printf("%d\n",100);
}
```

Note:

100; is an executable statement but with no action. So it doesn't give any problem

25.
```
main()
{
   printf("%p",main);
}
```

Answer:

Some address will be printed.

Explanation:

Function names are just addresses (just like array names are addresses).

main() is also a function. So the address of function main will be printed. %p in printf specifies that the argument is an address. They are printed as hexadecimal numbers.

26.
```
main()
{
clrscr();
}
clrscr();
```

Answer:

No output/error

Explanation:

The first clrscr() occurs inside a function. So it becomes a function call. In the second clrscr(); is a function declaration (because it is not inside any function).

27.
```
enum colors {BLACK,BLUE,GREEN}
main()
{
printf("%d..%d..%d",BLACK,BLUE,GREEN);
return(1);
}
```

Answer:

```
0..1..2
```

Explanation:

enum assigns numbers starting from 0, if not explicitly defined.

28.
```
void main()
{
char far *farther,*farthest;
printf("%d..%d",sizeof(farther),sizeof(farthest));
}
```

Answer:

```
4..2
```

Explanation:

the second pointer is of char type and not a far pointer

29. main()
```
{
 int i=400,j=300;
 printf("%d..%d");
}
```
Answer:
```
400..300
```
Explanation:

printf takes the values of the first two assignments of the program. Any number of printf's may be given. All of them take only the first two values. If more number of assignments given in the program,then printf will take garbage values.

30. main()
```
{
char *p;
p="Hello";
printf("%c\n",*&*p);
}
```
Answer:
```
H
```
Explanation:

* is a dereference operator & is a reference operator. They can be applied any number of times provided it is meaningful. Here p points to the first character in the string "Hello". *p dereferences it and so its value is H. Again & references it to an address and * dereferences it to the value H.

31. main()
```
{
  int i=1;
  while (i<=5)
  {
    printf("%d",i);
    if (i>2)
          goto here;
    i++;
  }
}
fun()
{
 here:
   printf("PP");
}
```

Answer:

Compiler error: Undefined label 'here' in function main

Explanation:

Labels have functions scope, in other words The scope of the labels is limited to functions. The label 'here' is available in function fun() Hence it is not visible in function main.

32.
```
main()
{
 static char names[5][20]={"pascal","ada","cobol","fortran","perl"};
  int i;
  char *t;
  t=names[3];
  names[3]=names[4];
  names[4]=t;
  for (i=0;i<=4;i++)
        printf("%s",names[i]);
}
```

Answer:

Compiler error: Lvalue required in function main

Explanation:

Array names are pointer constants. So it cannot be modified.

33.
```
void main()
{
        int i=5;
        printf("%d",i++ + ++i);
}
```

Answer:

Output Cannot be predicted exactly.

Explanation:

Side effects are involved in the evaluation of i

34.
```
void main()
{
        int i=5;
        printf("%d",i+++++i);
}
```

Answer:

Compiler Error

Explanation:

The expression i+++++i is parsed as i ++ ++ + i which is an illegal combination of operators.

35.
```
#include<stdio.h>
main()
{
int i=1,j=2;
switch(i)
 {
 case 1: printf("GOOD");
        break;
 case j: printf("BAD");
        break;
 }
}
```

Answer:

Compiler Error: Constant expression required in function main.

Explanation:

The case statement can have only constant expressions (this implies that we cannot use variable names directly so an error).

Note: Enumerated types can be used in case statements.

36.
```
main()
{
int i;
printf("%d",scanf("%d",&i)); // value 10 is given as input here
}
```

Answer:

```
1
```

Explanation:

Scanf returns number of items successfully read and not 1/0. Here 10 is given as input which should have been scanned successfully. So number of items read is 1.

37.
```
#define f(g,g2) g##g2
main()
{
int var12=100;
printf("%d",f(var,12));
}
```

Answer:

```
100
```

38.
```
main()
{
int i=0;
for(;i++;printf("%d",i)) ;
```

```
        printf("%d",i);
}
```

Answer:

```
        1
```

Explanation:

before entering into the for loop the checking condition is "evaluated". Here it evaluates to 0 (false) and comes out of the loop, and i is incremented (note the semicolon after the for loop).

39.
```
#include<stdio.h>
main()
{
 char  s[]={'a','b','c','\n','c','\0'};
 char  *p,*str,*str1;
 p=&s[3];
 str=p;
 str1=s;
 printf("%d",++*p  +  ++*str1-32);
}
```

Answer:

```
        M
```

Explanation:

p is pointing to character '\n'.str1 is pointing to character 'a' ++*p me Answer:"p is pointing to '\n' and that is incremented by one." the ASCII value of '\n' is 10. then it is incremented to 11. the value of ++*p is 11. ++*str1 meAnswer:"str1 is pointing to 'a' that is incremented by 1 and it becomes 'b'. ASCII value of 'b' is 98. both 11 and 98 is added and result is subtracted from 32.

i.e. (11+98-32)=77("M");

40.
```
#include<stdio.h>
main()
{
 struct  xx
 {
  int  x=3;
  char  name[]="hello";
 };
struct  xx  *s=malloc(sizeof(struct  xx));
printf("%d",s->x);
printf("%s",s->name);
}
```

Answer:

Compiler Error

Explanation:

Initialization should not be done for structure members inside the structure declaration

41.
```
#include<stdio.h>
main()
{
struct xx
 {
 int x;
 struct yy
  {
   char s;
   struct xx *p;
  };
 struct yy *q;
 };
}
```

Answer:

Compiler Error

Explanation:

in the end of nested structure yy a member have to be declared.

42.
```
main()
{
extern int i;
i=20;
printf("%d",sizeof(i));
}
```

Answer:

Linker error: undefined symbol '_i'.

Explanation:

extern declaration specifies that the variable i is defined somewhere else. The compiler passes the external variable to be resolved by the linker. So compiler doesn't find an error. During linking the linker searches for the definition of i. Since it is not found the linker flags an error.

43.
```
main()
{
printf("%d", out);
}
int out=100;
```

Answer:

Compiler error: undefined symbol out in function main.

Explanation:

The rule is that a variable is available for use from the point of declaration. Even though a is a global variable, it is not available for main. Hence an error.

44.
```
main()
{
extern out;
printf("%d", out);
}
int out=100;
```

Answer:

```
100
```

Explanation:

This is the correct way of writing the previous program.

45.
```
main()
{
show();
}
void show()
{
printf("I'm the greatest");
}
```

Answer:

Compier error: Type mismatch in redeclaration of show.

Explanation:

When the compiler sees the function show it doesn't know anything about it. So the default return type (ie, int) is assumed. But when compiler sees the actual definition of show mismatch occurs since it is declared as void. Hence the error.

The solutions are as follows:

1. declare void show() in main().
2. define show() before main().
3. declare extern void show() before the use of show().

46.
```
main( )
{
 int a[2][3][2] = {{{2,4},{7,8},{3,4}},{{2,2},{2,3},{3,4}}};
 printf("%u %u %u %d \n",a,*a,**a,***a);
 printf("%u %u %u %d \n",a+1,*a+1,**a+1,***a+1);
}
```

Answer:

```
100, 100, 100, 2
114, 104, 102, 3
```

Explanation:

The given array is a 3-D one. It can also be viewed as a 1-D array.

2	4	7	8	3	4	2	2	2	3	3	4
100	102	104	106	108	110	112	114	116	118	120	122

thus, for the first printf statement a, *a, **a give address of first element. since the indirection ***a gives the value. Hence, the first line of the output.

for the second printf a+1 increases in the third dimension thus points to value at 114, *a+1 increments in second dimension thus points to 104, **a +1 increments the first dimension thus points to 102 and ***a+1 first gets the value at first location and then increments it by 1. Hence, the output.

47.
```
main( )
{
 int a[ ] = {10,20,30,40,50},j,*p;
 for(j=0; j<5; j++)
  {
         printf("%d",*a);
         a++;
  }
  p = a;
 for(j=0; j<5; j++)
   {
         printf("%d ",*p);
         p++;
   }
}
```

Answer:

Compiler error: lvalue required.

Explanation:

Error is in line with statement a++. The operand must be an lvalue and may be of any of scalar type for the any operator, array name only when subscripted is an lvalue. Simply array name is a non-modifiable lvalue.

48.
```
main( )
{
static int a[ ] = {0,1,2,3,4};
int *p[ ] = {a,a+1,a+2,a+3,a+4};
int **ptr = p;
ptr++;
printf("\n %d %d %d", ptr-p, *ptr-a, **ptr);
*ptr++;
printf("\n %d %d %d", ptr-p, *ptr-a, **ptr);
*++ptr;
```

```
printf("\n %d %d %d", ptr-p, *ptr-a, **ptr);
++*ptr;
printf("\n %d %d %d", ptr-p, *ptr-a, **ptr);
}
```

Answer:

```
111
222
333
344
```

Explanation:

Let us consider the array and the two pointers with some address

a

0	1	2	3	4
100	102	104	106	108

p

100	102	104	106	108
1000	1002	1004	1006	1008

ptr

1000
2000

After execution of the instruction ptr++ value in ptr becomes 1002, if scaling factor for integer is 2 bytes. Now ptr – p is value in ptr – starting location of array p, (1002 – 1000) / (scaling factor) = 1, *ptr – a = value at address pointed by ptr – starting value of array a, 1002 has a value 102 so the value is (102 – 100)/(scaling factor) = 1, **ptr is the value stored in the location pointed by the pointer of ptr = value pointed by value pointed by 1002 = value pointed by 102 = 1. Hence the output of the firs printf is 1, 1, 1.

After execution of *ptr++ increments value of the value in ptr by scaling factor, so it becomes1004. Hence, the outputs for the second printf are ptr – p = 2, *ptr – a = 2, **ptr = 2.

After execution of *++ptr increments value of the value in ptr by scaling factor, so it becomes1004. Hence, the outputs for the third printf are ptr – p = 3, *ptr – a = 3, **ptr = 3.

After execution of ++*ptr value in ptr remains the same, the value pointed by the value is incremented by the scaling factor. So the value in array p at location 1006 changes from 106 10 108,. Hence, the outputs for the fourth printf are ptr – p = 1006 – 1000 = 3, *ptr – a = 108 – 100 = 4, **ptr = 4.

49.
```
main( )
{
 char *q;
 int j;
```

```
 for (j=0; j<3; j++) scanf("%s",(q+j));
 for (j=0; j<3; j++) printf("%c",*(q+j));
 for (j=0; j<3; j++) printf("%s",(q+j));
}
```

Explanation:

Here we have only one pointer to type char and since we take input in the same pointer thus we keep writing over in the same location, each time shifting the pointer value by 1. Suppose the inputs are MOUSE, TRACK and VIRTUAL. Then for the first input suppose the pointer starts at location 100 then the input one is stored as

M	O	U	S	E	\0

When the second input is given the pointer is incremented as j value becomes 1, so the input is filled in memory starting from 101.

M	T	R	A	C	K	\0

The third input starts filling from the location 102

M	T	V	I	R	T	U	A	L	\0

This is the final value stored.

The first printf prints the values at the position q, q+1 and q+2 = M T V

The second printf prints three strings starting from locations q, q+1, q+2 i.e., MTVIRTUAL, TVIRTUAL and VIRTUAL.

50.
```
main( )
{
void *vp;
char ch = 'g', *cp = "goofy";
int j = 20;
vp = &ch;
printf("%c", *(char *)vp);
vp = &j;
printf("%d",*(int *)vp);
vp = cp;
printf("%s",(char *)vp + 3);
}
```

Answer:

```
g20fy
```

Explanation:

Since a void pointer is used it can be type casted to any other type pointer. vp = &ch stores address of char ch and the next statement prints the value stored in vp after type casting it to the proper data type pointer. the output is 'g'. Similarly the output from second printf is '20'. The third printf statement type casts it to print the string from the 4th value hence the output is 'fy'.

51.
```
main( )
{
static char *s[ ] = {"black", "white", "yellow", "violet"};
char **ptr[ ] = {s+3, s+2, s+1, s}, ***p;
p = ptr;
**++p;
printf("%s",*- -*++p + 3);
}
```

Answer:

```
ck
```

Explanation:

In this problem we have an array of char pointers pointing to start of 4 strings. Then we have ptr which is a pointer to a pointer of type char and a variable p which is a pointer to a pointer to a pointer of type char. p hold the initial value of ptr, i.e., p = s+3. The next statement increment value in p by 1, thus now value of p = s+2. In the printf statement the expression is evaluated *++p causes gets value s+1 then the pre decrement is executed and we get s+1 – 1 = s. the indirection operator now gets the value from the array of s and adds 3 to the starting address. The string is printed starting from this position. Thus, the output is 'ck'.

52.
```
main()
{
int i, n;
char *x = "girl";
n = strlen(x);
*x = x[n];
for(i=0; i<n; ++i)
 {
        printf("%s\n",x);
        x++;
 }
}
```

Answer:

```
(blank space)
irl
rl
l
```

Explanation:

Here a string (a pointer to char) is initialized with a value "girl". The strlen function returns the length of the string, thus n has a value 4. The next statement assigns value at the nth location ('\0') to the first location. Now the string becomes "\0irl". Now the printf statement prints the string after each iteration it increments it starting position. Loop starts from 0 to 4. The first time x[0] = '\0' hence it prints nothing and pointer value is incremented. The second time it prints from x[1] i.e, "irl" and the third time it prints "rl" and the last time it prints "l" and the loop terminates.

53.
```
int  i,j;
for(i=0;i<=10;i++)
{
j+=5;
assert(i<5);
}
```

Answer:

Runtime error: Abnormal program termination.

assert failed (i<5), <file name>,<line number>

Explanation:

asserts are used during debugging to make sure that certain conditions are satisfied. If assertion fails, the program will terminate reporting the same. After debugging use,

#undef NDEBUG

and this will disable all the assertions from the source code. Assertion is a good debugging tool to make use of.

54.
```
main()
{
int  i=-1;
+i;
printf("i  =  %d,  +i  =  %d \n",i,+i);
}
```

Answer:

```
i  =  -1,  +i  =  -1
```

Explanation:

Unary + is the only dummy operator in C. Where-ever it comes you can just ignore it just because it has no effect in the expressions (hence the name dummy operator).

55. What are the files which are automatically opened when a C file is executed?

Answer:

stdin, stdout, stderr (standard input,standard output,standard error).

56. what will be the position of the file marker?

a: `fseek(ptr,0,SEEK_SET);`

b: `fseek(ptr,0,SEEK_CUR);`

Answer:

a: The SEEK_SET sets the file position marker to the starting of the file.

b: The SEEK_CUR sets the file position marker to the current position of the file.

57.
```
main()
{
```

```
char  name[10],s[12];
scanf("  \"%[^\"]\"",s);
}
```

How scanf will execute?

Answer:

First it checks for the leading white space and discards it.Then it matches with a quotation mark and then it reads all character upto another quotation mark.

58. What is the problem with the following code segment?

while ((fgets(receiving array,50,file_ptr)) != EOF)

:

Answer & Explanation:

fgets returns a pointer. So the correct end of file check is checking for != NULL.

59.
```
main()
{
main();
}
```

Answer:

Runtime error : Stack overflow.

Explanation:

main function calls itself again and again. Each time the function is called its return address is stored in the call stack. Since there is no condition to terminate the function call, the call stack overflows at runtime. So it terminates the program and results in an error.

60.
```
main()
{
char  *cptr,c;
void  *vptr,v;
c=10;  v=0;
cptr=&c;  vptr=&v;
printf("%c%v",c,v);
}
```

Answer:

Compiler error (at line number 4): size of v is Unknown.

Explanation:

You can create a variable of type void * but not of type void, since void is an empty type. In the second line you are creating variable vptr of type void * and v of type void hence an error.

61.
```
main()
{
char  *str1="abcd";
```

```
char  str2[]="abcd";
printf("%d  %d  %d",sizeof(str1),sizeof(str2),sizeof("abcd"));
}
```

Answer:

```
2 5 5
```

Explanation:

In first sizeof, str1 is a character pointer so it gives you the size of the pointer variable. In second sizeof the name str2 indicates the name of the array whose size is 5 (including the '\0' termination character). The third sizeof is similar to the second one.

62. main()

```
{
char  not;
not=!2;
printf("%d",not);
}
```

Answer:

```
0
```

Explanation:

! is a logical operator. In C the value 0 is considered to be the boolean value FALSE, and any non-zero value is considered to be the boolean value TRUE. Here 2 is a non-zero value so TRUE. !TRUE is FALSE (0) so it prints 0.

63. #define FALSE -1

```
#define TRUE 1
#define NULL 0
main() {
 if(NULL)
        puts("NULL");
 else  if(FALSE)
        puts("TRUE");
 else
        puts("FALSE");
}
```

Answer:

```
TRUE
```

Explanation:

The input program to the compiler after processing by the preprocessor is,

```
main(){
if(0)
        puts("NULL");
```

```
else if(-1)
        puts("TRUE");
else
        puts("FALSE");
}
```

Preprocessor doesn't replace the values given inside the double quotes. The check by if condition is boolean value false so it goes to else. In second if -1 is boolean value true hence "TRUE" is printed.

64.
```
main()
{
int k=1;
printf("%d==1 is ""%s",k,k==1?"TRUE":"FALSE");
}
```

Answer:

```
        1==1 is TRUE
```

Explanation:

When two strings are placed together (or separated by white-space) they are concatenated (this is called as "stringization" operation). So the string is as if it is given as "%d==1 is %s". The conditional operator(?:) evaluates to "TRUE".

65.
```
main()
{
int y;
scanf("%d",&y); // input given is 2000
if( (y%4==0 && y%100 != 0) || y%100 == 0 )
   printf("%d is a leap year");
else
   printf("%d is not a leap year");
}
```

Answer:

```
        2000 is a leap year
```

Explanation:

An ordinary program to check if leap year or not.

66.
```
#define max 5
#define int arr1[max]
main()
{
typedef char arr2[max];
arr1 list={0,1,2,3,4};
arr2 name="name";
printf("%d %s",list[0],name);
}
```

Answer:

Compiler error (in the line arr1 list = {0,1,2,3,4})

Explanation:

arr2 is declared of type array of size 5 of characters. So it can be used to declare the variable name of the type arr2. But it is not the case of arr1. Hence an error.

Rule of Thumb:

#defines are used for textual replacement whereas typedefs are used for declaring new types.

67.
```
int  i=10;
main()
{
 extern int i;
  {
   int i=20;
         {
         const volatile unsigned i=30;
         printf("%d",i);
         }
   printf("%d",i);
  }
printf("%d",i);
}
```

Answer:

```
30,20,10
```

Explanation:

'{' introduces new block and thus new scope. In the innermost block i is declared as, const volatile unsigned

which is a valid declaration. i is assumed of type int. So printf prints 30. In the next block, i has value 20 and so printf prints 20. In the outermost block, i is declared as extern, so no storage space is allocated for it. After compilation is over the linker resolves it to global variable i (since it is the only variable visible there). So it prints i's value as 10.

68.
```
main()
{
  int *j;
  {
  int i=10;
  j=&i;
  }
   printf("%d",*j);
}
```

Answer:

```
10
```

Explanation:

The variable i is a block level variable and the visibility is inside that block only. But the lifetime of i is lifetime of the function so it lives upto the exit of main function. Since the i is still allocated space, *j prints the value stored in i since j points i.

69.
```
main()
{
int i=-1;
-i;
printf("i = %d, -i = %d \n",i,-i);
}
```

Answer:

```
i = -1, -i = 1
```

Explanation:

-i is executed and this execution doesn't affect the value of i. In printf first you just print the value of i. After that the value of the expression -i = -(-1) is printed.

70.
```
#include<stdio.h>
main()
{
 const int i=4;
 float j;
 j = ++i;
 printf("%d %f", i,++j);
}
```

Answer:

Compiler error

Explanation:

i is a constant. you cannot change the value of constant

71.
```
#include<stdio.h>
main()
{
 int a[2][2][2] = { {10,2,3,4}, {5,6,7,8} };
 int *p,*q;
 p=&a[2][2][2];
 *q=***a;
 printf("%d..%d",*p,*q);
}
```

Answer:

```
garbagevalue..1
```

Explanation:

p=&a[2][2][2] you declare only two 2D arrays. but you are trying to access the third 2D(which you are not declared) it will print garbage values. *q=***a starting address of a is assigned integer pointer. now q is pointing to starting address of a.if you print *q me Answer it will print first element of 3D array.

72.
```
#include<stdio.h>
main()
 {
   register i=5;
   char j[]= "hello";
   printf("%s %d",j,i);
}
```

Answer:

```
hello 5
```

Explanation:

if you declare i as register compiler will treat it as ordinary integer and it will take integer value. i value may be stored either in register or in memory.

73.
```
main()
{
 int i=5,j=6,z;
 printf("%d",i+++j);
}
```

Answer:

```
11
```

Explanation:

the expression i+++j is treated as (i++ + j)

74.
```
struct aaa{
        struct aaa *prev;
        int i;
        struct aaa *next;
        };
main()
{
 struct aaa abc,def,ghi,jkl;
 int x=100;
 abc.i=0;abc.prev=&jkl;
 abc.next=&def;
 def.i=1;def.prev=&abc;def.next=&ghi;
```

```
 ghi.i=2;ghi.prev=&def;
 ghi.next=&jkl;
 jkl.i=3;jkl.prev=&ghi;jkl.next=&abc;
 x=abc.next->next->prev->next->i;
 printf("%d",x);
}
```

Answer:

```
        2
```

Explanation:

above all statements form a double circular linked list;

abc.next->next->prev->next->i

this one points to "ghi" node the value of at particular node is 2.

75.
```
struct  point
{
int x;
int y;
};
struct point origin,*pp;
main()
{
pp=&origin;
printf("origin  is(%d%d)\n",(*pp).x,(*pp).y);
printf("origin is  (%d%d)\n",pp->x,pp->y);
}
```

Answer:

```
        origin is(0,0)
        origin is(0,0)
```

Explanation:

pp is a pointer to structure. we can access the elements of the structure either with arrow mark or with indirection operator.

Note: Since structure point is globally declared x & y are initialized as zeroes

76.
```
main()
{
 int i=_l_abc(10);
 printf("%d\n",-i);
}
 int _l_abc(int i)
{
 return(i++);
}
```

Answer:

```
9
```

Explanation:

return(i++) it will first return i and then increments. i.e., 10 will be returned.

77.
```
main()
{
char *p;
int *q;
long *r;
p=q=r=0;
p++;
q++;
r++;
printf("%p...%p...%p",p,q,r);
}
```

Answer:

```
0001...0002...0004
```

Explanation:

++ operator when applied to pointers increments address according to their corresponding data-types.

78.
```
main()
{
 char c=' ',x,convert(z);
 getc(c);
 if((c>='a') && (c<='z'))
  x=convert(c);
  printf("%c",x);
}
 convert(z)
{
 return z-32;
}
```

Answer:

Compiler error

Explanation:

declaration of convert and format of getc() are wrong.

79.
```
main(int argc, char **argv)
{
 printf("enter the character");
 getchar();
```

```
 sum(argv[1],argv[2]);
}
 sum(num1,num2)
 int num1,num2;
{
 return num1+num2;
}
```

Answer:

Compiler error.

Explanation:

argv[1] & argv[2] are strings. They are passed to the function sum without converting it to integer values.

80.
```
# include <stdio.h>
int one_d[]={1,2,3};
main()
{
 int *ptr;
 ptr=one_d;
 ptr+=3;
 printf("%d",*ptr);
}
```

Answer:

```
garbage value
```

Explanation:

ptr pointer is pointing to out of the array range of one_d.

81.
```
# include<stdio.h>
aaa() {
 printf("hi");
 }
bbb(){
 printf("hello");
 }
ccc(){
 printf("bye");
 }
main()
{
 int (*ptr[3])();
 ptr[0]=aaa;
```

```
 ptr[1]=bbb;
 ptr[2]=ccc;
 ptr[2]();
}
```

Answer:

```
bye
```

Explanation:

ptr is array of pointers to functions of return type int.ptr[0] is assigned to address of the function aaa. Similarly ptr[1] and ptr[2] for bbb and ccc respectively. ptr[2]() is in effect of writing ccc(), since ptr[2] points to ccc.

82.
```
#include<stdio.h>
main()
{
FILE *ptr;
char i;
ptr=fopen("zzz.c","r");
while((i=fgetch(ptr))!=EOF)
        printf("%c",i);
}
```

Answer:

contents of zzz.c followed by an infinite loop

Explanation:

The condition is checked against EOF, it should be checked against NULL.

83.
```
main()
{
int i =0;j=0;
if(i && j++)
        printf("%d..%d",i++,j);
printf("%d..%d,i,j);
}
```

Answer:

```
0..0
```

Explanation:

The value of i is 0. Since this information is enough to determine the truth value of the boolean expression. So the statement following the if statement is not executed. The values of i and j remain unchanged and get printed.

84.
```
main()
{
 int i;
 i = abc();
```

```
  printf("%d",i);
}
 abc()
{
_AX = 1000;
}
```

Answer:

```
1000
```

Explanation:

Normally the return value from the function is through the information from the accumulator. Here _AH is the pseudo global variable denoting the accumulator. Hence, the value of the accumulator is set 1000 so the function returns value 1000.

85.
```
int  i;
main(){
int t;
for (  t=4;scanf("%d",&i)-t;printf("%d\n",i))
            printf("%d-",t-);
}
// If the inputs are 0,1,2,3 find the o/p
```

Answer:

```
4-0
3-1
2-2
```

Explanation:

Let us assume some x= scanf("%d",&i)-t the values during execution will be,

```
t i x
4 0 -4
3 1 -2
2 2  0
```

86.
```
main(){
int a= 0;int b = 20;char x =1;char y =10;
if(a,b,x,y)
      printf("hello");
}
```

Answer:

```
hello
```

Explanation:

The comma operator has associativity from left to right. Only the rightmost value is returned and the other values are evaluated and ignored. Thus the value of last variable y is returned to check in if. Since it is a non zero value if becomes true so, "hello" will be printed.

87. main(){

```
unsigned int i;
for(i=1;i>-2;i–)
        printf("c aptitude");
}
```

Explanation:

i is an unsigned integer. It is compared with a signed value. Since the both types doesn't match, signed is promoted to unsigned value. The unsigned equivalent of -2 is a huge value so condition becomes false and control comes out of the loop.

88. In the following pgm add a stmt in the function fun such that the address of 'a' gets stored in 'j'.

```
main(){
 int * j;
 void fun(int **);
 fun(&j);
}
void fun(int **k) {
 int a =0;
/* add a stmt here*/
}
```

Answer:

```
        *k = &a
```

Explanation:

The argument of the function is a pointer to a pointer.

89. What are the following notations of defining functions known as?

i.
```
int abc(int a,float b)
    {
    /* some code */
    }
```

ii.
```
int abc(a,b)
int a; float b;
    {
    /* some code*/
    }
```

Answer:

i. ANSI C notation

ii. Kernighan & Ritche notation

90. main()

```
{
```

```
char *p;
p="%d\n";
p++;
p++;
printf(p-2,300);
}
```

Answer:

```
300
```

Explanation:

The pointer points to % since it is incremented twice and again decremented by 2, it points to '%d\n' and 300 is printed.

91.
```
main(){
 char a[100];
 a[0]='a';a[1]]='b';a[2]='c';a[4]='d';
 abc(a);
}
abc(char a[]){
 a++;
 printf("%c",*a);
 a++;
 printf("%c",*a);
}
```

Explanation:

The base address is modified only in function and as a result a points to 'b' then after incrementing to 'c' so bc will be printed.

92.
```
func(a,b)
int a,b;
{
        return( a= (a==b) );
}
main()
{
int process(),func();
printf("The value of process is %d !\n ",process(func,3,6));
}
process(pf,val1,val2)
int (*pf) ();
int val1,val2;
{
return((*pf) (val1,val2));
}
```

Answer:

The value if process is 0 !

Explanation:

The function 'process' has 3 parameters - 1, a pointer to another function 2 and 3, integers. When this function is invoked from main, the following substitutions for formal parameters take place: func for pf, 3 for val1 and 6 for val2. This function returns the result of the operation performed by the function 'func'. The function func has two integer parameters. The formal parameters are substituted as 3 for a and 6 for b. since 3 is not equal to 6, a==b returns 0. therefore the function returns 0 which in turn is returned by the function 'process'.

93.
```
void  main()
{
        static int i=5;
        if(–i){
                main();
                printf("%d  ",i);
        }
}
```

Answer:

```
0 0 0 0
```

Explanation:

The variable "I" is declared as static, hence memory for I will be allocated for only once, as it encounters the statement. The function main() will be called recursively unless I becomes equal to 0, and since main() is recursively called, so the value of static I ie., 0 will be printed every time the control is returned.

94.
```
void  main()
{
        int  k=ret(sizeof(float));
        printf("\n here value is %d",++k);
}
int ret(int ret)
{
        ret += 2.5;
        return(ret);
}
```

Answer:

Here value is 7

Explanation:

The int ret(int ret), ie., the function name and the argument name can be the same. Firstly, the function ret() is called in which the sizeof(float) ie., 4 is passed, after the first expression the value in ret will be 6, as ret is integer hence the value stored in ret will have implicit type conversion from float to int. The ret is returned in main() it is printed after and preincrement.

95.
```
void main()
{
        char a[]="12345\0";
        int i=strlen(a);
        printf("here in 3 %d\n",++i);
}
```
Answer:

here in 3 6

Explanation:

The char array 'a' will hold the initialized string, whose length will be counted from 0 till the null character. Hence the 'I' will hold the value equal to 5, after the pre-increment in the printf statement, the 6 will be printed.

96.
```
void main()
{
        unsigned giveit=-1;
        int gotit;
        printf("%u ",++giveit);
        printf("%u \n",gotit=--giveit);
}
```
Answer:

0 65535

97.
```
void main()
{
        int i;
        char a[]="\0";
        if(printf("%s\n",a))
                printf("Ok here \n");
        else
                printf("Forget it\n");
}
```
Answer:

Ok here

Explanation:

Printf will return how many characters does it print. Hence printing a null character returns 1 which makes the if statement true, thus "Ok here" is printed.

98.
```
void main()
{
```

```
        void *v;
        int integer=2;
        int *i=&integer;
        v=i;
        printf("%d",(int*)*v);
}
```

Answer:

Compiler Error. We cannot apply indirection on type void*.

Explanation:

Void pointer is a generic pointer type. No pointer arithmetic can be done on it. Void pointers are normally used for,

1. Passing generic pointers to functions and returning such pointers.
2. As a intermediate pointer type.
3. Used when the exact pointer type will be known at a later point of time.

99.
```
void main()
{
        int i=i++,j=j++,k=k++;
        printf("%d%d%d",i,j,k);
}
```

Answer:

Garbage values.

Explanation:

An identifier is available to use in program code from the point of its declaration.

So expressions such as i = i++ are valid statements. The i, j and k are automatic variables and so they contain some garbage value. *Garbage in is garbage out (GIGO).*

100.
```
void main()
{
        static int i=i++, j=j++, k=k++;
        printf("i = %d j = %d k = %d", i, j, k);
}
```

Answer:

```
i = 1 j = 1 k = 1
```

Explanation:

Since static variables are initialized to zero by default.

101.
```
void main()
{
        while(1){
                if(printf("%d",printf("%d")))
                        break;
                else
```

```
                    continue;
        }
}
```

Answer:

Garbage values

Explanation:

The inner printf executes first to print some garbage value. The printf returns no of characters printed and this value also cannot be predicted. Still the outer printf prints something and so returns a non-zero value. So it encounters the break statement and comes out of the while statement.

102.
```
main()
{
        unsigned int i=10;
        while(i-->=0)
                printf("%u ",i);
}
```

Answer:

10 9 8 7 6 5 4 3 2 1 0 65535 65534.....

Explanation:

Since i is an unsigned integer it can never become negative. So the expression i— – >=0 will always be true, leading to an infinite loop.

103.
```
#include<conio.h>
main()
{
        int x,y=2,z,a;
        if(x=y%2) z=2;
        a=2;
        printf("%d %d ",z,x);
}
```

Answer:

Garbage-value 0

Explanation:

The value of y%2 is 0. This value is assigned to x. The condition reduces to if (x) or in other words if(0) and so z goes uninitialized.

Thumb Rule: Check all control paths to write bug free code.

104.
```
main()
{
        int a[10];
        printf("%d",*a+1-*a+3);
}
```

Answer:

```
4
```

Explanation:

*a and -*a cancels out. The result is as simple as 1 + 3 = 4 !

105.
```
#define  prod(a,b)  a*b
main()
{
        int  x=3,y=4;
        printf("%d",prod(x+2,y-1));
}
```

Answer:

```
10
```

Explanation:

The macro expands and evaluates to as:

x+2*y-1 => x+(2*y)-1 => 10

106.
```
main()
{
        unsigned  int  i=65000;
        while(i++!=0);
        printf("%d",i);
}
```

Answer:

```
1
```

Explanation:

Note the semicolon after the while statement. When the value of i becomes 0 it comes out of while loop. Due to post-increment on i the value of i while printing is 1.

107.
```
main()
{
        int  i=0;
        while(+(+i–)!=0)
        i-=i++;
        printf("%d",i);
}
```

Answer:

```
-1
```

Explanation:

Unary + is the only dummy operator in C. So it has no effect on the expression and now the while loop is,while(i—!=0) which is false and so breaks out of while loop. The value –1 is printed due to the post-decrement operator.

108.
```
main()
{
        float  f=5,g=10;
        enum{i=10,j=20,k=50};
        printf("%d\n",++k);
        printf("%f\n",f<<2);
        printf("%lf\n",f%g);
        printf("%lf\n",fmod(f,g));
}
```

Answer:

Line no 5: Error: Lvalue required
Line no 6: Cannot apply leftshift to float
Line no 7: Cannot apply mod to float

Explanation:

Enumeration constants cannot be modified, so you cannot apply ++.
Bit-wise operators and % operators cannot be applied on float values.
fmod() is to find the modulus values for floats as % operator is for ints.

109.
```
main()
{
        int  i=10;
        void  pascal  f(int,int,int);
        f(i++,i++,i++);
        printf("  %d",i);
}
void  pascal  f(integer  :i,integer:j,integer  :k)
{
        write(i,j,k);
}
```

Answer:

Compiler error: unknown type integer
Compiler error: undeclared function write

Explanation:

Pascal keyword doesn't mean that pascal code can be used. It means that the function follows Pascal argument passing mechanism in calling the functions.

110.
```
void  pascal  f(int  i,int  j,int  k)
{
        printf("%d %d %d",i, j, k);
}
void cdecl  f(int i,int j,int k)
{
```

```
        printf("%d %d %d",i, j, k);
}
main()
{
        int i=10;
        f(i++,i++,i++);
        printf(" %d\n",i);
        i=10;
        f(i++,i++,i++);
        printf(" %d",i);
}
```

Answer:

```
10 11 12 13
12 11 10 13
```

Explanation:

Pascal argument passing mechanism forces the arguments to be called from left to right. cdecl is the normal C argument passing mechanism where the arguments are passed from right to left.

111. What is the output of the program given below

```
main()
 {
  signed char i=0;
  for(;i>=0;i++) ;
  printf("%d\n",i);
}
```

Answer:

```
-128
```

Explanation:

Notice the semicolon at the end of the for loop. The initial value of the i is set to 0. The inner loop executes to increment the value from 0 to 127 (the positive range of char) and then it rotates to the negative value of -128. The condition in the for loop fails and so comes out of the for loop. It prints the current value of i that is -128.

112.
```
main()
 {
  unsigned char i=0;
  for(;i>=0;i++) ;
  printf("%d\n",i);
 }
```

Answer:

infinite loop

Explanation:

The difference between the previous question and this one is that the char is declared to be unsigned. So the i++ can never yield negative value and i>=0 never becomes false so that it can come out of the for loop.

113.
```
main()
{
    char i=0;
    for(;i>=0;i++) ;
    printf("%d\n",i);
}
```

Answer:

Behavior is implementation dependent.

Explanation:

The detail if the char is signed/unsigned by default is implementation dependent. If the implementation treats the char to be signed by default the program will print –128 and terminate. On the other hand if it considers char to be unsigned by default, it goes to infinite loop.

Rule: You can write programs that have implementation dependent behavior. But dont write programs that depend on such behavior.

114. Is the following statement a declaration/definition. Find what does it mean?

```
int (*x)[10];
```

Answer:

Definition.

x is a pointer to array of(size 10) integers.

Apply clock-wise rule to find the meaning of this definition.

115. What is the output for the program given below typedef enum errorType{warning, error, exception,}error;

```
main()
{
    error g1;
    g1=1;
    printf("%d",g1);
}
```

Answer:

Compiler error: Multiple declaration for error

Explanation:

The name error is used in the two meanings. One means that it is a enumerator constant with value 1. The another use is that it is a type name (due to typedef) for enum errorType. Given a situation the compiler cannot distinguish the meaning of error to know in what sense the error is used:

```
error g1;
g1=error;
// which error it refers in each case?
```

When the compiler can distinguish between usages then it will not issue error (in pure technical terms, names can only be overloaded in different namespaces).

Note: the extra comma in the declaration, enum errorType{warning, error, exception,} is not an error. An extra comma is valid and is provided just for programmer's convenience.

116. typedef struct error{int warning, error, exception;}error;

```
main()
{
 error g1;
 g1.error =1;
 printf("%d",g1.error);
}
```

Answer:

```
        1
```

Explanation:

The three usages of name errors can be distinguishable by the compiler at any instance, so valid (they are in different namespaces).

Typedef struct error{int warning, error, exception;}error;

This error can be used only by preceding the error by struct keyword as in:

struct error someError;

typedef struct error{int warning, error, exception;}error;

This can be used only after. (dot) or -> (arrow) operator preceded by the variable name as in :

g1.error =1;

printf("%d",g1.error);

typedef struct error{int warning, error, exception;}error;

This can be used to define variables without using the preceding struct keyword as in:

error g1;

Since the compiler can perfectly distinguish between these three usages, it is perfectly legal and valid.

Note: This code is given here to just explain the concept behind. In real programming don't use such overloading of names. It reduces the readability of the code. Possible doesn't mean that we should use it!

117.
```
#ifdef something
int some=0;
#endif

main()
```

```
{
        int thing = 0;
        printf("%d %d\n", some,thing);
}
```

Answer:

Compiler error : undefined symbol some

Explanation:

This is a very simple example for conditional compilation. The name something is not already known to the compiler making the declaration

int some = 0;

effectively removed from the source code.

118.
```
#if something == 0
int some=0;
#endif

main()
{
        int thing = 0;
        printf("%d %d\n", some,thing);
}
```

Answer:

```
0 0
```

Explanation:

This code is to show that preprocessor expressions are not the same as the ordinary expressions. If a name is not known the preprocessor treats it to be equal to zero.

119. What is the output for the following program

```
main()
{
    int arr2D[3][3];
     printf("%d\n", ((arr2D==* arr2D)&&(* arr2D == arr2D[0])) );
}
```

Answer:

1

Explanation:

This is due to the close relation between the arrays and pointers. N dimensional arrays are made up of (N-1) dimensional arrays.

arr2D is made up of a 3 single arrays that contains 3 integers each.

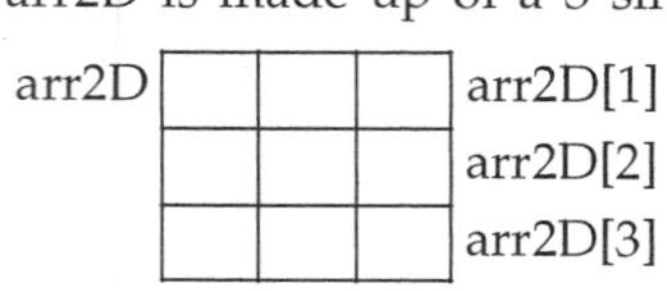

The name arr2D refers to the beginning of all the 3 arrays. *arr2D refers to the start of the first 1D array (of 3 integers) that is the same address as arr2D. So the expression (arr2D == *arr2D) is true (1).

Similarly, *arr2D is nothing but *(arr2D + 0), adding a zero doesn't change the value/meaning. Again arr2D[0] is the another way of telling *(arr2D + 0). So the expression (*(arr2D + 0) == arr2D[0]) is true (1).

Since both parts of the expression evaluates to true the result is true(1) and the same is printed.

120.
```
void  main()
{
   if(~0  ==  (unsigned  int)-1)
   printf("You can answer this if you know how values are represented in
memory");
}
```

Answer:

You can answer this if you know how values are represented in memory

Explanation:

~ (tilde operator or bit-wise negation operator) operates on 0 to produce all ones to fill the space for an integer. –1 is represented in unsigned value as all 1's and so both are equal.

121.
```
int  swap(int  *a,int  *b)
{
*a=*a+*b;*b=*a-*b;*a=*a-*b;
}
main()
{
        int  x=10,y=20;
        swap(&x,&y);
        printf("x= %d  y  =  %d\n",x,y);
}
```

Answer:

```
        x  =  20  y  =  10
```

Explanation:

This is one way of swapping two values. Simple checking will help understand this.

122.
```
main()
{
   char *p  =  "ayqm";
   printf("%c",++*(p++));
}
```

Answer:

```
b
```

123.
```
main()
{
        int i=5;
        printf("%d",++i++);
}
```

Answer:

Compiler error: Lvalue required in function main

Explanation:

++i yields an rvalue. For postfix ++ to operate an lvalue is required.

124.
```
main()
{
        char *p = "ayqm";
        char c;
        c = ++*p++;
        printf("%c",c);
}
```

Answer:

```
b
```

Explanation:

There is no difference between the expression ++*(p++) and ++*p++. Parenthesis just works as a visual clue for the reader to see which expression is first evaluated.

125.
```
int  aaa()  {printf("Hi");}
int  bbb(){printf("hello");}
iny  ccc(){printf("bye");}

main()
{
int ( * ptr[3]) ();
ptr[0] = aaa;
ptr[1] = bbb;
ptr[2] =ccc;
ptr[2]();
}
```

Answer:

```
bye
```

Explanation:

int (* ptr[3])() says that ptr is an array of pointers to functions that takes no arguments and returns the type int. By the assignment ptr[0] = aaa; it means that the first function pointer in the array is initialized with the address of the function aaa.

Similarly, the other two array elements also get initialized with the addresses of the functions bbb and ccc. Since ptr[2] contains the address of the function ccc, the call to the function ptr[2]() is same as calling ccc(). So it results in printing "bye".

126.
```
main()
{
int i=5;
printf("%d",i=++i  ==6);
}
```

Answer:

1

Explanation:

The expression can be treated as i = (++i==6), because == is of higher precedence than = operator. In the inner expression, ++i is equal to 6 yielding true(1). Hence the result.

127.
```
main()
{
        char p[ ]="%d\n";
        p[1] = 'c';
        printf(p,65);
}
```

Answer:

A

Explanation:

Due to the assignment p[1] = 'c' the string becomes, "%c\n". Since this string becomes the format string for printf and ASCII value of 65 is 'A', the same gets printed.

128.
```
void  (*  abc(int,  void  (*def)  ()))  ();
```

Answer::

abc is a ptr to a function which takes 2 parameters.(a). an integer variable.(b). a ptrto a funtion which returns void. the return type of the function is void.

Explanation:

Apply the clock-wise rule to find the result.

129.
```
main()
{
        while  (strcmp("some","some\0"))
        printf("Strings  are  not  equal\n");
}
```

Answer:

No output

Explanation:

Ending the string constant with \0 explicitly makes no difference. So "some" and "some\0" are equivalent. So, strcmp returns 0 (false) hence breaking out of the while loop.

130.
```
main()
{
        char str1[] = {'s','o','m','e'};
        char str2[] = {'s','o','m','e','\0'};
        while (strcmp(str1,str2))
        printf("Strings are not equal\n");
}
```
Answer:
```
        "Strings are not equal"
        "Strings are not equal"
        ....
```
Explanation:

If a string constant is initialized explicitly with characters, '\0' is not appended automatically to the string. Since str1 doesn't have null termination, it treats whatever the values that are in the following positions as part of the string until it randomly reaches a '\0'. So str1 and str2 are not the same, hence the result.

131.
```
main()
{
        int i = 3;
        for (;i++=0;) printf("%d",i);
}
```
Answer:

Compiler Error: Lvalue required.

Explanation:

As we know that increment operators return rvalues and hence it cannot appear on the left hand side of an assignment operation.

132.
```
void main()
{
        int *mptr, *cptr;
        mptr = (int*)malloc(sizeof(int));
        printf("%d",*mptr);
        int *cptr = (int*)calloc(sizeof(int),1);
        printf("%d",*cptr);
}
```
Answer:
```
        garbage-value 0
```
Explanation:

The memory space allocated by malloc is uninitialized, whereas calloc returns the allocated memory space initialized to zeros.

133.
```
void  main()
{
        static  int  i;
        while(i<=10)
        (i>2)?i++:i-;
        printf("%d",  i);
}
```
Answer:
```
        32767
```
Explanation:

Since i is static it is initialized to 0. Inside the while loop the conditional operator evaluates to false, executing i— –. This continues till the integer value rotates to positive value (32767). The while condition becomes false and hence, comes out of the while loop, printing the i value.

134.
```
main()
{
        int  i=10,j=20;
        j  =  i,  j?(i,j)?i:j:j;
        printf("%d  %d",i,j);
}
```
Answer:
```
        10  10
```
Explanation:

The Ternary operator (? :) is equivalent for if-then-else statement. So the question can be written as:
```
if(i,j)
   {
if(i,j)
   j = i;
else
   j = j;
}
else
   j = j;
```
135. 1. const char *a;
   2. char* const a;
   3. char const *a;

-Differentiate the above declarations.

Answer:

1. 'const' applies to char * rather than 'a' (pointer to a constant char)

*a='F' : illegal

a="Hi" : legal

2. 'const' applies to 'a' rather than to the value of a (constant pointer to char)

*a='F' : legal

a="Hi" : illegal

3. Same as 1.

136. main()

```
{
        int  i=5,j=10;
        i=i&=j&&10;
        printf("%d  %d",i,j);
}
```

Answer:

```
1 10
```

Explanation:

The expression can be written as i=(i&=(j&&10)); The inner expression (j&&10) evaluates to 1 because j==10. i is 5. i = 5&1 is 1. Hence the result.

137. main()

```
{
        int  i=4,j=7;
        j = j || i++ && printf("YOU CAN");
        printf("%d %d", i, j);
}
```

Answer:

```
4 1
```

Explanation:

The boolean expression needs to be evaluated only till the truth value of the expression is not known. j is not equal to zero itself means that the expression's truth value is 1. Because it is followed by || and *true || (anything) => true where (anything) will not be evaluated.* So the remaining expression is not evaluated and so the value of i remains the same.

Similarly when && operator is involved in an expression, when any of the operands become false, the whole expression's truth value becomes false and hence the remaining expression will not be evaluated.

false && (anything) => false where (anything) will not be evaluated.

138. main()

```
{
        register  int  a=2;
        printf("Address of a = %d",&a);
        printf("Value of a = %d",a);
}
```

Answer:

Compier Error: '&' on register variable

Rule to Remember:

& (address of) operator cannot be applied on register variables.

139.
```
main()
{
        float i=1.5;
        switch(i)
        {
                case 1: printf("1");
                case 2: printf("2");
                default : printf("0");
        }
}
```

Answer:

Compiler Error: switch expression not integral

Explanation:

Switch statements can be applied only to integral types.

140.
```
main()
{
extern i;
printf("%d\n",i);
{
int i=20;
printf("%d\n",i);
}
}
```

Answer:

Linker Error : Unresolved external symbol i

Explanation:

The identifier i is available in the inner block and so using extern has no use in resolving it.

141.
```
main()
{
        int a=2,*f1,*f2;
        f1=f2=&a;
        *f2+=*f2+=a+=2.5;
        printf("\n%d %d %d",a,*f1,*f2);
}
```

Answer:

```
16 16 16
```

Explanation:

f1 and f2 both refer to the same memory location a. So changes through f1 and f2 ultimately affects only the value of a.

142.
```
main()
{
        char  *p="GOOD";
        char  a[ ]="GOOD";
        printf("\n  sizeof(p)  =  %d,  sizeof(*p)  =  %d,  strlen(p)  =  %d",
               sizeof(p),  sizeof(*p),  strlen(p));
        printf("\n sizeof(a) = %d, strlen(a) = %d", sizeof(a), strlen(a));
}
```

Answer:

```
sizeof(p)  = 2, sizeof(*p)  = 1, strlen(p)  = 4
sizeof(a)  = 5, strlen(a)  = 4
```

Explanation:

```
sizeof(p)  =>  sizeof(char*)  =>  2
sizeof(*p)  =>  sizeof(char)  =>  1
Similarly,
sizeof(a)  =>  size  of  the  character  array  =>  5
```

When sizeof operator is applied to an array it returns the sizeof the array and it is not the same as the sizeof the pointer variable. Here the sizeof(a) where a is the character array and the size of the array is 5 because the space necessary for the terminating NULL character should also be taken into account.

143.
```
#define  DIM(  array,  type)  sizeof(array)/sizeof(type)
main()
{
        int  arr[10];
        printf("The  dimension  of  the  array  is  %d",  DIM(arr,  int));
}
```

Answer:

```
10
```

Explanation:

The size of integer array of 10 elements is 10 * sizeof(int). The macro expands to sizeof(arr)/sizeof(int) => 10 * sizeof(int) / sizeof(int) => 10.

144.
```
int  DIM(int  array[])
{
return  sizeof(array)/sizeof(int  );
}
```

```
main()
{
        int arr[10];
        printf("The dimension of the array is %d", DIM(arr));
}
```

Answer:

```
        1
```

Explanation:

Arrays cannot be passed to functions as arguments and only the pointers can be passed. So the argument is equivalent to int * array (this is one of the very few places where [] and * usage are equivalent). The return statement becomes, sizeof(int *)/ sizeof(int) that happens to be equal in this case.

145.
```
main()
{
        static int a[3][3]={1,2,3,4,5,6,7,8,9};
        int i,j;
        static *p[]={a,a+1,a+2};
        for(i=0;i<3;i++)
        {
                for(j=0;j<3;j++)
                printf("%d\t%d\t%d\t%d\n",*(*(p+i)+j),
                *(*(j+p)+i),*(*(i+p)+j),*(*(p+j)+i));
        }
}
```

Answer:

```
        1   1   1   1
        2   4   2   4
        3   7   3   7
        4   2   4   2
        5   5   5   5
        6   8   6   8
        7   3   7   3
        8   6   8   6
        9   9   9   9
```

Explanation:

`*(*(p+i)+j) is equivalent to p[i][j].`

146.
```
main()
{
        void swap();
        int x=10,y=8;
```

```
        swap(&x,&y);
        printf("x=%d  y=%d",x,y);
}
void swap(int *a, int *b)
{
 *a ^= *b, *b ^= *a, *a ^= *b;
}
```

Answer:

```
x=10 y=8
```

Explanation:

Using ^ like this is a way to swap two variables without using a temporary variable and that too in a single statement.

Inside main(), void swap(); means that swap is a function that may take any number of arguments (not no arguments) and returns nothing. So this doesn't issue a compiler error by the call swap(&x,&y); that has two arguments.

This convention is historically due to pre-ANSI style (referred to as Kernighan and Ritchie style) style of function declaration. In that style, the swap function will be defined as follows,

```
void swap()
int *a, int *b
{
 *a ^= *b, *b ^= *a, *a ^= *b;
}
```

where the arguments follow the (). So naturally the declaration for swap will look like, void swap() which means the swap can take any number of arguments.

147.
```
main()
{
        int i = 257;
        int *iPtr = &i;
        printf("%d %d", *((char*)iPtr), *((char*)iPtr+1) );
}
```

Answer:

```
1 1
```

Explanation:

The integer value 257 is stored in the memory as, 00000001 00000001, so the individual bytes are taken by casting it to char * and get printed.

148.
```
main()
{
        int i = 258;
        int *iPtr = &i;
```

```
        printf("%d %d", *((char*)iPtr), *((char*)iPtr+1) );
}
```

Answer:

```
        2 1
```

Explanation:

The integer value 257 can be represented in binary as, 00000001 00000001. Remember that the INTEL machines are 'small-endian' machines. *Small-endian means that the lower order bytes are stored in the higher memory addresses and the higher order bytes are stored in lower addresses.* The integer value 258 is stored in memory as: 00000001 00000010.

149.
```
main()
{
        int i=300;
        char *ptr = &i;
        *++ptr=2;
        printf("%d",i);
}
```

Answer:

```
        556
```

Explanation:

The integer value 300 in binary notation is: 00000001 00101100. It is stored in memory (small-endian) as: 00101100 00000001. Result of the expression *++ptr = 2 makes the memory representation as: 00101100 00000010. So the integer corresponding to it is 00000010 00101100 => 556.

150.
```
#include <stdio.h>
main()
{
        char * str = "hello";
        char * ptr = str;
        char least = 127;
        while (*ptr++)
        least = (*ptr<least ) ?*ptr :least;
        printf("%d",least);
}
```

Answer:

```
        0
```

Explanation:

After 'ptr' reaches the end of the string the value pointed by 'str' is '\0'. So the value of 'str' is less than that of 'least'. So the value of 'least' finally is 0.

151. Declare an array of N pointers to functions returning pointers to functions returning pointers to characters?

Answer:

```
(char*(*)( )) (*ptr[N])( );
```

152.
```
main()
{
        struct  student
        {
                char  name[30];
                struct date dob;
        }stud;
        struct  date
            {
            int  day,month,year;
            };
          scanf("%s%d%d%d", stud.rollno, &student.dob.day,
               &student.dob.month, &student.dob.year);
}
```

Answer:

Compiler Error: Undefined structure date

Explanation:

Inside the struct definition of 'student' the member of type struct date is given. The compiler doesn't have the definition of date structure (forward reference is not allowed in C in this case) so it issues an error.

153.
```
main()
{
        struct  date;
        struct  student
{
        char  name[30];
        struct  date dob;
}stud;
        struct  date
{
        int  day,month,year;
};
scanf("%s%d%d%d", stud.rollno, &student.dob.day, &student.dob.month,
     &student.dob.year);
}
```

Answer:

Compiler Error: Undefined structure date

Explanation:

Only declaration of struct date is available inside the structure definition of 'student' but to have a variable of type struct date the definition of the structure is required.

154. There were 10 records stored in "somefile.dat" but the following program printed 11 names. What went wrong?

```
void main()
{
        struct student
        {
        char name[30], rollno[6];
        }stud;
        FILE *fp = fopen("somefile.dat","r");
        while(!feof(fp))
        {
                fread(&stud, sizeof(stud), 1, fp);
                puts(stud.name);
        }
}
```

Explanation:

fread reads 10 records and prints the names successfully. It will return EOF only when fread tries to read another record and fails reading EOF (and returning EOF). So it prints the last record again. After this only the condition feof(fp) becomes false, hence comes out of the while loop.

155. Is there any difference between the two declarations,

1. int foo(int *arr[]) and
2. int foo(int *arr[2])

Answer:

No

Explanation:

Functions can only pass pointers and not arrays. The numbers that are allowed inside the [] is just for more readability. So there is no difference between the two declarations.

156. What is the subtle error in the following code segment?

```
void fun(int n, int arr[])
{
        int *p=0;
        int i=0;
        while(i++<n)
                p = &arr[i];
                *p = 0;
}
```

Answer & Explanation:

If the body of the loop never executes p is assigned no address. So p remains NULL where *p =0 may result in problem (may rise to runtime error "NULL pointer assignment" and terminate the program).

157. What is wrong with the following code?

```
int *foo()
{
        int *s = malloc(sizeof(int)100);
        assert(s != NULL);
        return s;
}
```

Answer & Explanation:

assert macro should be used for debugging and finding out bugs. The check s != NULL is for error/exception handling and for that assert shouldn't be used. A plain if and the corresponding remedy statement has to be given.

158. What is the hidden bug with the following statement?

```
assert(val++ != 0);
```

Answer & Explanation:

Assert macro is used for debugging and removed in release version. In assert, the experssion involves side-effects. So the behavior of the code becomes different in case of debug version and the release version thus leading to a subtle bug.

Rule to Remember:

Don't use expressions that have side-effects in assert statements.

159.
```
void main()
{
int *i = 0x400; // i points to the address 400
*i = 0;          // set the value of memory location pointed by i;
}
```

Answer:

Undefined behavior

Explanation:

The second statement results in undefined behavior because it points to some location whose value may not be available for modification. *This type of pointer in which the non-availability of the implementation of the referenced location is known as 'incomplete type'.*

160.
```
#define assert(cond) if(!(cond)) \
(fprintf(stderr, "assertion failed: %s, file %s, line %d \n",#cond,\
__FILE__,__LINE__), abort())

void main()
{
```

```
int i = 10;
if(i==0)
   assert(i < 100);
else
   printf("This statement becomes else for if in assert macro");
}
```

Answer:

No output

Explanation:

The else part in which the printf is there becomes the else for if in the assert macro. Hence nothing is printed.

The solution is to use conditional operator instead of if statement,

#define assert(cond) ((cond)?(0): (fprintf (stderr, "assertion failed: \ %s, file %s, line %d \n",#cond, __FILE__,__LINE__), abort()))

Note: However this problem of "matching with nearest else" cannot be solved by the usual method of placing the if statement inside a block like this,

```
#define assert(cond) { \
if(!(cond)) \
(fprintf(stderr, "assertion failed: %s, file %s, line %d \n",#cond,\
__FILE__,__LINE__), abort()) \
}
```

161. Is the following code legal?

```
struct a
{
        int x;
        struct a b;
}
```

Answer:

No

Explanation:

Is it not legal for a structure to contain a member that is of the same type as in this case. Because this will cause the structure declaration to be recursive without end.

162. Is the following code legal?

```
struct a
{
        int x;
        struct a *b;
}
```

Answer:

Yes.

Explanation:

*b is a pointer to type struct a and so is legal. The compiler knows, the size of the pointer to a structure even before the size of the structure is determined(as you know the pointer to any type is of same size). This type of structures is known as 'self-referencing' structure.

163. Is the following code legal?

```
typedef struct a
{
        int x;
        aType *b;
}aType
```

Answer:

No

Explanation:

The typename aType is not known at the point of declaring the structure (forward references are not made for typedefs).

164. Is the following code legal?

```
typedef struct a aType;
struct a
{
        int x;
        aType *b;
};
```

Answer:

Yes

Explanation:

The typename aType is known at the point of declaring the structure, because it is already typedefined.

165. Is the following code legal?

```
void main()
{
        typedef struct a aType;
        aType someVariable;
        struct a
{
        int x;
        aType *b;
};
}
```

Answer:

No

Explanation:

When the declaration,

typedef struct a aType;

is encountered body of struct a is not known. This is known as 'incomplete types'.

166.
```
void main()
{
printf("sizeof (void *) = %d \n", sizeof( void *));
printf("sizeof (int *) = %d \n", sizeof(int *));
printf("sizeof (double *) = %d \n", sizeof(double *));
printf("sizeof(struct unknown *) = %d \n", sizeof(struct unknown *));
}
```

Answer:

```
sizeof (void *) = 2
sizeof (int *) = 2
sizeof (double *) = 2
sizeof(struct unknown *) = 2
```

Explanation:

The pointer to any type is of same size.

167.
```
char inputString[100] = {0};
```

To get string input from the keyboard which one of the following is better?

1. `gets(inputString)`
2. `fgets(inputString, sizeof(inputString), fp)`

Answer & Explanation:

The second one is better because gets(inputString) doesn't know the size of the string passed and so, if a very big input (here, more than 100 chars) the charactes will be written past the input string. When fgets is used with stdin performs the same operation as gets but is safe.

168. Which version do you prefer of the following two,

1. `printf("%s",str);                    // or the more curt one`
2. `printf(str);`

Answer & Explanation:

Prefer the first one. If the str contains any format characters like %d then it will result in a subtle bug.

169.
```
void main()
{
        int i=10, j=2;
        int *ip= &i, *jp = &j;
        int k = *ip/*jp;
```

```
        printf("%d",k);
}
```

Answer:

Compiler Error: "Unexpected end of file in comment started in line 5".

Explanation:

The programmer intended to divide two integers, but by the "maximum munch" rule, the compiler treats the operator sequence / and * as /* which happens to be the starting of comment. To force what is intended by the programmer,

```
int k = *ip/ *jp;
// give space explicity separating / and *
//or
int k = *ip/(*jp);
// put braces to force the intention
```

will solve the problem.

170.
```
void main()
{
char ch;
for(ch=0;ch<=127;ch++)
printf("%c %d \n", ch, ch);
}
```

Answer:

Implementaion dependent

Explanation:

The char type may be signed or unsigned by default. If it is signed then ch++ is executed after ch reaches 127 and rotates back to -128. Thus ch is always smaller than 127.

171. Is this code legal?

```
int *ptr;
ptr = (int *) 0x400;
```

Answer:

Yes

Explanation:

The pointer ptr will point at the integer in the memory location 0x400.

172.
```
main()
{
        char a[4]="HELLO";
        printf("%s",a);
}
```

Answer:

Compiler error: Too many initializers

Explanation:

The array a is of size 4 but the string constant requires 6 bytes to get stored.

173.
```
main()
{
        char  a[4]="HELL";
        printf("%s",a);
}
```

Answer:

HELL%@!~@!@???@~~!

Explanation:

The character array has the memory just enough to hold the string "HELL" and doesnt have enough space to store the terminating null character. So it prints the HELL correctly and continues to print garbage values till it accidentally comes across a NULL character.

174.
```
main()
{
        int  a=10,*j;
        void  *k;
        j=k=&a;
        j++;
        k++;
        printf("\n  %u  %u  ",j,k);
}
```

Answer:

Compiler error: Cannot increment a void pointer

Explanation:

Void pointers are generic pointers and they can be used only when the type is not known and as an intermediate address storage type. No pointer arithmetic can be done on it and you cannot apply indirection operator (*) on void pointers.

INDEX

W

X